McGraw-Hill Ryerson
Principles of Mathematics 9
Exercise and Homework Book

AUTHOR

Mary Card
B.A., B.Ed.
Toronto District School Board

REVIEWERS

Bryce Bates
Toronto District School Board

Rob Gleeson
Bluewater District School Board

Carol Miron
Toronto District School Board

Andrzej Pienkowski
Toronto District School Board

Sunil Singh
Toronto District School Board

McGraw-Hill Ryerson

Toronto   Montréal   Boston   Burr Ridge, IL   Dubuque, IA   Madison, WI   New York
San Francisco   St. Louis   Bangkok   Bogotá   Caracas   Kuala Lumpur   Lisbon   London
Madrid   Mexico City   Milan   New Delhi   Santiago   Seoul   Singapore   Sydney   Taipei

McGraw-Hill Ryerson

McGraw-Hill Ryerson
Principles of Mathematics 9 Exercise and Homework Book

ISBN-13: 978-0-07-097346-6
ISBN-10: 0-07-097346-6

http://www.mcgrawhill.ca

6 7 8 9 0 MP 1 9 8 7 6

Printed and bound in Canada

The Geometer's Sketchpad®, Key Curriculum Press, 1150 65th Street, Emeryville, CA 94608, 1-800-995-MATH.

Statistics Canada information is used with the permission of Statistics Canada. Users are forbidden to copy the data and redisseminate them, in an original or modified form, for commercial purposes, without permission from Statistics Canada. Information on the availability of the wide range of data from Statistics Canada can be obtained from Statistics Canada's Regional Offices, its World Wide Web site at http://www.statcan.ca, and its toll-free number 1-800-263-1136.

PUBLISHER: Linda Allison
ASSOCIATE PUBLISHER: Kristi Clark
PROJECT MANAGER: Maggie Cheverie, Janice Dyer
DEVELOPMENTAL EDITOR: Julia Cochrane, Jackie Lacoursiere
MANAGER, EDITORIAL SERVICES: Crystal Shortt
SUPERVISING EDITOR: Janie Deneau
EDITORIAL ASSISTANT: Erin Hartley
MANAGER, PRODUCTION SERVICES: Yolanda Pigden
PRODUCTION COORDINATOR: Zonia Strynatka
COVER DESIGN: Pronk & Associates; Dianna Little
ELECTRONIC PAGE MAKE-UP: Jackie Lacoursiere
COVER IMAGE: Paul Rapson/Science Photo Library

Contents

Prerequisite Skills 1

Chapter 1 Mathematical Processes

    1.1 Focus on Problem Solving..27

    1.2 Focus on Communicating 28

    1.3 Focus on Connecting..29

    1.4 Focus on Representing 30

    1.5 Focus on Selecting Tools and Computational Strategies...................31

    1.6 Focus on Reasoning and Proving..32

    1.7 Focus on Reflecting 33

    Chapter 1 Review...34

Chapter 2 Relations

    2.1 Hypotheses and Sources of Data..35

    2.2 Sampling Principles 37

    2.3 Use Scatter Plots to Analyse Data 39

    2.4 Trends, Interpolation, and Extrapolation 41

    2.5 Linear and Non-Linear Relations...44

    2.6 Distance-Time Graphs 47

    Chapter 2 Review...49

Chapter 3 Polynomials

    3.1 Build Algebraic Models Using Concrete Materials............................51

    3.2 Work With Exponents...53

    3.3 Discover the Exponent Laws 55

    3.4 Communicate With Algebra 57

    3.5 Collect Like Terms 60

    3.6 Add and Subtract Polynomials...62

    3.7 The Distributive Property 65

    Chapter 3 Review...67

Chapter 4 Equations

4.1 Solve Simple Equations 69

4.2 Solve Multi-Step Equations 71

4.3 Solve Equations Involving Fractions 73

4.4 Modelling With Formulas 75

4.5 Modelling With Algebra 77

Chapter 4 Review 79

Chapter 5 Modelling With Graphs

5.1 Direct Variation 81

5.2 Partial Variation 83

5.3 Slope 85

5.4 Slope as a Rate of Change 87

5.5 First Differences 90

5.6 Connecting Variation, Slope, and First Differences 93

Chapter 5 Review 95

Chapter 6 Analyse Linear Relations

6.1 The Equation of a Line in Slope y-Intercept Form: $y = mx + b$ 97

6.2 The Equation of a Line in Standard Form: $Ax + By + C = 0$ 100

6.3 Graph a Line Using Intercepts 102

6.4 Parallel and Perpendicular Lines 104

6.5 Find an Equation for a Line Given the Slope and a Point 107

6.6 Find an Equation for a Line Given Two Points 109

6.7 Linear Systems 112

Chapter 6 Review 115

Chapter 7 Geometric Relationships

7.1 Angle Relationships in Triangles 117

7.2 Angle Relationships in Quadrilaterals 119

7.3 Angle Relationships in Polygons 122

7.4 Midpoints and Medians in Triangles 125

7.5 Midpoints and Diagonals in Quadrilaterals 127

Chapter 7 Review...129

Chapter 8 Measurement Relationships

    8.1 Apply the Pythagorean Theorem 131

    8.2 Perimeter and Area of Composite Figures.................................134

    8.3 Surface Area and Volume of Prisms and Pyramids.....................137

    8.4 Surface Area of a Cone...139

    8.5 Volume of a Cone 141

    8.6 Surface Area of a Sphere 144

    8.7 Volume of a Sphere 146

    Chapter 8 Review...149

Chapter 9 Optimizing Measurements

    9.1 Investigate Measurement Concepts 151

    9.2 Perimeter and Area Relationships of a Rectangle........................154

    9.3 Minimize the Surface Area of a Square-Based Prism 156

    9.4 Maximize the Volume of a Square-Based Prism.........................159

    9.5 Maximize the Volume of a Cylinder 161

    9.6 Minimize the Surface Area of a Cylinder.................................163

    Chapter 9 Review...165

Challenge Questions 167

Answers..177

Prerequisite Skills: Lowest Common Denominator

Principles of Mathematics 9, Student Skills Book, pages 1–2

Practise

1. Use multiples to find the LCD for each pair of fractions.

   a) $\dfrac{1}{3}, \dfrac{1}{4}$

   b) $\dfrac{1}{2}, \dfrac{1}{5}$

   c) $\dfrac{1}{8}, \dfrac{1}{9}$

2. Use multiples to find the LCD for each pair of fractions.

   a) $\dfrac{1}{5}, \dfrac{1}{6}$

   b) $\dfrac{1}{7}, \dfrac{1}{8}$

   c) $\dfrac{1}{5}, \dfrac{1}{10}$

3. Use prime factors to find the LCD for each pair of fractions.

   a) $\dfrac{1}{3}, \dfrac{1}{5}$

   b) $\dfrac{1}{4}, \dfrac{1}{8}$

   c) $\dfrac{1}{8}, \dfrac{1}{12}$

4. Use prime factors to find the LCD for each pair of fractions.

   a) $\dfrac{1}{6}, \dfrac{1}{9}$

   b) $\dfrac{1}{10}, \dfrac{1}{12}$

   c) $\dfrac{1}{10}, \dfrac{1}{16}$

5. Find the LCD for each set of fractions.

   a) $\dfrac{1}{2}, \dfrac{1}{3}, \dfrac{1}{6}$

   b) $\dfrac{1}{3}, \dfrac{1}{5}, \dfrac{1}{15}$

6. Find the LCD for each set of fractions.

   a) $\dfrac{1}{6}, \dfrac{1}{9}, \dfrac{1}{18}$

   b) $\dfrac{1}{3}, \dfrac{1}{4}, \dfrac{1}{5}$

7. Use the LCD to write equivalent fractions.

   a) $\dfrac{3}{4}, \dfrac{5}{6}$

   b) $\dfrac{5}{8}, \dfrac{4}{10}$

8. Use the LCD to write equivalent fractions.

   a) $\dfrac{1}{3}, \dfrac{3}{4}, \dfrac{5}{8}$

   b) $\dfrac{1}{2}, \dfrac{2}{3}, \dfrac{3}{8}$

Prerequisite Skills: Add and Subtract Fractions
Principles of Mathematics 9, Student Skills Book, pages 3–4

Practise

1. Find each sum or difference. Express your answers in lowest terms.

a) $\dfrac{3}{7} + \dfrac{4}{7}$

b) $\dfrac{5}{6} + \dfrac{4}{6}$

c) $\dfrac{4}{5} - \dfrac{1}{5}$

d) $\dfrac{7}{8} - \dfrac{5}{8}$

2. Find each sum.

a) $\dfrac{5}{8} + \dfrac{1}{4}$

b) $\dfrac{7}{12} + \dfrac{5}{6}$

c) $\dfrac{5}{14} + \dfrac{3}{7}$

3. Find each sum.

a) $\dfrac{3}{4} + \dfrac{5}{6}$

b) $\dfrac{3}{4} + \dfrac{2}{5}$

c) $\dfrac{2}{3} + \dfrac{2}{7}$

4. Find each difference.

a) $\dfrac{5}{6} - \dfrac{2}{3}$

b) $\dfrac{5}{14} - \dfrac{1}{7}$

c) $\dfrac{7}{10} - \dfrac{2}{5}$

5. Find each difference.

a) $\dfrac{5}{6} - \dfrac{2}{5}$

b) $\dfrac{5}{7} - \dfrac{1}{3}$

c) $\dfrac{7}{9} - \dfrac{1}{4}$

6. Find each difference.

a) $4\dfrac{3}{5} - 2\dfrac{2}{3}$

b) $5\dfrac{1}{4} - 3\dfrac{1}{6}$

c) $2\dfrac{2}{7} - 1\dfrac{4}{5}$

7. During one week, Diwani studied for $3\dfrac{1}{2}$ h on Monday, $2\dfrac{1}{4}$ h on Tuesday, and $2\dfrac{5}{6}$ h on Wednesday.

a) Find the total number of hours that Diwani studied for this week.

b) For how much longer did she study on Monday than on Wednesday?

c) For how much longer did she study on Wednesday than on Tuesday?

Prerequisite Skills: Multiply and Divide Fractions
Principles of Mathematics 9, Student Skills Book, pages 5–6

Practise
Express your answers in lowest terms.

1. Multiply.

   a) $\dfrac{2}{7} \times \dfrac{3}{5}$

   b) $\dfrac{4}{7} \times \dfrac{7}{9}$

   c) $\dfrac{3}{8} \times \dfrac{4}{5}$

   d) $\dfrac{2}{3} \times \dfrac{7}{10}$

2. Multiply.

   a) $\dfrac{3}{4} \times 1\dfrac{2}{3}$

   b) $2\dfrac{3}{5} \times \dfrac{1}{6}$

   c) $5\dfrac{1}{7} \times 2\dfrac{1}{6}$

   d) $3\dfrac{4}{5} \times 4\dfrac{1}{2}$

3. Divide.

   a) $\dfrac{5}{8} \div \dfrac{5}{6}$

   b) $\dfrac{6}{7} \div \dfrac{4}{5}$

   c) $\dfrac{3}{14} \div \dfrac{7}{10}$

   d) $\dfrac{3}{4} \div \dfrac{5}{18}$

4. Divide.

   a) $1\dfrac{2}{3} \div \dfrac{3}{4}$

   b) $\dfrac{5}{8} \div 2\dfrac{1}{2}$

   c) $1\dfrac{5}{9} \div 4\dfrac{2}{3}$

   d) $3\dfrac{2}{7} \div 4\dfrac{1}{3}$

5. A bowl filled with lollipops is $\dfrac{3}{4}$ full. $\dfrac{2}{3}$ of these lollipops are green. What fraction of the full bowl are the green lollipops?

6. A box of blueberries is $\dfrac{2}{5}$ full. Janet and her friends had each eaten $\dfrac{1}{10}$ of a box of blueberries. How many people ate blueberries?

Prerequisite Skills: Add Integers

Principles of Mathematics 9, Student Skills Book, **page 7**

Practise

1. Use a number line to model each sum.
   a) $-3 + 5$
   b) $-4 + 2$
   c) $5 + (-4)$
   d) $4 + (-6)$

2. Use a number line to model each sum.
   a) $-1 + (-3)$
   b) $-2 + 2$
   c) $3 + (-3)$
   d) $0 + (-5)$

3. Find each sum.
   a) $5 + (-7)$
   b) $-3 + 6$
   c) $-3 + 2$
   d) $-5 + (-2)$

4. Find each sum.
   a) $-5 + 5$
   b) $6 + (-6)$
   c) $0 + (-3)$
   d) $-8 + 0$

5. Find each sum.
   a) $-6 + (-4)$
   b) $3 + (-1)$
   c) $4 + (-5)$
   d) $0 + (-2)$

6. Find each sum.
   a) $-4 + (-5) + 3$
   b) $6 + (-3) + 3$
   c) $3 + (-2) + (-4)$
   d) $-5 + 4 + (-3)$

7. Find each sum.
   a) $-2 + 6 + (-3)$
   b) $-5 + (-4) + (-3)$
   c) $3 + (-8) + 7$
   d) $4 + (-12) + 3$

8. Find each sum.
   a) $-3 + 2 + (-4) + 1$
   b) $6 + (-2) + (-5) + 3$
   c) $-8 + 4 + (-5) + (-3)$
   d) $5 + (-7) + 3 + (-9)$

9. Find each sum.
   a) $9 + (-5) + (-1) + 4$
   b) $-2 + 6 + (-3) + (-7)$
   c) $6 + (-8) + 4 + (-3)$
   d) $-2 + 1 + (-9) + 8$

10. The temperature in Stratford starts at $-5°C$, rises $18°C$, and then falls $8°C$. What is the final temperature?

11. On Monday the price of a company's stock is $35 per share. On Tuesday the price drops $4, on Wednesday it rises $7, on Thursday it drops $6, and on Friday it rises $7. What was the price of the stock per share at the end of the week?

Practise

1. Subtract.
   a) $7 - 5$
   b) $6 - 8$
   c) $4 - (-3)$
   d) $5 - (-2)$

2. Subtract.
   a) $4 - 4$
   b) $(-5) - (-5)$
   c) $0 - 9$
   d) $0 - (-6)$

3. Subtract.
   a) $0 - 4$
   b) $0 - (-8)$
   c) $-8 - 2$
   d) $-5 - 3$

4. Subtract.
   a) $-3 - (-8)$
   b) $-4 - (-2)$
   c) $-6 - (-6)$
   d) $-7 - 0$

5. Copy each question and fill in the ☐ with the correct integer.
   a) $-4 - \boxed{} = -7$
   b) $\boxed{} - 5 = 4$
   c) $0 - \boxed{} = -7$

6. Copy each equation and fill in the ☐ with the correct integer.
   a) $\boxed{} - (-3) = 5$
   b) $0 - \boxed{} = 3$
   c) $6 - \boxed{} = -2$

7. Evaluate.
   a) $10 - 8 - 5$
   b) $2 - 9 - (-1)$
   c) $-3 - (-4) - 11$
   d) $-15 - (-5) - (-7)$

8. Evaluate.
   a) $16 - 12 - 5$
   b) $5 - 12 - (-4)$
   c) $-4 - (-2) - 8$
   d) $-18 - (-3) - (-13)$

9. Which expressions have the same result?
   a) $9 - 4$
   b) $-5 - (-2)$
   c) $-8 - (-3)$
   d) $-2 - (-7)$
   e) $-8 - (-5)$
   f) $-9 - (-4)$

10. The average low temperature in Tobermorey in October is 5°C. In February it is 23°C lower. What is the average low temperature in Tobermorey in February?

11. The air temperature is –8°C. With the wind blowing at a speed of 18 km/h, this temperature feels like –15°C. How many degrees does the temperature change because of the wind chill?

Prerequisite Skills: Multiply and Divide Integers

Principles of Mathematics 9, Student Skills Book, **page 9**

Practise

1. Find each product.
   a) 5×7
   b) $4 \times (-3)$
   c) $(-3) \times 6$
   d) $(-2) \times (-8)$

2. Find each product.
   a) $0(9)$
   b) $(-4)(7)$
   c) $6(-7)$
   d) $(-6)(-8)$

3. Find each quotient.
   a) $18 \div 6$
   b) $12 \div (-3)$
   c) $(-16) \div 2$
   d) $(-15) \div (-5)$

4. Find each quotient.
   a) $\dfrac{0}{-4}$
   b) $\dfrac{35}{-7}$
   c) $\dfrac{-24}{6}$
   d) $\dfrac{-28}{-4}$

5. Multiply.
   a) $(-8) \times 3 \times 2$
   b) $5 \times (-2) \times 0$
   c) $6 \times (-1) \times (-3)$

6. Multiply.
   a) $(-3) \times (-5) \times (-4)$
   b) $(-6) \times 2 \times (-4)$
   c) $4 \times (-3) \times (-2)$

7. List all integers that divide evenly into each.
   a) 18
   b) −15

8. List all integers that divide evenly into each.
   a) 24
   b) −30

9. Write a multiplication expression and a division expression that would have each result.
   a) −8
   b) −15

10. Determine how each multiplication or division pattern is formed. Then, write the next two numbers.
    a) 1, 4, 16, …
    b) −400, −200, −100, …

Prerequisite Skills: Distributive Property

Principles of Mathematics 9, Student Skills Book, page 10

Practise

1. Use the distributive property to evaluate.
   a) $5(70 + 1)$
   b) $3(60 - 1)$
   c) $4(20 + 3)$
   d) $6(30 - 4)$

2. Use the distributive property to evaluate.
   a) $0.4(10 + 0.2)$
   b) $0.3(10 - 0.4)$
   c) $0.5(20 + 0.7)$
   d) $0.2(30 - 0.9)$

3. Use the distributive property to evaluate.
   a) $6(100 + 30 + 8)$
   b) $5(100 + 20 + 9)$
   c) $3(200 + 50 + 4)$
   d) $2(400 + 10 + 7)$

4. Use the distributive property to evaluate.
   a) $5(4 + 0.3 + 0.02)$
   b) $2(3 + 0.4 + 0.03)$
   c) $4(6 + 0.5 + 0.03)$
   d) $7(5 + 0.6 + 0.08)$

5. Evaluate using the distributive property.
   a) $5(41)$
   b) $3(97)$
   c) $8(43)$
   d) $9(86)$

6. Evaluate using the distributive property.
   a) $3(104)$
   b) $6(202)$
   c) $5(410)$
   d) $9(360)$

7. Evaluate using the distributive property.
   a) $7(198)$
   b) $4(227)$
   c) $3(514)$
   d) $3(799)$

8. Evaluate using the distributive property.
   a) $3(3.2)$
   b) $5(7.8)$
   c) $6(4.1)$

9. Evaluate using the distributive property.
   a) $7(8.09)$
   b) $4(6.03)$
   c) $8(9.04)$

10. Evaluate using the distributive property and mental math.
    a) $2(3.17)$
    b) $4(5.24)$
    c) $9(8.63)$

11. Evaluate using the distributive property and mental math.
    a) $30(21)$
    b) $40(29)$
    c) $50(47)$

12. Evaluate using the distributive property and mental math.
    a) $60(310)$
    b) $50(420)$
    c) $40(670)$

Prerequisite Skills: Order of Operations

Principles of Mathematics 9, Student Skills Book, page 11

Practise

1. Evaluate.

a) $3^2 + 2(3+1)^2$

b) $2^3 - 3(4-2)^2$

c) $5 + 4(9 - 3 \times 2)$

d) $7 - 3(8 - 2^2 \times 1)$

2. Evaluate.

a) $5 + 3 \times (2^4 - 2^3)$

b) $9 - 2^2 \times 3(4 - 6)$

c) $5(4^2 - 3^2) + 8$

d) $6[11 - (3+1)^2 + 3]$

3. Evaluate.

a) $(15 + 3) \div (10 - 2^3)$

b) $4 \times 3(24 \div 2^2) + 5$

c) $(5^2 - 3^2) \div 4 + 8 \times 2$

d) $6[4^3 \div (3+1)^2 - 3]$

4. Evaluate.

a) $5(-4) + (-4)^2$

b) $-20 \div (-4) - 3$

c) $(-3)(-4) + (1-3)^2$

d) $(1-5)^2 \div (1-3)$

5. Evaluate.

a) $(-1)^5 - 8 \div (-4)$

b) $(3-5)^3 \div (6-8)^2$

c) $(2^3 - 3^2)^5 - (-16) \div (-8)$

d) $[(-5)^2 - (-7)^2] \times 3 \div (-2)$

6. Evaluate.

a) $5 - 2 \times 3.1 + 4.2$

b) $(2.5 + 3^2) - 1.6$

c) $0.2(11 - 7) + (0.4)^2$

d) $2(0.7 + 0.2)^2 + 4.6$

7. Evaluate.

a) $3.2 + 0.5 \times 3 - 4$

b) $(2^2 + 4.3) - 1.2 \times 2$

c) $(0.5)^2 + 0.4(9 - 5)$

d) $8.2 + 2(1 + 2)^2$

8. Insert brackets to make each equation true.

a) $16 \div 4 - 5 \times 2^2 = -4$

b) $16 \div 4 - 5 \times 2^2 = -16$

c) $16 \div 4 - 5 \times 2^2 = -64$

9. Copy each equation and use the symbols +, −, ×, ÷, and ( ) to make it true.

a) $4 \boxed{} 2 \boxed{} 3 = -2$

b) $20 \boxed{} 5 \boxed{} 9 = -5$

c) $-12 \boxed{} 3 \boxed{} -6 = 2$

d) $10 \boxed{} 3 \boxed{} -2 = -14$

Prerequisite Skills: Bar Graphs
Principles of Mathematics 9, Student Skills Book, pages 12–13

Practise

1. This bar graph shows the number of people that visited a shopping mall during one week.

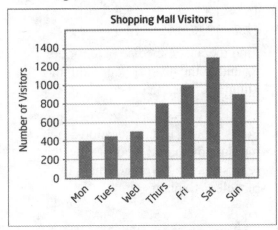

a) On which day did the fewest people visit the shopping mall? On which day did the most people visit the shopping mall?

b) Describe any trends in the number of customers during this week at the shopping mall.

2. This table shows the number of members attending a golf club during one week.

Day of the Week	Number of Members
Monday	238
Tuesday	245
Wednesday	220
Thursday	264
Friday	270
Saturday	350
Sunday	325

a) Make a bar graph of the data.

b) Describe any trends in member attendance during this week at the golf club.

3. This bar graph shows the number of visitors during the year 2005 to museum.

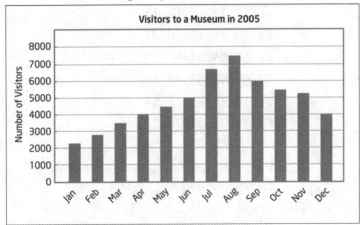

a) In which month were the fewest visitors in the museum? In which month were the most visitors in the museum?

b) Describe any trends in the number of visitors during this year at the museum.

4. This table shows the average cost of 1 L of milk in various cities across Canada for one week in July in 2006.

City	Average Cost of Milk ($/L)
St. John's, NL	1.15
Charlottetown, PE	1.11
Halifax, NS	1.15
Saint John, MB	1.17
Montreal, QC	1.08
Toronto, ON	1.05
Winnipeg, MB	1.03
Regina, SK	1.04
Calgary, AB	1.06
Vancouver, BC	1.08

a) Make a bar graph of the data.

b) In what regions was the average cost of milk the least? Why?

Prerequisite Skills: Measures of Central Tendency

Principles of Mathematics 9, Student Skills Book, **pages 14**

Practise

1. Find the mean, median, and mode for each set of data.
   a) 13, 15, 17, 14, 15
   b) 30, 35, 32, 30, 31
   c) 52, 55, 54, 55, 56
   d) 40, 42, 43, 43, 46
   e) 88, 83, 85, 88, 84
   f) 21, 25, 24, 26, 21

2. Find the mean, median, and mode for each set of data.
   a) 31, 32, 34, 32, 35, 37
   b) 51, 54, 56, 55, 57, 54
   c) 81, 85, 84, 82, 85, 87
   d) 60, 67, 68, 68, 62, 65
   e) 46, 45, 47, 44, 41, 47
   f) 90, 95, 94, 90, 93, 96

3. Find the mean, median, and mode for each set of data. Round to one decimal place, when necessary.
   a) 19, 23, 26, 21, 24, 17, 23
   b) 41, 34, 36, 34, 37, 34, 40
   c) 74, 65, 64, 72, 75, 66, 64
   d) 40, 54, 48, 48, 52, 45, 53

4. Find the mean, median, and mode for each set of data. Round to two decimal places, when necessary.
   a) 2.3, 2.1, 1.9, 1.9, 2.6
   b) 4.5, 4.3, 3.4, 3.8, 4.3
   c) 6.4, 6.5, 6.4, 7.4, 7.6, 6.4
   d) 8.0, 9.4, 8.8, 8.8, 9.2, 8.4

5. The masses, in kilograms, of twelve different models of bicycles are shown.

14.8	15.1	12.5	13.7
15.2	12.7	13.5	12.3
12.7	13.8	14.7	13.9

   Find the mean, median, and mode. Round to the nearest hundredth of kilogram, when necessary.

6. For the mass data in question 5, which measure of central tendency best represents the "average" mass of bicycles? Explain.

7. The weights, to the nearest kilogram, of a group of 16-year-olds are shown.

67.2	68.3	59.7	67.5
58.3	70.3	62.3	69.4
72.5	58.2	62.5	71.3
68.4	90.2	69.4	72.3
69.4	71.4	72.4	67.5

   Find the mean, median, and mode.

8. For the weight data in question 7, which measure of central tendency represents the "average" weight of 16-year-olds? Explain.

Practise

1. This table shows the ages and weekly incomes of 15 employees at a company.

Age (years)	Weekly Income ($)
27	692
29	705
30	650
32	725
33	700
35	740
38	600
42	750
45	780
46	760
47	800.
50	850
51	840
55	860
59	900

Make a scatter plot of the data. Put age on the horizontal axis and income on the vertical axis.

2. This table shows the lengths, from the nose to the end of the tail, and the masses of different types of cats.

Type of Cat	Length (cm)	Mass (kg)
Lion	300	180
Lioness	270	140
Cheetah	180	45
Mountain Lion	240	90
Jaguar	260	140
Leopard	265	70
Tiger	270	190
Tigress	240	135
Lynx	90	30

Make a scatter plot of the data. Put length on the horizontal axis and mass on the vertical axis.

3. This table shows approximate driving distances and times from North Bay, Ontario to various cities in Ontario.

City	Distance (km)	Driving Time (h)
Barrie	237	3.0
Haileybury	147	1.5
Kapuskasing	478	5.0
London	498	6.0
New Liskeard	149	1.5
Ottawa	365	4.0
Sault Ste Marie	434	4.5
Sudbury	125	1.5
Thunder Bay	1032	11.0
Timmins	350	4.0
Toronto	330	3.5
Windsor	675	8.0

Make a scatter plot of the data. Put distance on the x-axis and driving time on the y-axis. Label the axes, and include a title for the scatter plot.

4. This table shows the height and the circumference of a tree at different ages.

Age (years)	Height (m)	Circumference (cm)
1	1.1	15.2
2	1.1	18.2
3	2.4	20.7
4	2.5	23.2
5	3.1	27.0
6	4.3	29.5
7	4.5	32.0
8	5.3	33.9

Make a scatter plot of the data. Put height on the x-axis and circumference on the y-axis. Label the axes, and include a title for the scatter plot.

Prerequisite Skills: Linear Relationships
Principles of Mathematics 9, Student Skills Book, pages 17–18

Practise

1. This graph shows that the relationship between the cost of oranges and quantity of oranges, in kilograms, is linear.

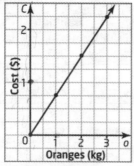

a) Copy and complete the table.

Oranges (kg)	Cost ($)
1	
2	
3	

b) Identify the coordinates where the graph crosses the vertical axis. Explain the meaning of this point.

2. This graph shows that the relationship between the cost of parking a car and the time, in hours, is linear.

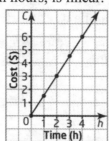

a) Copy and complete the table.

Time (h)	Cost ($)
1	
	3.00
3	
	6.00

b) Identify the coordinates where the graph crosses the vertical axis. Explain the meaning of this point.

3. Jean records the height of a bean plant after planting it in her garden.

Time (weeks)	Height (cm)
1	10
2	14
3	18
4	22
7	34

a) Graph this linear relationship.

b) When does the height of the tomato plant reach 30 cm?

c) Identify the coordinates where the graph crosses the vertical axis. Explain the meaning of this point.

4. This table shows how the distance a person walks changes with time.

Time (h)	Distance (km)
1	4
2	8
3	12
4	16

a) Graph this linear relationship.

b) How many hours does the person take to walk 14 km?

c) How far does the person walk in 1.5 h?

d) Identify the coordinates where the graph crosses the vertical axis. Explain the meaning of this point.

Prerequisite Skills: Rational Numbers

Principles of Mathematics 9, Student Skills Book, pages 19–20

Practise

1. In each part, decide which rational number is not equivalent to the others.

   a) $\dfrac{3}{5}$, 0.6, $\dfrac{-3}{-5}$, $\dfrac{3}{-5}$

   b) $-\dfrac{5}{8}$, $\dfrac{-5}{-8}$, -0.625, $\dfrac{-5}{8}$

   c) -0.25, $-\dfrac{1}{4}$, $\dfrac{-1}{-4}$, $\dfrac{-1}{4}$

   d) $\dfrac{-12}{5}$, 2.4, $2\dfrac{2}{5}$, , $\dfrac{-12}{-5}$

2. Express each rational number in decimal form.

   a) $\dfrac{4}{5}$

   b) $-\dfrac{7}{10}$

   c) $\dfrac{-3}{8}$

   d) $\dfrac{11}{4}$

3. Express each rational number as a quotient of two integers.

   a) $1\dfrac{2}{5}$

   b) 0.9

   c) $-3\dfrac{2}{9}$

   d) -4.3

4. Write three equivalent rational numbers for each number.

   a) $\dfrac{-5}{8}$

   b) $\dfrac{-4}{-3}$

   c) -0.75

5. Write three equivalent rational numbers for each number.

   a) $\dfrac{-6}{4}$

   b) $-\dfrac{4}{12}$

   c) $\dfrac{-12}{-10}$

6. Graph the rational numbers on a number line. Then, write the numbers in order, from least to greatest.

   -3.2, 4, $1\dfrac{3}{10}$, 2.5, -3, $-\dfrac{9}{5}$

7. Copy each math sentence. Fill in each ☐ with the symbols <, >, or = to make the statement true.

   a) $\dfrac{2}{-5}$ ☐ $\dfrac{-3}{8}$

   b) $\dfrac{5}{-3}$ ☐ $\dfrac{-7}{2}$

   c) $\dfrac{5}{-4}$ ☐ $\dfrac{-15}{12}$

Prerequisite Skills: Rates
Principles of Mathematics 9, Student Skills Book, **page 21**

Practise

1. Calculate each unit rate.
   a) A car travelled 750 km in 8 h.
   b) Janeena ran 10 km in 2 h.
   c) Jane swam 100 m in 80 s.

2. Calculate each unit rate.
   a) Sushil walked 8 km in 4 h.
   b) A bus travelled 450 km in 5 h.
   c) A train travelled 380 km in 4 h.

3. Calculate each unit rate.
   a) Five limes cost $1.30.
   b) Two pairs of jeans cost $70.00.
   c) Twelve cornmeal muffins cost $15.00.

4. Calculate each unit rate.
   a) Eight bottles of water cost $9.60.
   b) Four apples cost $2.40.
   c) Three mugs cost $13.50.

5. Calculate each unit rate.
   a) A bag of cookies costs $3.20 for 800g.
   b) A box of crackers costs $2.25 for 750 g.
   c) A box of raisins costs $1.95 for 425 g.

6. Calculate each unit rate.
   a) A cookie recipe calls for 400 mL of chocolate chips to make 80 cookies.
   b) A photocopy machine prints 400 pages in 2 min.
   c) A ceiling fan makes 150 rotations in 5 min.

7. Which brand of jam is a better buy?
   Brand A: $3.55 for 300 g
   Brand B: $5.92 for 450 g

8. Which brand of corn syrup is a better buy?
   Brand A: $13.75 for 400 mL
   Brand B: $16.25 for 550 mL

9. Which brand of popcorn is a better buy?
   Brand A: $5.25 for 500 g
   Brand B: $4.80 for 450 g

10. Which brand of laundry soap is a better buy?
    Brand A: $17.00 for 2.2 kg
    Brand B: $13.95for 1.9 kg

11. Terri and José work part-time jobs at different convenience stores.
    Terri earns $38 for 4 h of work.
    Jose earns $90 for 10 h of work.
    a) Which person receives the better hourly rate of pay?
    b) How much better is the hourly rate of pay?

12. Colette and Glen work part-time jobs at different bookstores.
    Colette earns $45 for 6 h of work.
    Glen earns $29 for 4 h of work.
    a) Which person receives the better hourly rate of pay?
    b) How much better is the hourly rate of pay?

Prerequisite Skills: Ratio and Proportion
Principles of Mathematics 9, Student Skills Book, **page 22–23**

Practise

1. Write each ratio in simplest form.
   a) 4:14   b) 6:18
   c) 25:40   d) 100:40

2. Write each ratio in simplest form.
   a) 24:36   b) 140:49
   c) 44:121   d) 90:81

3. To make 1000 mL of lemonade Maanasa uses 350 mL of frozen concentrate and 650 mL of water.
   a) Write a ratio in simplest form, to compare the amount of frozen concentrate to the total amount of lemonade.
   b) Write a ratio, in simplest form, to compare the amount of water to the total amount of lemonade.
   c) Write a ratio, in simplest form, to compare the amount of frozen concentrate to the amount of water.

4. How much frozen concentrate and water are needed to make 1500 mL of the lemonade in question 3?

5. One recipe for fresh limeade uses 900 mL of lime juice, 3000 mL of water, and 500 mL of sugar.
   a) Write a ratio, in simplest form, to compare the amount of lime juice to the amount of water.
   b) Write a ratio, in simplest form, to compare the amount of lime juice to the amount of sugar.
   c) Write a ratio, in simplest form, to compare the amount of water to the amount of sugar.

6. Refer to the limeade recipe in question 5.
   a) Write a ratio, in simplest form, to compare the amount of lime juice to the total amount of limeade.
   b) Write a ratio, in simplest form, to compare the amount of water to the total amount of limeade.
   c) Write a ratio, in simplest form, to compare the amount of sugar to the total amount of limeade.

7. Use the limeade recipe in question 5.
   a) How much sugar is needed to mix with 540 mL of lime juice?
   b) How much water is needed to mix with 200 mL of sugar.

8. Three out of five people prefer Choco chocolate chip cookies. How many would prefer Choco chocolate chip cookies in a group of 200 people?

9. Five out of seven people prefer Cranba cranberry juice. How many would prefer Cranba cranberry juice in a group of 350 people?

10. Seven out of nine dogs prefer Crunch Chow dry dog food. How many dogs would prefer Crunch Chow dry dog food in a group of 180 dogs?

Prerequisite Skills: Percents

Principles of Mathematics 9, Student Skills Book, page 24–25

Practise

1. Express as a percent.
   a) 0.05
   b) 0.125
   c) 0.6
   d) 0.35
   e) 1.24

2. Express as a percent.
   a) $\dfrac{3}{4}$
   b) $\dfrac{5}{8}$
   c) $\dfrac{3}{5}$
   d) $\dfrac{8}{5}$

3. Express as a percent. Round to one decimal place, if necessary.
   a) $\dfrac{5}{11}$
   b) $\dfrac{1}{3}$
   c) $\dfrac{4}{9}$
   d) $\dfrac{2}{7}$
   e) $\dfrac{5}{3}$

4. Write as a decimal.
   a) 29%
   b) 38.5%
   c) 8%
   d) 115%

5. Amanda's height increased from 140 cm to 148 cm in one year.
   a) Find Amanda's increase in height as a percent. Round to one decimal place.
   b) How tall would Amanda have to grow to have a 4% increase in height over the year? Round to the nearest centimetre.

6. A coat was originally priced at $149.99. The coat is on sale for $104.99.
   a) Find the percent discount, to the nearest whole number.
   b) What sale price would represent a 25% discount?

7. The mass of a compound is made up of the following four elements.
   - oxygen 75%
   - carbon 15%
   - hydrogen 8%
   - nitrogen 2%
   a) Find the mass of each element in a compound with a mass of 8 kg.
   b) Find the mass of each element in a compound with a mass of 20 kg.

8. A retailer buys a sweater for $20, and sells the sweater for $47.99.
   a) Find the percent markup, to the nearest whole number.
   b) What selling price would represent a 120% markup?

Prerequisite Skills: Powers

Principles of Mathematics 9, Student Skills Book, page 26–27

Practise

1. Write each as a power in exponential form.
   a) $4 \times 4 \times 4 \times 4 \times 4 \times 4$
   b) $7 \times 7 \times 7 \times 7 \times 7 \times 7 \times 7 \times 7$
   c) $3 \times 3 \times 3 \times 3$
   d) $11 \times 11 \times 11$

2. Write each as a power in exponential form.
   a) $2.8 \times 2.8 \times 2.8 \times 2.8 \times 2.8$
   b) $6.1 \times 6.1 \times 6.1$
   c) $3.4 \times 3.4 \times 3.4 \times 3.4 \times 3.4$
   d) $1.7 \times 1.7 \times 1.7 \times 1.7 \times 1.7 \times 1.7$

3. Write each as a power in exponential form.
   a) $(-1) \times (-1) \times (-1)$
   b) $(-6) \times (-6) \times (-6) \times (-6) \times (-6)$
   c) $(-3) \times (-3) \times (-3) \times (-3)$
   d) $(-7) \times (-7) \times (-7) \times (-7) \times (-7) \times (-7)$

4. Write each as a power in exponential form.
   a) $x \times x \times x \times x \times x$
   b) $y \times y$
   c) $m \times m \times m$
   d) $d \times d \times d \times d \times d$

5. Expand each power and then evaluate.
   a) 7^2
   b) 4^5
   c) 10^4
   d) 1^{13}
   e) 5^3
   f) 2^8

6. Evaluate.
   a) 2.3^4
   b) 1.4^5
   c) 0.3^3
   d) 0.25^2

7. Evaluate.
   a) 12.1^2
   b) 10.5^3
   c) 15.4^3
   d) 20.7^2

8. Express 16 as
   a) a power of 4
   b) a power of 2

9. Express 729 as
   a) a power of 27
   b) a power of 9
   c) a power of 3

10. Write each power.
   a) 512 as a power of 8
   b) 2401 as a power of 7
   c) 1 000 000 000 as a power of 10

11. Copy each equation. Find the correct number to make the equation true.
   a) $3^5 = \square$

   b) $2^{\square} = 256$

   c) $\square^4 = 6561$

Prerequisite Skills: Classify Triangles
Principles of Mathematics 9, Student Skills Book, page 28–29

Practise

1. Classify each triangle using its side lengths.

   a)
   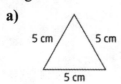
   5 cm, 5 cm, 5 cm

   b)
   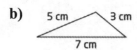
   5 cm, 3 cm, 7 cm

   c)
   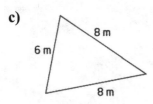
   8 m, 6 m, 8 m

2. Classify each triangle as acute, right or obtuse.

   a)
   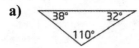
   38°, 32°, 110°

   b)
   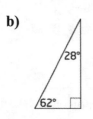
   28°, 62°

   c)
   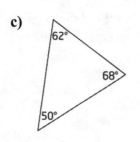
   62°, 68°, 50°

3. Classify each triangle in two ways.

   a)
   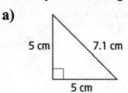
   5 cm, 7.1 cm, 5 cm

   b)
   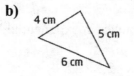
   4 cm, 5 cm, 6 cm

   c)
   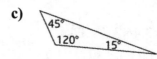
   45°, 120°, 15°

   d)
   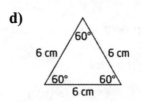
   60°, 6 cm, 6 cm, 60°, 60°, 6 cm

4. a) Name all triangles in the figure.
   b) Classify each triangle by its angle measures.

   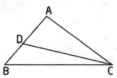

5. a) Name all triangles in the figure.
   b) Classify each triangle in two ways.

Prerequisite Skills: Classify Polygons

Principles of Mathematics 9, Student Skills Book, page 30–31

Practise

1. Classify each polygon according to its number of sides and tell whether it is regular or irregular.

   a)

   b)

   c)

   d)

   e)

   f)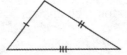

   g)

2. Classify each quadrilateral. Give reasons for your answer.

   a)

   b)

   c)

   d)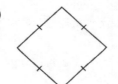

   e)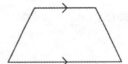

3. Name and classify the two quadrilaterals found in each of the following figures.

   a)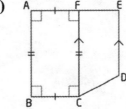

   b)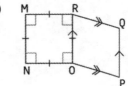

Prerequisite Skills: Angle Properties
Principles of Mathematics 9, Student Skills Book, **page 32-34**

Practise

1. Find the measure of angle *x*.

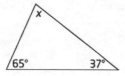

2. Find the measure of ∠ABC.

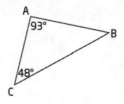

3. Find the measure of ∠PQR.

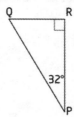

4. Find the measure of each unknown angle.

a)

b)

c)

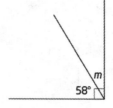

5. Find the measure of each unknown angle.

a)

b)

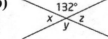

6. Find the measure of each unknown angle.

a)

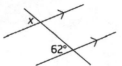

b)

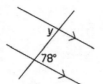

c)

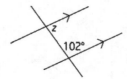

7. Find the measures of angles *x*, *y*, and *z*. Give reasons for each answer.

a)

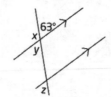

b)

Prerequisite Skills: Calculate Perimeter and Circumference
Principles of Mathematics 9, Student Skills Book, page 35–36

Practise

1. Find the perimeter of each shape.

a)

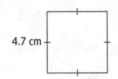

4.7 cm

b)

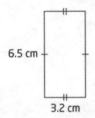

6.5 cm

3.2 cm

c) 2.5 m

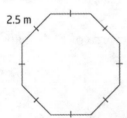

d) 16 mm

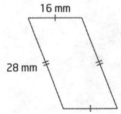

28 mm

e)

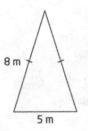

8 m

5 m

f) 4.2 cm

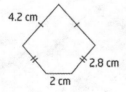

2.8 cm

2 cm

2. Calculate the circumference of each circle. Round answers to the nearest tenth of a unit.

a)

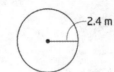

2.4 m

b)

9.1 mm

c)

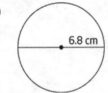

6.8 cm

d)

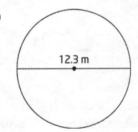

12.3 m

3. A parking area has the dimensions shown.

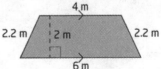

4 m

2.2 m

2 m

5 m

Find the perimeter of the parking area.

4. A patio has the dimensions shown.

4 m

2.2 m
2 m
2.2 m

6 m

Find the perimeter of the patio.

Prerequisite Skills: Apply Area Formulas

Principles of Mathematics 9, Student Skills Book, page 37–38

Practise

1. Determine the area of each shape.

a)
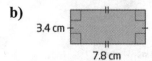
7.3 cm

b)
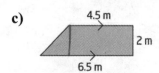
3.4 cm
7.8 cm

c)
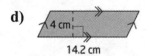
4.5 m
2 m
6.5 m

d)
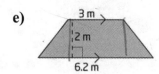
4 cm
14.2 cm

e)
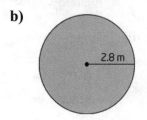
3 m
2 m
6.2 m

2. Determine the area of each shape. Round answers to the nearest tenth of a square unit.

a)

5.8 cm
5.2 cm

b)

2.8 m

3. Determine the area of each shape. Round answers to the nearest tenth of a square unit.

a)
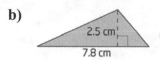
8.6 cm

b)
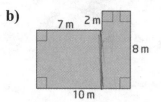
2.5 cm
7.8 cm

4. Determine the area of each shape.

a)

4 m
1.8 m
2 m
6 m

b)

7 m   2 m
8 m
10 m

c)

57 mm
57 mm
40 mm

d)
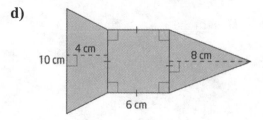
4 cm
8 cm
10 cm
6 cm

Prerequisite Skills: Calculate Surface Area and Volume
Principles of Mathematics 9, Student Skills Book, page 39–40

Practise

1. Determine the surface area of each three-dimensional figure. If necessary, round answers to the nearest square unit.

a)

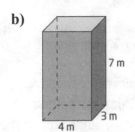

5 cm
5 cm
5 cm

b)

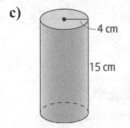

7 m
3 m
4 m

c)

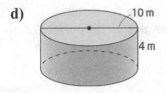

4 cm
15 cm

d)

10 m
4 m

2. Determine the volume of each three-dimensional figure in question 1. If necessary, round answers to the nearest cubic unit.

3. Calculate the surface area and volume of each three-dimensional figure. Round answers to the nearest tenth of a square unit or cubic unit.

a)

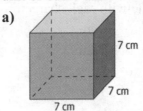

7 cm
7 cm
7 cm

b)

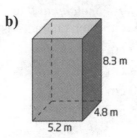

8.3 m
4.8 m
5.2 m

c)

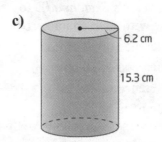

6.2 cm
15.3 cm

d)

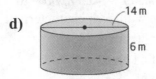

14 m
6 m

4. Determine the surface area and the volume of the triangular prism.

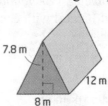

7.8 m
12 m
8 m

Prerequisite Skills: Use *The Geometer's Sketchpad*®
Principles of Mathematics 9, Student Skills Book, page 41–42

Practise

*Either draw a sketch of your results or choose **Print** from the **File** menu.*

1. Use *The Geometer's Sketchpad*® to create a triangle with each characteristic.
   a) a perimeter of 28 cm
   b) a perimeter of 15 cm
   c) a perimeter of 18 cm
   d) a perimeter of 30 cm

2. Use *The Geometer's Sketchpad*® to create a triangle with each characteristic.
   a) an area of 20 cm^2
   b) an area of 38 cm^2
   c) an area of 40 cm^2
   d) an area of 45 cm

3. Use *The Geometer's Sketchpad*® to create a circle with each characteristic.
   a) a circumference of 14 cm
   b) a circumference of 20 cm
   c) a circumference of 28 cm
   d) a circumference of 21 cm

4. Use *The Geometer's Sketchpad*® to create a circle with each characteristic.
   a) an area of 30 cm^2
   b) an area of 42 cm^2
   c) an area of 26 cm^2
   d) an area of 15 cm^2

5. Use *The Geometer's Sketchpad*® to create a quadrilateral with each characteristic.
   a) a perimeter of 16 cm
   b) a perimeter of 22 cm
   c) a perimeter of 36 cm
   d) a perimeter of 17 cm

6. Use *The Geometer's Sketchpad*® to create a quadrilateral with each characteristic.
   a) an area of 32 cm^2
   b) an area of 16 cm^2
   c) an area of 26 cm^2
   d) an area of 27 cm^2

7. Use *The Geometer's Sketchpad*® to create any triangle.
   a) Measure its perimeter and area.
   b) Create a quadrilateral that has approximately the same area as the triangle.
   c) Compare the perimeters of the two figures.

8. Use *The Geometer's Sketchpad*® to create any quadrilateral.
   a) Measure its perimeter and area.
   b) Create a circle that has approximately the same circumference as the perimeter of the quadrilateral.
   c) Compare the areas of the two figures.

Prerequisite Skills: Compare Figures

Principles of Mathematics 9, Student Skills Book, **page 43–44**

Practise

1. **a)** Calculate the surface area and volume of the two open-topped containers.

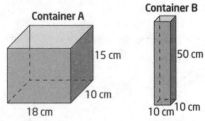

   b) Which container has the larger surface area?

   c) Which container has the larger volume?

2. **a)** Calculate the surface area and volume of the two open-topped containers.

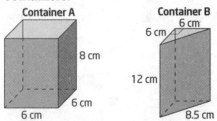

   b) Which container has the larger surface area?

   c) Which container has the larger volume?

3. **a)** Calculate the surface area and volume of the two open-topped containers. Round to the nearest square unit or cubic unit.

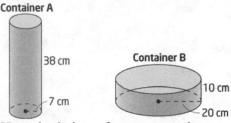

   b) How do their surface areas and volumes compare?

4. **a)** Calculate the surface area and volume of the two open-topped containers.

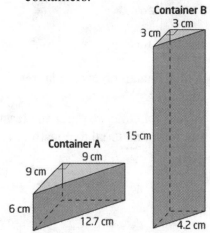

   b) Which container has the larger surface area?

   c) Which container has the larger volume?

5. **a)** Calculate the surface area and volume of the two open-topped containers. Round to the nearest square unit or cubic unit, if necessary.

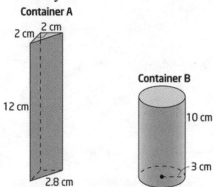

   b) Which container has the larger surface area?

   c) Which container has the larger volume?

6. Compare the surface area and volume of the two open-topped containers. Round to the nearest square unit or cubic unit, if necessary.

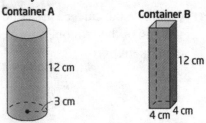

Container A

12 cm

3 cm

Container B

12 cm

4 cm 4 cm

a) Which container has the largest capacity?

b) Which container requires the least amount of material to construct it?

1.1 Focus on Problem Solving
Principles of Mathematics 9, pages 6–9

A

1. Continue each pattern for three more terms. Describe how to find successive terms.
   a) 3, 8, 13
   b) 2, 6, 18
   c) 1, 2, 2, 4, 8
   d) 2, 3, 5, 7, 11, 13

2. You have a toonie, a loonie, and three quarters. How many different sums of money can you make?

3. a) Use a calculator to evaluate each quotient.

   $1 \div 37 = ?$

   $2 \div 37 = ?$

   $3 \div 37 = ?$
   b) Continue and identify a pattern in the results.
   c) Use the pattern to evaluate $25 \div 37$.

B

4. a) Express the fractions $\frac{1}{11}, \frac{2}{11}, \frac{3}{11}$, and so on as decimals. Describe the pattern.
   b) How does the pattern change if the denominator is 111?
   c) What if the denominator is 11 111?

5. How many perfect cubes divide evenly into 13 824?

6. How many diagonals are there in each polygon?
   a) square
   b) pentagon
   c) hexagon
   d) 12-sided polygon (dodecagon)
   e) n-sided polygon

7. a) On what day of the week were you born? Explain how you found out.
   b) Describe a method of determining the day of the week for any date.

8. How many times does the digit 3 occur in the numbers from 1 to 1000?

C

9. In the following sum, each letter represents a different digit. T is three times A, W is one third of H, and Y = 1. Find the value of each letter.

   T H A T
   + W A S
   E A S Y

10. A Sudoku is a Japanese number puzzle that follows a simple set of rules. Each three by three square, each row, and each column must contain each of the numerals 1 through 9 only once. Here is a Sudoku that is almost completed. What must the missing digits be?

5	3	2	1	6	8	4	7	9
7	1	8	4	5	9	3	6	2
6	4	9	3	7	2	1	5	8
9	5	4	7	8	3	2	1	6
2	7	3	5	1	6	8	9	4
8	6	1	2	9	4	5	3	7
3	9	6	8	4	5	7	2	1
4	2	7	6	3	1	9	8	5
1	8	5	9	2	7	6	4	3

1.2 Focus on Communicating
Principles of Mathematics 9, pages 10–13

A

1. Describe the pattern in each sequence. Give the next two terms.

    a) 18, 15, 12

    b) −8, −10, −12

    c) $\dfrac{1}{6}, \dfrac{1}{3}, \dfrac{1}{2}$

    d) 4, −12, 36, −108

    e) 4, 4, 8, 12, 20

    f)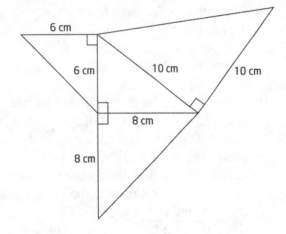

B

2. Is there a relationship between the areas of the isosceles right triangles placed on each side of a right triangle? Use the diagram to help you explain your answer.

    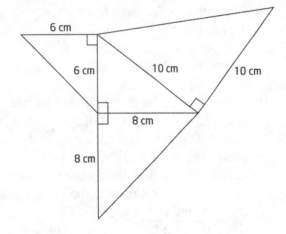

    6 cm 6 cm 10 cm 10 cm 8 cm 8 cm

3. **a)** Explain how the diagram illustrates the fact that $\dfrac{3}{5} \times \dfrac{2}{3} = \dfrac{6}{15}$.

    b) What product is modelled by the number line diagram?

    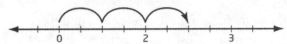

    0   2   3

4. Anna, Bryce, Coral, and Deepak chose their favourite sport on a survey. Their choices are tennis, swimming, baseball, and hockey, but not in that order. Anna and Deepak do not like team sports. Both Anna and Bryce only like sports with balls. Coral does not play any of the sports with double letters in their names. Match each student with the correct sport. Justify your reasoning.

C

5. In a recycling depot, there are eight recycling checkpoints equally spaced along a 7-m section of the recycling line. A recycling bin is to be located 4 m away from the assembly line. Where is the best location for a recycling bin to be placed so that the workers will have to go the least distance to take the materials to be recycled?

1.3 Focus on Connecting
Principles of Mathematics 9, pages 14–18

A

1. Raza has five Canadian stamps in his wallet. If the wallet contains any combination of 50¢, 2¢, and 1¢ stamps, what are the possible total values of the stamps?

2. How many portable CD players would fit inside your classroom? Explain your reasoning.

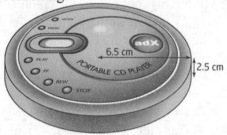

B

3. How many parallelograms of all sizes are there in the diagram?

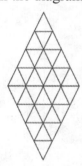

4. Six friends ate 15 pieces of birthday cake. Kees ate four times as many pieces as Rae. Rae ate one third as many pieces as Jason. Kees ate twice as many pieces as Anil. Anil and Edgar ate the same number of pieces. Ming and Jason ate the same number of pieces. Kees ate the most pieces. What fraction of the 15 pieces of birthday cake did each person eat?

5. How many books are there in all the public libraries in Ontario?

6. A polygon has seven sides. How many diagonals does it have?

C

7. Each small cube measures 1 cm by 1 cm by 1 cm. What is the approximate volume of this 3-D arrow?

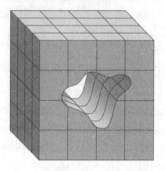

8. Each three by three square, each row, and each column must contain each of the numerals from 1 to 9 only once. Copy and complete this Sudoku puzzle.

					5		1	4
	5	3					8	9
				2	9			3
	7		2		1	3		
		1		9		4		
		2	5		8		9	
4			8	5				
5	8				6	1		
2	3		9					

1.4 Focus on Representing

Principles of Mathematics 9, pages 19–22

A

1. On a bicycle ride to a store, Faiza rode 3 km east, then 5 km south, then 5 km west, and finally 5 km north. Where is the store relative to her starting point?

2. The bottom floor of an office building has 12 offices. Each of the other floors above it has $\frac{1}{2}$ as many offices as the floor below. Use a diagram and a numeric representation to help determine the maximum number of floors that this building can have.

B

3. There are 30 people at a party, not including the host. Each person gets introduced to each other person once by the host. How many introductions are there?

4. The gear ratio on a toy truck compares the number of teeth on the *driver* cog to the number of teeth on the *driving* cog. The driver cog on the toy truck has 50 teeth and the driving cog has 40 teeth.

   a) If the driver cog rotates four turns, how many turns does the driving cog make?

   b) How many turns of the driver cog are required for the driving cog to turn three times?

5. Plot each set of points on a grid. Describe the pattern and plot the next three points.
   a) A(0, 0), B(2, –1), C(4, –2)
   b) P(1, 2), Q(–1, –2), R(1, 2)
   c) D(1, 2), E(2, 4), F(3, 6)

6. The points A(−3, 2) and B(1, 2) are two vertices of right isosceles triangle △ABC. AB is not one of the equal sides. Find all possible locations of the third vertex so that the area of the triangle is 10 square units.

C

7. The points A(1, 2) and B(−3, −2) are two vertices of an isosceles triangle. Find all possible whole-number coordinates of the other vertex.

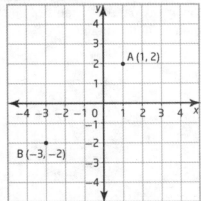

1.5 Focus on Selecting Tools and Computational Strategies

Principles of Mathematics 9, pages 23–28

A

1. a) Draw a diagram to illustrate that
$8 \div 2 = 4$.

b) Draw a diagram to illustrate that
$15 \div 5 = 3$.

2. Use an appropriate tool and strategy to find the two missing values in each sequence.

a) $5, 8, 11, \ldots, \square, \square, 41$

b) $3, 12, 48, \ldots, \square, \square, 49\,152$

c) $6, 4, 2, \ldots, \square, \square, -12$

d) $4, -36, \ldots, \square, \square, -26\,244$

B

3. Find each sum. Express your answers in lowest terms.

a) $-\dfrac{3}{5} + \left(-\dfrac{1}{5}\right)$

b) $-\dfrac{2}{5} + \dfrac{3}{4}$

c) $\dfrac{2}{9} + \left(-\dfrac{2}{3}\right)$

d) $\dfrac{1}{7} + \dfrac{2}{21}$

4. Find each difference.

a) $\dfrac{1}{4} - \left(-\dfrac{1}{4}\right)$

b) $\dfrac{3}{5} - \dfrac{3}{4}$

c) $\dfrac{1}{8} - \left(-\dfrac{1}{16}\right)$

d) $\dfrac{2}{5} - \dfrac{3}{10}$

5. Evaluate.

a) $\left(-\dfrac{3}{8}\right) \times \dfrac{2}{5}$

b) $\dfrac{3}{4} \div \left(-\dfrac{5}{6}\right)$

c) $\dfrac{1}{8} \times \left(-\dfrac{2}{5}\right)$

d) $\dfrac{1}{8} \div \left(-\dfrac{1}{16}\right)$

6. Use an appropriate tool to help determine the thousandth term in the sequence $-25, -21, -17, -13, \ldots$.

C

7. A string winds around the cylindrical part of a water bottle a total of five times. The cylindrical part of the water bottle has a circumference of 22 cm and a height of 19 cm. How long is the string?

8. If you fold a piece of string in half, in half again, and so on, up to *n* folds, and then cut it through the last fold with a pair of scissors, how many pieces of string will you have?

1.6 Focus on Reasoning and Proving
Principles of Mathematics 9, pages 29–33

A

1. Prove that the sum of five consecutive whole numbers is always divisible by 5.

2. Prove that a mathematics textbook always has an even number of pages.

B

3. Give a counter-example to prove each statement false.

   a) All even numbers are evenly divisible by 4.

   b) The sum of any two odd numbers is always odd.

   c) The product of any two fractions is always positive.

4. The integer -7 can be expressed as a difference of cubes.

   $$1^3 - 2^3$$
   $$= 1 - 8$$
   $$= -7$$

   How many integers between 1 and 100 can be expressed as a difference of cubes of whole numbers?

5. a) Copy and complete each sum.

   $$1 = ?$$
   $$1 + 3 = ?$$
   $$1 + 3 + 5 = ?$$
   $$1 + 3 + 5 + 7 = ?$$

   b) Describe the pattern in the sums.

   c) What is the sum of the first n odd numbers?

6. What is the mass of a subway train, including passengers, during rush hour?

C

7. a) Calculate 2^1.

   b) Calculate $2^2 - 2$.

   c) Calculate $2^1 + 2^2$.

   d) Calculate $2^3 - 2$.

   e) Calculate $2^1 + 2^2 + 2^3$.

   f) Calculate $2^4 - 2$.

   g) Describe a rule that this seems to illustrate.

   h) Verify your rule by trying it with two more examples.

   i) Did your examples work? If not, try to develop a different rule and verify it.

8. For the sequence 1, 1, -2, -2, -2, 3, 3, 3, 3, -4, -4, -4, -4, -4, 5, 5, 5, 5, 5, 5, ...

   a) what is the 50th term?

   b) what is the sum of the first 50 terms?

   c) what is the 100th term?

   d) what is the sum of the first 100 terms?

1.7 Focus on Reflecting
Principles of Mathematics 9, pages 34–36

A

1. If you multiply a number by −5 and then add 13, the result is −7. What is the number?

2. One third of a number, decreased by $\frac{3}{4}$, gives $\frac{1}{3}$. What is the number?

B

3. **a)** How many numbers between 1 and 100 are divisible by 3?

    b) How many numbers between 1 and 100 are divisible by 4?

    c) How many numbers between 1 and 100 are divisible by both 3 and 4?

    d) How many numbers between 1 and 100 are divisible by either 3 or 4?

    e) Explain your strategy and verify that it works.

4. **a)** How many numbers between 1 and 1000 contain the digit 5?

    b) How many numbers between 1 and 1000 contain the digit 0?

    c) How many numbers between 1 and 1000 contain the digit 5 and the digit 0?

    d) How many numbers between 1 and 1000 contain either the digit 5 or the digit 0?

    e) Explain your strategy and verify that it works.

5. In a video game, a character has been programmed to start at 40 pixels to the left of centre. The character moves 70 pixels to the right, then 55 pixels to the left, then 40 pixels to the right, then 25 pixels to the left, and so on.

    a) The character disappears when it lands on zero, the centre. After how many moves will this occur?

    b) Verify that your answer is correct.

6. What number to the exponent 12 is 2 176 782 336?

C

7. How many litres of bottled water are consumed in Ontario in a month?

8. Each three by three square, each row, and each column must contain each of the numerals 1 through 9 only once. Copy and complete this Sudoku puzzle.

2	3	1		7				
	7		4			1		
5					9			
4		2			8	3		7
	5					9		
6		3	9			5		4
			5					1
	7			4		3		
				9		6	5	2

1. Continue each pattern for three more terms. Describe how to find successive terms.

   a) 6, 9, 12

   b) 8, 16, 32

   c) 9, 10, 13, 18

   d) 13, 11, 7, 1

2. Plot each set of points on a grid. Describe the pattern and plot the next three points.

   a) A(1, 2), B(4, 4), C(7, 6)

   b) G(4, 5), H(0, 3), I(−4, 1)

   c) P(−6, −1), Q(−9, −3), R(−12, −5)

3. Use appropriate tools or strategies to find the next three terms in each sequence.

   a) $\dfrac{3}{8}, \dfrac{1}{2}, \dfrac{5}{8}$

   b) $0, -\dfrac{1}{4}, -\dfrac{1}{2}$

4. How many quarters will fill up a 4-L milk jug?

5. How many squares of all sizes are on a chessboard? What strategies did you use?

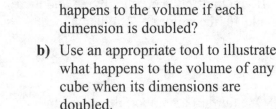

6. a) A cubical box measures 2 cm by 2 cm by 2 cm. What happens to the volume if each dimension is doubled?

   b) Use an appropriate tool to illustrate what happens to the volume of any cube when its dimensions are doubled.

7. Copy the numbers in the order shown. Replace each ☐ with the symbol +, −, ×, ÷, or =, and insert brackets to make a true mathematical statement.

   a) 12 ☐ 3 ☐ 5 ☐ 2 ☐ 1

   b) $\dfrac{1}{3}$ ☐ $\dfrac{1}{4}$ ☐ $\dfrac{5}{6}$ ☐ $\dfrac{1}{2}$ ☐ $\dfrac{5}{12}$ ☐ $\dfrac{1}{12}$

8. Evaluate. Express your answers in lowest terms.

   a) $-\dfrac{2}{5} + \dfrac{3}{4}$

   b) $\dfrac{3}{5} - \left(-\dfrac{2}{3}\right)$

   c) $\left(-\dfrac{2}{3}\right) \times \left(-\dfrac{4}{7}\right)$

   d) $\left(-2\dfrac{1}{5}\right) \div \left(-3\dfrac{1}{2}\right)$

9. a) Use an appropriate tool to determine the hundredth term in the sequence 5, 8, 11, 14, ….

   b) Use an appropriate tool to determine which term in the sequence 144, 139, 134, 129, … is −416.

10. The number 614 656 is what number raised to the exponent 4? Which tool did you use?

2.1 Hypotheses and Sources of Data

Principles of Mathematics 9, pages 42–47

A

1. State the opposite of each hypothesis.

   a) Most people's favourite colour is blue.

   b) Teenagers spend more time listening to rock music than to classical music.

   c) Bob's favourite type of ice cream is chocolate.

   d) Most students study mathematics.

2. State a hypothesis about a relationship between the variables in each pair. Then, state the opposite of each hypothesis.

   a) a father's shoe size and the shoe sizes of his children

   b) the cost of a movie ticket and the number of people renting DVDs

   c) the altitude of a city and the length of time it takes for water to boil

   d) a university student's age and the average of the student's marks

B

3. Which of the following data are primary and which are secondary? Explain.

   a) The Student Council President surveys students about a school dance.

   b) A student downloads data from a comparison-shopping Web site about the prices of running shoes at sporting goods stores across the country.

   c) A researcher interviews 100 people to determine their favourite airline.

   d) A teacher finds data on the 2006 Census in a report published by Statistics Canada.

4. Identify each data source as primary or secondary. State one advantage of each source of data.

   a) A researcher interviews 100 employees about the length of time they spend travelling to the workplace.

   b) An airline company searches on the Internet for data on the places Canadians have travelled recently.

   c) A ferry company surveys 800 recent customers about possible changes to the ferry schedule.

   d) A volunteer searches reference books at a library to check the values of cars made in 2005.

5. a) Make a hypothesis about whether the students at your school prefer to spend time rollerblading or ice skating in their leisure time.

   b) Describe how you could test your hypothesis. Explain whether you would use primary or secondary data.

6. Anoja prepared the following table using data volunteered by eight students in her math class.

Name	Eye Colour	Favourite Subject
Kelvin	brown	History
Dajanth	green	Math
Tanzilah	blue	French
Debbie	blue	English
Tanveer	brown	History
Doug	blue	History
Matt	blue	English
Jamal	blue	Math
Jack	brown	Math
Sanjay	brown	History

a) Is Anoja using primary or secondary data? Explain.

b) Make two hypotheses based on these data.

c) How could you test your hypotheses?

7. Elliot prepared the following table using data collected by a researcher at a company.

Employee's Name	Favourite Colour	Favourite Animal
Sandeep	orange	dog
John	red	horse
Azra	green	cat
Sanjay	blue	dog
Kim	yellow	dog
Anneli	green	cat
Janet	green	dog
Faiza	blue	horse
Freshta	orange	cat
Vidak	blue	dog
Vedrana	purple	dog
Zoë	green	cat
Janet	blue	dog

a) Is Elliot using primary or secondary data? Explain.

b) Make two hypotheses based on these data.

c) How could you test your hypotheses?

C

8. a) Make a hypothesis about the relationship between the resolution of a digital camera and its price.

b) Use an Internet search engine to collect data about digital camera prices. Compare the results when you use the key words "camera stores," "digital camera resolution," and "digital camera prices."

c) Did you conduct primary or secondary research? Explain.

d) Describe another method for gathering data about computer speeds and prices.

9. a) Make a hypothesis about the relationship between the altitude of a mountain and the temperature at the top of the mountain.

b) Use data from a reference book in the library or an on-line source to test your hypothesis.

10. a) Make a hypothesis about how the difference between Olympic records for men and women in the 100-m freestyle swimming race has changed over the years.

b) Use the Internet or other sources to collect data to test your hypothesis.

c) Explain how the data you found prove or disprove your hypothesis.

2.2 Sampling Principles
Principles of Mathematics 9, pages 48–55

A

1. Identify the population in each sample.

   a) Generally, girls learn to talk before boys do.

   b) As cars age, their value decreases.

   c) Most sporting goods stores charge more for ice skates than for hockey sticks.

   d) Generally, teenage boys learn to drive cars before teenage girls do.

2. Describe the data required to answer each question. Explain whether you would use a census or a sample to collect each set of data.

   a) How are a person's height and weight related?

   b) What is the most common colour of car at a car dealership?

   c) What is the most common size of painting in an art gallery?

   d) Is the mean mark on an exam greater than 70%?

3. Describe how you could choose a random sample to determine each of the following.

   a) the type of soft drink preferred by students at a local school

   b) Ontario teenagers' favourite radio station

   c) countries of origin for citizens of Toronto

   d) Ontario residents' favourite TV program

B

4. Identify the type of sample in each situation. Comment on any possible bias in these samples.

   a) A business studies class interviews newly qualified Chartered Accountants at a single company to learn about their choices for career specialization.

   b) A market research company randomly selects phone numbers from a city directory to survey citizen's opinions on a new brand of toothpaste.

   c) Every fourth person entering a provincial park is asked to fill out a questionnaire about the park.

   d) Visitors leaving a museum are interviewed to find out what restaurants people like to dine at.

5. List three ways you could divide workers in a company into groups for selecting a stratified random sample.

6. A recording company wants to survey Canadian musicians.

   a) Identify the population.

   b) Suggest a stratified random sampling technique that the company could use.

7. A health club wants to select 100 of its 415 members for a survey.

   a) Identify the population.

   b) Describe a systematic random sampling technique that the company could use.

8. The student council at a school wants to survey members of school clubs.

    a) Identify the population.

    b) Describe a method of randomly selecting 20% of the members of the clubs.

9. This table lists the enrolment at a university.

Year	Number of Students
1	1270
2	1138
3	987
4	880

The university administration wants to interview a random sample of 500 students, stratified by year. How many students should the administration select from each year?

10. Identify the population for each of the following. Then, describe how you would select an appropriate sample of each population.

    a) the popularity of various sports teams in your school

    b) the popularity of various sports teams in your community

    c) the effectiveness of a national campaign to convince people not to drink and drive

    d) the spending habits of teenagers in Ontario

    e) the quality of photo prints from various digital imaging companies

    f) the mean cost of propane in your community

C

11. a) Design and conduct a survey to determine how much sleep students get.

    b) Present your results in a table and a graph.

    c) Explain your choice of sampling technique.

12. a) Design and conduct a survey to determine

    • the percent of students in your school who are taking math at the grade 12 level

    • the reasons for their choice

    b) Present your data in a table and a bar graph.

    c) Explain your choice of sampling technique.

13. In a *voluntary sample*, people choose to answer the survey, rather than being selected by the person doing the survey. For example, a research company could mail out surveys and ask recipients to fill them in and mail them back. Discuss whether this voluntary sample accurately represents a population.

14. A survey selects 10 employees from each department at 200 companies across Ontario.

    a) Explain why this sample is not completely random.

    b) How does this sampling method bias the results of the survey?

2.3 Use Scatter Plots to Analyse Data

Principles of Mathematics 9, pages 56–67

A

1. Identify the independent and the dependent variable in each pair.

  a) physical activity and heart rate

  b) cost of postage and mass of a letter

  c) age of a tree and height of a tree

  d) value of a car and age of a car

2. This table shows the value of an initial investment of $1000 in a mutual fund for 3 years. The values have been rounded to the nearest dollar.

Time (years)	0	1	2	3
Value ($)	1000	1092	1142	1249

  a) Make a scatter plot of the data.

  b) Describe the relationship between the variables.

3. This table lists the number of hours of driving instruction received by students at a driving school and their driving-test scores.

Instructional Hours	10	15	21	6	18	20	12
Student's Score	78	85	96	75	84	45	82

  a) Identify the independent variable and the dependent variable.

  b) Make a scatter plot of the data.

  c) Describe the relationship between the variables.

  d) Are there any outliers? If so, explain how they differ from the rest of the data.

B

4. This table lists data from the monthly sales of T-shirts for a rock band.

Price ($)	Monthly Sales
10	2500
12	2200
15	1600
18	1200
20	800
24	250

  a) Identify the independent variable and the dependent variable.

  b) Make a scatter plot of the data.

  c) Describe the relationship between the variables.

5. This table shows the minimum stopping distances on wet asphalt at various speeds.

Speed (km/h)	Stopping Distance (m)
10	0.9
20	3.2
30	7.3
40	13.0
50	20.1
60	28.6
70	39.1
80	51.3
90	64.8
100	80.0
110	96.5

  a) Identify the independent variable and the dependent variable.

  b) Make a scatter plot of the data.

  c) Describe the relationship between the speed of the car and its stopping distance on wet asphalt.

6. This table shows the average fuel economy of a particular car, in litres per 100 km, at various constant speeds, measured at a test track.

Speed (km/h)	Fuel Economy (L/100 km)
10	14.26
20	12.85
30	11.70
40	10.65
50	10.25
60	10.10
70	10.24
80	10.84
90	11.38
100	12.14
110	14.59
120	15.64
130	16.88
140	19.26
150	22.50

a) Identify the independent variable and the dependent variable.

b) Make a scatter plot of the data.

c) At what speed does this car have the best fuel economy?

7. This table gives the total number of passengers, in thousands, of Canadian air-carriers, every 2 years for the period from 1990 to 1998.

Year	Passengers (1000s)
1990	36 777
1992	37 202
1994	38 868
1996	40 176
1998	42 104

a) Make a scatter plot of the data.

b) Describe the relationship between the year and the total number of passengers.

C

8. a) Make a hypothesis about the relationship between a person's arm length and leg length.

b) Design and carry out an experiment to investigate the relationship. What conclusions can you make from the data you collected?

c) Compare your hypothesis with the results of your experiment.

d) How could you improve your experiment?

9. This table shows the fat and energy content in typical servings of cookies.

Item	Serving Size (g)	Fat (g)	Energy (kJ)
Chocolate Chunk Cookies	31	8.2	670
Butterfly Wing Cookies	19	5.5	420
Digestive Biscuits	40	8.5	830
Pure Butter Shortbreads	33	10	750
Vanilla Wafers	30	7	574

a) Calculate the amount of fat, in milligrams, per gram of each item. Round to the nearest milligram. Then, calculate the energy content per gram of each item. Round to the nearest tenth of a kilojoule. List the results of your calculations in a table.

b) Make a scatter plot of the two sets of data you calculated in part a).

c) Identify and explain any outliers.

d) Describe what you can learn from the scatter plot.

2.4 Trends, Interpolation, and Extrapolation
Principles of Mathematics 9, pages 68–76

A

1. This table shows the mean monthly rent for a three-bedroom house in Sault Ste. Marie, Ontario, from 1998 to 2003.

Year	1998	1999	2000	2001	2002	2003
Rent ($)	900	954	1011	1072	1136	1204

   a) Make a bar graph of the data.

   b) Describe the trend in rents.

   c) Predict the mean rent for a three-bedroom house in Sault Ste. Marie in 2008.

2. This table shows the number of math graduates from a university from 1999 to 2004.

Year	Graduates
1999	152
2000	170
2001	176
2002	183
2003	190
2004	196

   a) Make a scatter plot of the data.

   b) Describe the trend in the number of math students graduating from the university.

   c) Predict the number of math students graduating from the university in 2008.

B

3. This table summarizes data about cell phone and dishwasher use in Canada.

Cell Phone and Dishwasher Use in Canada					
Year	2000	2001	2002	2003	2004
Cell Phone (%)	41.8	47.6	51.6	54	58.9
Dishwasher (%)	51.2	52	54.3	55	56

Adapted from Statistics Canada, Cansim Database, Table 203-0020.

   a) Use a graph to compare the trend in cell phone use in Canada with the trend in dishwasher use in Canada.

   b) Predict the cell phone use and the dishwasher use in Canada in 2010.

4. This table shows the yearly taxes for a cottage in Sydenham, Ontario, from 2001 to 2005.

Year	2001	2002	2003	2004	2005
Taxes ($)	1400	1600	1800	2000	3000

   a) Identify the independent variable and the dependent variable.

   b) Make a scatter plot of the data.

   c) Describe the trend in taxes.

   d) Identify any outliers. Explain whether you would include any of these outliers in the data set.

5. This table shows the population of Ontario from 1990 to 2000.

Year	Population (1000s)
1990	10 299.6
1991	10 472.6
1992	10 570.5
1993	10 690.4
1994	10 827.5
1995	10 964.9
1996	11 100.9
1997	11 249.5
1998	11 384.4
1999	11 513.8
2000	11 669.3

a) Make a scatter plot of the data.

b) Describe the trend in population.

c) Estimate the population of Ontario in 2010.

6. The following table relates mean word length and recommended age level for a set of children's books.

Recommended Age	Mean Word Length
4	3.5
6	5.5
5	4.6
6	5.0
7	5.2
9	6.5
8	6.1
5	4.9

a) Create a scatter plot of the data.

b) Predict the average word length in books for 12-year-olds.

7. This table gives the average annual pet expenses of individuals with certain incomes.

Income ($)	Pet Expenses ($)
15 000	104
25 000	195
35 000	250
45 000	350
55 000	477

a) Identify the independent variable and the dependent variable.

b) Create a scatter plot of the data.

c) Describe the trend in pet expenses. Suggest two reasons to explain this trend.

d) Estimate the pet expenses for an individual with an annual average income of $40 000.

e) Estimate the pet expenses for an individual with an annual average income of $60 000.

f) Estimate the yearly income for a person with average annual pet expenses of $400.

8. This table shows the distance travelled by a car from 0 s to 14 s.

Time (s)	0	2	4	6	8	10	12
Distance (m)	0	6	22	50	90	140	190

a) Make a scatter plot of the data.

b) Use the scatter plot to predict the distance travelled by the car after 9 s.

C

9. An object is thrown straight up into the air. This table shows the height of the object as it ascends.

Time (s)	0	0.2	0.4	0.6	0.8	1.0	1.2
Height (m)	0	1.7	3.0	3.9	4.4	4.5	4.2

a) Make a scatter plot of the data.

b) Use the scatter plot to predict how long the object will be in the air.

10. This table summarizes data about the average weekly earnings in Canada.

Average Weekly Earnings ($)			
Year	Canada	Ontario	Alberta
2001	667.27	712.88	683.49
2002	680.93	726.21	698.85
2003	690.57	734.78	707.31
2004	706.03	748.10	730.81
2005	728.17	768.59	769.13

Adapted from Statistics Canada, CANSIM Database, Table 281-0044

a) Use a graph to compare the trend in average weekly earnings in Canada with the trends in Ontario and Alberta. Summarize the trends in one or two sentences.

b) Estimate the average weekly earnings in Canada, Ontario, and Alberta in 2006.

2.5 Linear and Non-Linear Relations
Principles of Mathematics 9, pages 77–87

A

1. Does each graph show a linear relationship? Explain.

   a)
   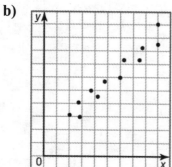

   b)

2. Does each set of points have a linear relationship? Justify your answer.

   a) (−2, −2), (−2, −1), (−1, −1), (0, 0), (1, 0), (1, 1), (2, 2), (2, 3), (3, 3), (4, 3), (4, 4), (5, 5)

   b) (−3, −1), (−2, −1), (−2, −2), (−1, −2), (0, −1), (1, −1), (1, −2), (2, 0), (2, 1), (3, 1), (3, 2), (3, 3)

3. State whether each of these lines of best fit is a good model for the data. Justify your answers.

   a)
   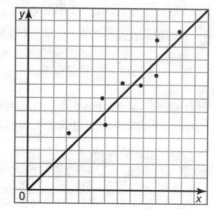

   b)
   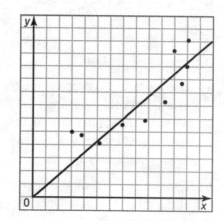

4. State whether each of these lines of best fit is a good model for the data. Justify your answers.

a)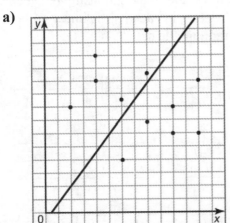

b)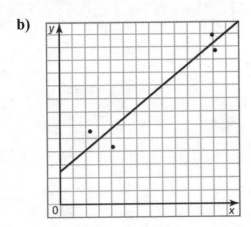

5. Plot each set of points on a grid. If your plot shows a linear relationship, draw a line of best fit. If the relation appears non-linear, sketch a curve of best fit.

a) (−4, −3), (−3, −1), (−2, −1), (−1, −1), (0, 1), (1, 2), (2, 2), (3, 5), (4, 5), (5, 6)

b)

x	4	3	6	5	2	7	1	7
y	1	1	4	3	2	5	3	6

B

6. This table represents the distance that a ball travels when dropped from the top of a 4-m ladder.

Time (s)	0.1	0.2	0.3	0.4	0.5	0.6	0.7	0.8
Distance (m)	0.05	0.2	0.4	0.8	1.2	1.7	2.4	3.1

a) Make a scatter plot of the data.

b) Draw a line or curve of best fit.

c) Describe the relationship between the variables.

7. This table represents data from a survey to determine the relationship between a student's age and the number of books they have read in the past year.

Age (years)	16	15	18	17	16	15	14	17
Books Read	5	3	8	6	4	4	5	15

a) Make a scatter plot of the data.

b) Describe the relationship between the variables.

c) Are there any outliers? If so, explain how they differ from the rest of the data.

8. This table shows the pressure of salt water at various depths.

Depth (m)	Pressure (kPa)
5	150.385
10	199.315
15	248.425
20	297.458
25	346.491
30	395.525
35	444.558
40	493.591

a) Make a scatter plot of the data.

b) Draw a line or curve of best fit.

c) Describe the relationship between the variables.

d) Estimate the water pressure at a depth of 38 m.

e) Extrapolate to estimate the water pressure at a depth of 60 m.

9. Design and carry out an experiment to see if there is a linear relationship between the armspan and height of students in your class.

Write a report on your experiment. This report should include

a) the objective of the experiment

b) your hypothesis

c) a description of your procedure

d) your observations

e) your conclusions

f) an evaluation of the experiment

C

10. Consider each set of data. How can you tell whether the relationship between the variables in each pair is linear without graphing the data?

a)

x	−3	−2	−1	0	1	2	3
y	−4	−2	0	2	4	6	8

b)

t	0	1	2	3	4	5	6
h	−4	−2	−1	4	3	5	7

c)

t	−3	−2	−1	0	1	2	3
d	8	−4	3	0	−3	−4	−5

2.6 Distance-Time Graphs
Principles of Mathematics 9, pages 88–94

A

1. Describe the motion shown in each distance-time graph.

   a)

   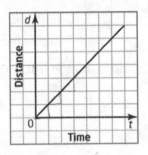

   b)

   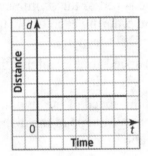

   c)

   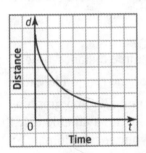

   d)

   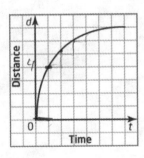

2. Describe a situation that corresponds to each distance-time graph.

   a)

   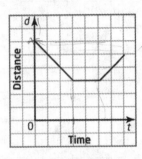

   b)

   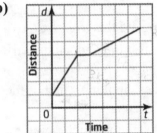

B

3. Draw a distance-time graph for each situation.

   a) A student leaves school at lunch, walking at a decreasing speed. He slows down, and then stops to talk to a friend. He turns around and walks back to school at an increasing speed.

   b) A student leaves home, walking at a constant speed. She slows down, and then stops for a few seconds to look in a store window. She turns around and walks back home at a decreasing speed.

4. Sketch a distance-time graph for a cyclist that slowly speeds up after stopping at a stop sign.

5. A swimmer starts out from shore and swims to a dock directly across the lake and back. This graph shows the swimmer's distance from shore during this trip.

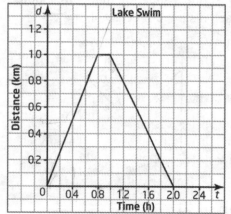

a) How long did this trip take?

b) How far is it to the dock directly across the lake?

c) What does the flat portion of the graph represent?

d) Was the swimmer swimming faster on the way to the dock or on the way back?

6. a) You are holding a rangefinder pointed at a wall. Describe how you would move to match the graph.

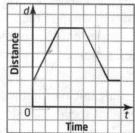

b) How would the distance-time graph change if you walked faster?

c) How would the distance-time graph change if you walked slower?

d) If a rangefinder and graphing calculator are available, use them to check your answers to parts b) and c).

7. This graph shows how far a car has travelled from its starting point.

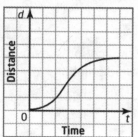

Describe the car's motion in a few sentences.

C

8. a) Find the speed of the swimmer in question 5 during each of the three segments of the swim.

b) Draw a speed-time graph for the swimmer's swim.

c) How is the speed of the swimmer related to the shape of the distance-time graph?

d) What does negative speed represent in this situation?

9. a) Sketch three distance-time graphs.

b) Describe the motion in each graph.

c) If a rangefinder and graphing calculator are available, use them to check your answer to part b).

Chapter 2 Review

1. State a hypothesis about a relationship between the variables in each pair. Then, state the opposite hypothesis.

   a) the temperature in a city during the winter and the amount of electricity used by the city's residents

   b) a person's shoe size and his or her marks in English

2. State the opposite of each hypothesis.

   a) Internet use has more than tripled in the past 20 years.

   b) The more you practise, the worse you will do in a game.

3. State whether each data source is primary or secondary. Then, explain whether the source is a good choice.

   a) To determine the number of each size of T-shirt to buy for student volunteers, a teacher surveyed 100 of the school's students by phone.

   b) To find data on the sizes of fish in Ontario, a student searched the Internet.

4. A chain store wishes to survey a representative sample of its employees.

   a) Identify the population.

   b) Describe a suitable stratified random sample for this survey.

   c) Give an example of a non-random sample.

   d) Explain why the non-random sample might not be representative of the population.

5. An office manager wants to survey employees' opinions about the working conditions at the office.

   a) Identify the population.

   b) Describe how the office manager could use a stratified random sample for the survey.

6. A travel company wants to determine how its clients feel about electronic tickets for airlines.

   a) Identify the population.

   b) Describe how the travel company could use a systematic random sample for its survey.

7. This table shows the lengths of five boats and the number of passengers each one can carry.

Length (feet)	17	19	21	23	25
Capacity (passengers)	6	8	10	11	13

   a) Make a scatter plot of the data.

   b) Describe the relationship between the length of a boat and its capacity.

   c) Estimate the number of passengers that a 20-foot boat could carry.

   d) Predict the number of passengers that a 29-foot boat could carry.

8. Graph each set of points on a grid. Then, draw a line or curve of best fit for each set of data. Explain.

a)

x	–3	–1	2	1	–5	–2	0	–4
y	0	2	5	4	–2	1	3	–1

b)

Time (days)	0	1	2	3	4	5
Height (cm)	0.2	0.4	0.8	1.2	2.0	2.6

9. Design and carry out an experiment to see if there is a linear relationship between the height of a pile of quarters and the number of quarters in the pile. This report should include

a) the objective of your experiment

b) your hypothesis

c) a description of your procedure

d) your observations

e) your conclusions

f) an evaluation of the experiment

10. Draw a distance-time graph to represent each situation.

a) A student leaves school and walks to a store directly across the street at a speed of 4 m/s for 20 s, stops for 30 s to talk to a friend, and then walks back to the entrance of the school at a speed of 5 m/s for 16 s.

b) A ball dropped from a height of 8 m steadily increases in speed until it hits the ground.

11. Describe the motion in each distance-time graph.

a)
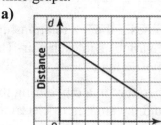

b)
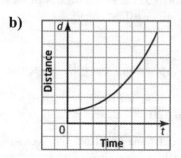

c)
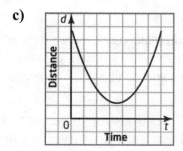

12. Which of the graphs in question 11 show linear functions between distance and time? Justify your answer.

3.1 Build Algebraic Models Using Concrete Materials

Principles of Mathematics 9, pages 104–109

A

1. Use algebra tiles to represent each area.

   a) 4 square units

   b) 9 square units

   c) $2x^2$ square units

   d) $4x^2$ square units

2. Use tiles to model each algebraic expression.

   a) $x^2 + 5x$

   b) $3x^2 - 4x$

   c) $2x^2 + 3x + 4$

   d) $x^2 - 5x - 3$

3. Write the algebraic expression represented by each model.

   a)

   b)

   c)

   d)

4. Each unit tile represents 1 m that Jacinth walked on a hike. Find each distance.

   a)

   b)

   c)

   d)

   e)

B

5. a) Build an area model to represent a square with length and width both equal to 5 cm. Sketch the model and label the length and width.

   b) What is the area? Write this as a power.

6. a) Build a volume model to represent a cube with length, width, and height all equal to 3 cm. Sketch the model and label the length, width, and height..

   b) What is the volume? Write this as a power.

7. a) Build a volume model to represent a cube with length, width, and height all equal to 5 cm. Sketch the model and label the length, width, and height.

   b) What is the volume? Write this as a power.

   c) Write an expression for the area of one face as a power. Evaluate the area of one face.

8. The area of one face of a cube is 64 cm^2.

   a) What side length of the cube would give this area?

   b) Determine the volume of the cube. Write this as a power.

9. **a)** A cube has a volume of 125 cm^3. Find the total surface area of all six faces.

   b) A cube has a volume of 343 cm^3. Find the total surface area of all six faces.

10. The total surface area of all six faces of a cube is 96 cm^2.

   a) Determine the area of one face of the cube.

   b) What side length of the cube would give this area?

   c) Determine the volume of the cube. Write this as a power.

11. Use tiles to build an area model that has length and width as indicated.

   a) length $= x$, width $= x + 2$

   b) length $= x + 1$, width $= x + 3$

   c) length $= x + 4$, width $= x$

   d) length $= x + 2$, width $= x + 3$

C

12. Two cubes have a total volume of 72 cm^3. Both cubes have whole-number side lengths.

   a) Find the side length of each cube.

   b) Find the total surface area of both cubes.

13. What is the final digit in the number 2687^{398}? Hint: First compute 7^1, 7^2, 7^3, 7^4, 7^5, ..., until you see a pattern. Why are the final digits of these numbers the same as the final digits of 2687^1, 2687^2, 2687^3, ...?

3.2 Work With Exponents
Principles of Mathematics 9, **pages 110–118**

A

1. Write each as a power.
   a) $5 \times 5 \times 5 \times 5 \times 5 \times 5$
   b) $(-3) \times (-3) \times (-3) \times (-3)$
   c) $2.03 \times 2.03 \times 2.03 \times 2.03 \times 2.03$
   d) $\left(-\dfrac{2}{3}\right) \times \left(-\dfrac{2}{3}\right) \times \left(-\dfrac{2}{3}\right)$

2. Write each power in expanded form.
   a) 2^4 b) $(-4)^5$
   c) 0.7^3 d) $\left(-\dfrac{3}{4}\right)^2$

3. Evaluate.
   a) 2^3
   b) $(-4)^2$
   c) -4^2
   d) $(-6)^3$
   e) $\left(\dfrac{3}{4}\right)^4$

4. Evaluate.
   a) $\left(-\dfrac{2}{3}\right)^3$
   b) 2.3^3
   c) 1^5
   d) $(-1)^{99}$
   e) -1^{28}

5. Evaluate. Remember to use the correct order of operations.
   a) $2^3 + 2^4$ b) $4^5 - 4^3$
   c) $4^2 \times 2^4$ d) $2^6 \div 4^3$

6. Evaluate. Remember to use the correct order of operations.
   a) $2^4 + 2^2 - 2^3$
   b) $2^4 - 2^2 + 2^3$
   c) $(5^2 - 3^2) + (5^2 - 3^2)$
   d) $\left(\dfrac{3}{4}\right)^2 \times \left(-\dfrac{2}{3}\right)^3$
   e) $30(2)^3$
   f) $-5(-3)^2$

7. Substitute the given values into each expression. Then, evaluate the expression. Round your answers to the nearest tenth where necessary.
   a) $5a^2$; $a = 3$
   b) πr^2; $r = 2.5$
   c) $c^2 - b^2$; $b = 5$, $c = 13$
   d) $\dfrac{1}{3}\pi r^2 h$; $r = 6$, $h = 4$
   e) $4\pi r^2$; $r = 1.2$
   f) $x^2 - 3x - 10$; $x = -2$

B

8. a) Evaluate each power.
      $3^1 \quad 3^2 \quad 3^3 \quad 3^4 \quad 3^5 \quad 3^6$
   b) Examine the final digit of each of your answers. What pattern do you notice?
   c) Use the pattern that you found in part b) to determine the final digit in the number 3243^{3243}.

9. Staphylococcus aureus is a type of bacteria that can cause dangerous health problems. It doubles every 60 min. The initial population of a sample of Staphylococcus aureus is 200.

   a) Copy and complete the table.

Time (min)	Population of Staphylococcus aureus
0	200
60	400
120	
180	
240	

   b) Construct a graph of population versus time. Use a smooth curve to connect the points. Describe the shape of the graph.

   c) What will the population be after
   • 12 h?   • 1 day?

10. Bronchial pneumonia can be caused by the bacterium Streptococcus pneumoniae. The doubling time of Streptococcus pneumoniae is 20 min.

    a) Copy and complete the table.

Time (min)	Population of Streptococcus pneumoniae
0	100
20	200
40	400
60	
80	
100	

    b) Construct a graph of population versus time. Use a smooth curve to connect the points. Describe the shape of the graph.

C

11. The radius of a hydrogen atom is 0.000 000 6 mm. This number can be written in scientific notation as 6.0×10^{-7}.

    a) How many hydrogen atoms placed in a row will make 3 mm?

    b) How many balls, each with a diameter of 60 cm, placed in a row would have a length of 3000 km?

12. Iodine-131 is a radioactive isotope of iodine that is used in a sodium salt to diagnose thyroid disease. The half-life of Iodine-131 is 8 days, which means that it takes 8 days for the sample to decay to half its original amount.

    a) Suppose you started with a 200-mg sample of Iodine-131. Copy and complete the table.

Number of Half-Life Periods	Time (days)	Amount of Iodine-131 Remaining (mg)
0	0	200
1	8	$200\left(\dfrac{1}{2}\right)^{1} = 100$
2	16	
3		
4		

    b) Construct a graph of the amount, in milligrams, of Iodine-131 remaining versus time, in days. Describe the shape of the graph.

    c) Approximately how much Iodine-131 will remain after 48 days?

    d) How long will it take until only 1 mg of Iodine-131 remains?

13. Write each number in scientific notation.

    a) 34 500 000 000

    b) 0.000 000 005 12

3.3 Discover the Exponent Laws
Principles of Mathematics 9, pages 119–129

A

1. Apply the product rule to write each as a single power. Then, evaluate the expression.
   a) $4^3 \times 4^2$
   b) $(-2)^2 \times (-2)^4$
   c) $2.5^3 \times 2.5^3$
   d) $(-1)^{15} \times (-1)^{25}$
   e) $\left(\dfrac{2}{3}\right)^4 \times \left(\dfrac{2}{3}\right)^3$
   f) $\left(-\dfrac{3}{5}\right)^2 \times \left(-\dfrac{3}{5}\right)^3$

2. Apply the quotient rule to write each as a single power. Then, evaluate the expression.
   a) $8^5 \div 8^3$
   b) $(-5)^4 \div (-5)$
   c) $3.2^5 \div 3.2^2$
   d) $(-1)^{35} \div (-1)^{20}$
   e) $\left(\dfrac{3}{4}\right)^6 \div \left(\dfrac{3}{4}\right)^3$
   f) $\left(-\dfrac{2}{5}\right)^5 \div \left(-\dfrac{2}{5}\right)^3$

3. Apply the power rule to write each as a single power. Then, evaluate the expression.
   a) $(5^3)^2$
   b) $(-4^3)^2$
   c) $(0.2^2)^3$
   d) $(-1^6)^3$
   e) $\left[\left(\dfrac{1}{5}\right)^2\right]^2$
   f) $\left[\left(-\dfrac{5}{6}\right)^3\right]^2$

4. Simplify using the exponent laws. Then, evaluate.
   a) $3^2 \times 3^4 \times 3^1$
   b) $4^5 \div 4^2 \div 4$
   c) $(2^3)^2 \times (2^2)^3$
   d) $(2^6)^3 \div (2^4)^4$

5. Simplify using the exponent laws. Then, evaluate.
   a) $3^5 \times 3^2 \div 3^4$
   b) $4^6 \div 4^3 \times 4^2$
   c) $\dfrac{0.2^4 \times 0.2^3}{(0.2^2)^2}$
   d) $\dfrac{(-3)^5 \div (-3)^2}{(-3)^2}$
   e) $(6^2)^5 \times (6^3)^5 \div (6^5)^3$
   f) $[(-5)^2]^3 \div (-5)^4 \times (-5)^2$

6. Simplify.
   a) $x^5 \times x^3$
   b) $y^8 \div y^6$
   c) $(m^4)^3$
   d) $(d^2)^4$
   e) $a^3b \times ab^3$
   f) $c^5d^4 \div cd$

B

7. Simplify.
   a) $3x^3y^2 \times 5x^4y^3$
   b) $8a^5b^3 \div 4ab^2$
   c) $(2m^3n^2)^4 \div (-4mn)^2$
   d) $(-c^3)^2 \times (-2c)^3$

8. Simplify.
   a) $\dfrac{3d^4m^3 \times 8d^2m^5}{2d^2m^2 \times 6d^3m^2}$
   b) $\dfrac{2g^2h^3 \times (-3g^2h^2)^2}{3gh \times 6g^2h^2}$
   c) $\dfrac{33x^5y^7 \div 11xy^2}{12x^5y^3 \div 4x^2y^2}$

9. Consider the expression $\dfrac{3x^3y \times 6xy^3}{(-3xy)^2}$.

   a) Substitute $x = -1$ and $y = 2$ into the expression. Then, evaluate the expression.

   b) Simplify the original expression using the exponent laws. Then, substitute the given values and evaluate the expression.

   c) Describe the advantages and disadvantages of each method.

10. The probability of tossing tails with a standard coin is $\dfrac{1}{2}$, because it is one of two possible outcomes. The probability of tossing four tails in a row is

   $\left(\dfrac{1}{2}\right)^4$ or $\dfrac{1}{16}$.

   a) What is the probability of tossing
   • 9 tails in a row?
   • 12 tails in a row?

   b) Write each answer in part a) as a power of a power.

11. a) What is the probability of rolling a 5 with a standard number cube?

   b) What is the probability of rolling five 5s in a row with a standard number cube?

   c) What is the probability of rolling a prime number with a standard number cube?

   d) What is the probability of not rolling a 2 with a standard number cube?

12. A triangular pyramid has the numbers 1, 2, 3, and 4 on its sides.

   a) What is the probability of rolling a 3?

   b) What is the probability of rolling four 3s in a row? Write as a power. Then, evaluate the expression.

   c) What is the probability of rolling seven 3s in a row? Write as a power. Then, evaluate the expression.

C

13. Evaluate each of the following. Express each answer in scientific notation and then in standard notation.

   a) $4 \times 10^4 \times 2 \times 10^3$

   b) $1.4 \times 10^3 \times 5 \times 10^2$

   c) $(8 \times 10^9) \div (4 \times 10^5)$

   d) $(4.6 \times 10^{11}) \div (2 \times 10^9)$

14. If $x^3 = \dfrac{1}{8}$, place the following values in order from least to greatest:

   $x, x^2, \dfrac{1}{x}, \dfrac{1}{x^2}$

15. a) Predict the screen output of your scientific or graphing calculator when you enter the following calculations: $(4 \times 10^9) \div (8 \times 10^5)$.

   b) Is the answer what you predicted? Explain the answer that the calculator provided.

3.4 Communicate With Algebra

Principles of Mathematics 9, pages 130–139

A

1. Identify the coefficient and the variable part of each term.

   a) $3x$

   b) $-5y$

   c) dm

   d) $-4ab$

2. Identify the coefficient and the variable part of each term.

   a) $-w^3y^2$

   b) $-0.2e^5f$

   c) $\dfrac{2}{3}x^5$

   d) $-\dfrac{3}{8}y^4$

3. Classify each polynomial by the number of terms.

   a) $4x^3$

   b) $-5ab + c$

   c) $7a^6 + b^5 - 10$

   d) $-3m^7 n^4$

   e) $x^2 - 3x + 4$

   f) $x^2 - y$

4. State the degree of each term.

   a) $6x$

   b) $-5x^3$

   c) $7y$

   d) u^5v^3

   e) $0.4m^3n$

   f) $\dfrac{2}{3}x^3y^5$

   g) 5

   h) -3

5. State the degree of each polynomial.

   a) $2x + 5$

   b) $a^2 - 3a - 5$

   c) $d + 3e^3$

   d) $m^4n^3 - 6m^5n^4$

   e) $3xy + \dfrac{1}{2}x^3y^2$

   f) $4x^2y^3 - \dfrac{2}{5}x^5y^3$

6. A soccer team earns 2 points for a win and 1 point for a tie. Let w represent the number of wins and t represent the number of ties. Write an expression that describes the team's total points.

B

7. The students at Northdale High School sell coupon books to raise money for a school trip. The school receives 45% of the money paid for the coupon books.

   a) Choose a variable to represent the money paid for the coupon books.

   b) Using your variable from part a), write the expression for the amount of money the school will receive.

   c) Shannon sold one coupon book to her grandmother for $20. Calculate the amount of money the school receives on this sale.

   d) The sum of all coupon book orders was $14 000. Use your formula to calculate how much the school will receive for this fundraiser.

8. In a basketball game, each player on the team receives 2 points for a basket and 1 point for a free throw.

   a) Write an expression to represent a player's total score for the game.

   b) In the game, Mohamed scored six baskets and five free throws. Use your expression to find Mohamed's total score.

9. On a multiple-choice test, you earn 1 point for each correct answer and lose 2 points for each incorrect answer.

   a) Write an expression for a student's total score.

   b) Tim answered 22 questions correctly and 3 incorrectly. Find Tim's score.

10. Elizabeth has a summer job at a camera store. She earns a $10 bonus for each gold membership and a $5 bonus for each silver membership.

    a) Write a polynomial expression that describes Elizabeth's total bonus.

    b) Identify the variable and the coefficient of each term and explain what they mean.

    c) How much will Elizabeth's bonus be if she sells 20 gold memberships and 30 silver memberships?

11. A theatre charges $80 for orchestra seats, $50 for dress circle seats, and $25 for balcony seats.

    a) Write an expression that describes the total earnings from seat sales.

    b) Identify the variable and the coefficient of each term and explain what they mean.

    c) How much will the theatre earn if it sells 100 orchestra seats, 200 dress circle seats, and 150 balcony seats?

    d) How much with the theatre earn if it sells 80 orchestra seats, 250 dress circle seats, and 200 balcony seats?

C

12. Protect-a-Boat Insurance Company charges $400 for liability, plus 15% of the value of the boat, plus $200 per passenger.

    a) Write an expression to model the insurance cost.

    b) Find the cost of insurance for a $120 000 boat that can carry 60 passengers.

13. Judy is training for an Ironman triathlon race. During her training program, she finds that she can swim at 1.5 km/h, cycle at 30 km/h, and run at 12 km/h. To estimate her time for an upcoming race, Judy rearranges the formula distance = speed × time to find that time = $\dfrac{\text{distance}}{\text{speed}}$.

    a) Choose a variable to represent the distance travelled for each part of the race. For example, choose c for cycle.

    b) Copy and complete the table. The second row is done for you.

Part of the Race	Speed (km/h)	Distance (km)	Time (h)
swim			
cycle	30	c	$\dfrac{c}{30}$
run			

    c) Write a trinomial to model Judy's time.

    d) The upcoming Ironman race is a triathlon composed of a 3.8-km swim, a 180.2-km cycle, and a full marathon run of 42.2 km. Using your expression from part c), calculate how long it will take Judy to finish the race.

3.5 Collect Like Terms
Principles of Mathematics 9, pages 144–153

A

1. Classify each pair of terms as either like or unlike.
   a) $5x$ and $-4x$
   b) $4a$ and $4b$
   c) $-x^3$ and $-3x$
   d) $5m^2$ and $4m^2$
   e) $4xy$ and $3yx$
   f) $4a^2b$ and $-3ab^2$

2. Write two like terms for each.
   a) $10d$
   b) $-m$
   c) $5a^2$
   d) $-4ab$
   e) $4x^2y^2$
   f) 8

3. Copy the two columns of terms into your notebook. Connect each term in the first column with the like term in the second column.

$5x$	$-3a^2b^2$
$-3mn$	$2x^3$
8	$-3x$
$4a^5$	-5
$-2x^3$	$5mn$
$6a^2b^2$	$7a^5$

4. Simplify by collecting like terms.
   a) $5x + 2 + 3x + 4$
   b) $4y + 5 - 2y - 3$
   c) $4m - 3 - m + 4$
   d) $6n - 4 - 5n - 2$
   e) $3x^2 + 5 + 2x^2 + 4$
   f) $7a + 3b - 4a - 5b$

5. Simplify.
   a) $3x^2 + 5x + 4x^2 + 2x$
   b) $5a - 1 + 3 - 2a - 4 - a$
   c) $4m^2 + 3m + 2 - 2m^2 - 5m - 3$
   d) $5w^3 + 4w^2 - 3w - w^3 + 2w^2 + 2w$

6. Simplify.
   a) $3a^2 - 2ab - 2b^2 - 2a^2 - ab + b^2$
   b) $2m^3n^2 + 3m^2n^3 - m^3n^2 - 2m^2n^3$
   c) $-4x^2y + 5x - 3 - 3x^2y - 8x + 5$
   d) $5r^4 + 3r^2 - 4 + 2r^4 - 2r^2 + 1$

B

7. The length of a rectangular garden is five times its width.
   a) Write an expression for the perimeter of the garden.
   b) Find the perimeter if the garden is 20 m wide.
   c) Find the length and width if the perimeter is 180 m.
   d) Write an expression for the area of the garden.
   e) Find the area if the garden is 30 m wide.
   f) Find the length and width if the area is 500 m^2.

8. Use algebra tiles, virtual algebra tiles, or a diagram to model and simplify each expression.
   a) $2x + 3 + 4x + 1$
   b) $5y + 2 - 3y - 1$
   c) $2c^2 + 3c + 4c^2 - 4c$

9. A square has an unknown side length, x.

   a) Write a simplified expression for its perimeter.

   b) Write a simplified expression for its area.

   c) If the area of the square is 25 m², find the perimeter of the square.

10. Kathe's Kitchen Stores estimates its profits at its five stores for the next x months as follows.

Store	Profit ($)
North End	$1500x - 3200$
South End	$1300x - 900$
West End	$2150x - 1100$
East End	$1700x - 5000$
Central	$1850x - 800$

   a) Copy the table, and add a column titled **Profit (or Loss) After 2 Months ($)**. Complete the table and find the sum of the profits (or losses).

   b) Write a polynomial representing the total profit (or loss) at all five stores.

   c) Use your polynomial from part b) to calculate the sum of the profits (or losses) from all five stores after 2 months. Compare this to your answer from part a).

   d) Calculate the total profit (or loss) after 1 year.

11. A regular pentagon has an unknown side length, x. Write a simplified expression for its perimeter.

C
12. John simplified the following expression:
$$x^2 + 3x + x^2 + 2x$$
$$= x^4 + 6x^2$$

   a) Describe the error that John made.

   b) How can you convince John that these two expressions are not equal?

   c) Simplify the expression properly. How can you convince John that your answer is correct?

13. When asked his birth year, the 19th-century British mathematician Augustus De Morgan said that he was x years old in the year x^2. In what year was he born?

3.6 Add and Subtract Polynomials
Principles of Mathematics 9, pages 154–159

A

1. Simplify by removing brackets and collecting like terms.

   a) $(3x + 2) + (5x + 3)$

   b) $(7m - 5) + (3m + 4)$

   c) $(-3n + 5) + (n - 4)$

   d) $(3k + 2) + (5k + 4) + (2k + 3)$

   e) $(6r + 5) + (4r - 1) + (3r - 2)$

2. Simplify by adding the opposite polynomial.

   a) $(3x + 5) - (2x + 3)$

   b) $(7m + 4) - (3m + 3)$

   c) $(5s - 2) - (3s + 5)$

   d) $(4d - 5) - (2d - 3)$

   e) $(3r + 7) - (2r - 5)$

   f) $(6t - 5) - (3t + 7)$

3. Simplify.

   a) $(3x + 5) + (4x - 3)$

   b) $(5y - 4) + (7y - 3)$

   c) $(4p^2 + 8p + 2) + (2p^2 - 3p - 4)$

   d) $(6m^2 - 5mn - 5n^2) - (m^2 + mn - 4n^2)$

   e) $(4a + 5b) + (2a - 3b) - (3a - b)$

   f) $(3p^2 - 2p) + (3p + 5q) - (2q - 2p^2)$

B

4. A soccer team gives each player a bonus on top of his or her base salary for every goal the player scores. Data for some of the team's players are given.

Player	Base Salary ($1000s)	Goals
Gerros	60	70
Makaros	50	20
Smith	70	80

   a) Find a simplified expression for the total earnings for these three players if b represents the bonus, in dollars.

   b) Find the total earnings for these three players when $b = \$300$.

5. Winson is building a dock at his cottage. The length of the dock is twice the width, plus 3 m.

   a) Draw a diagram of the dock and label the width and length with algebraic expressions.

   b) Find a simplified algebraic expression for the perimeter of the dock.

   c) Find an algebraic expression for the area of the dock.

   d) If the width of the dock is 2 m, find the perimeter and area of the dock.

6. A group of employees at a shoe store are paid a yearly salary according to the following rate, where n is the amount of sales.

Employee	Fixed Yearly Salary ($)	Commission
Susan	40 000	$0.10n$
Kelvin	35 000	$0.20n$
Jean	25 000	$0.14n$
Luxana	20 000	$0.16n$

a) Write a simplified expression for the total amount paid to the group of employees.

b) This table shows the sales achievement levels for the company.

Status	Sales ($)
Silver	50 000
Gold	75 000
Platinum	100 000

Determine the total annual salary for the group if their sales achievement level

- reaches silver status

- reaches gold status

- reaches platinum status

c) Which employee makes the highest salary at each achievement level?

7. Copy and complete the addition cascade.

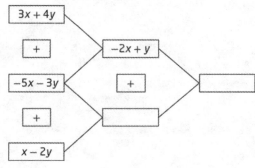

8. Copy and complete the subtraction cascade.

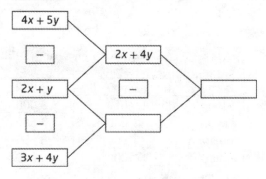

C

9. A women's hockey team gives players a bonus on top of their base salary for every goal and for every assist they score. Data for some of the team's players are given.

Player	Base Salary ($1000s)	Goals	Assists
Cruz	80	35	25
Gortan	60	20	18
McKinnon	100	42	30

a) Write an algebraic expression for the earnings of each of these three players, where g represents the bonus for goals and a represents the bonus for assists.

b) Find a simplified expression for the total earnings for these three players.

c) Find the total earnings for these three players if $g = 200$ and $a = 100$.

10. A group of employees at a store are paid a weekly salary and a commission of 5% of their total weekly sales. The sales for last week are listed in the table.

Employee	Fixed Weekly Salary ($)	Total Sales ($)
Jack	700	10 000
Yaling	650	8 000
Stacia	800	6 500
Meisrain	900	8 500
Janet	1000	5 000

a) Determine the weekly earnings for each employee.

b) Find a simplified expression for the total amount paid to the group of employees, if c represents the commission, expressed as a decimal.

3.7 The Distributive Property
Principles of Mathematics 9, pages 160–169

A

1. Expand, using the distributive property.
   a) $3(x + 2)$
   b) $4(x - 5)$
   c) $-2(x + 4)$
   d) $-5(x - 4)$

2. Expand, using the distributive property.
   a) $4(2a + 3)$
   b) $6(3b - 4)$
   c) $-(6m + 5)$
   d) $-(4r - 3)$

3. Expand.
   a) $x(x + 4)$
   b) $a(a - 5)$
   c) $z(-z + 3)$
   d) $b(-2b + 1)$

4. Expand.
   a) $-w(3w + 5)$
   b) $-m(3m - 2)$
   c) $4q(3q + 7)$
   d) $-7d(-2d - 5)$

5. Expand, using the distributive property.
   a) $(m + 2) \times 3$
   b) $(d - 3) \times 5$
   c) $(3h + 5) \times (-2)$
   d) $(4r - 1) \times (-3)$

6. Expand, using the distributive property.
   a) $(q - 4) \times 5$
   b) $(b - 6) \times 7$
   c) $(5t + 7) \times (-4)$
   d) $(7c - 3) \times (-5)$

7. Expand.
   a) $3(x^2 + 5x + 4)$
   b) $5(x^2 - 3x + 2)$
   c) $4m(m^2 + 3m + 5)$
   d) $5a(a^2 + a - 4)$
   e) $(x^2 + 7x + 3)(3)$

8. Expand.
   a) $(x^2 + x - 1)(-4)$
   b) $(a^2 - a + 4)(5)$
   c) $(r^2 + r - 5)(-1)$
   d) $5[x + 3(x + 2)]$
   e) $-4[5(b - 3) - b]$

B

9. Expand and simplify.
   a) $5(x + 4) + 3(x - 6)$
   b) $3(a - 5) - 2(a + 4)$
   c) $0.3(c + 2) + 0.5(2c - 5)$
   d) $-4(4d - 3) - 2(3d + 4)$
   e) $3k(k + 5) + 4k(k - 3)$

10. An electrician charges $75 per visit plus $25/h for house calls.

a) Write an algebraic expression that describes the service charge for one household visit.

b) Use your expression to find the total service charge for a 3.5-h repair job.

c) Suppose all charges are double for evenings, weekends, and holidays. Write a simplified expression for these service charges.

d) Use your simplified expression from part c) to calculate the cost for a 3.5-h repair job on the weekend. Does this answer make sense?

11. Expand and simplify.

   a) $-0.4h(3h-2) - 0.3h(2h+3)$

   b) $3(a+2) + 5(a-3) - 2(a+4)$

   c) $4(r-3) - 3(r+2) + 2(r-5)$

   d) $3a(2a+3) + 4(a^2 + 2a - 4)$

   e) $5g(2g-3) - 3(2g^2 - 4g + 3)$

12. A room has dimensions as shown.

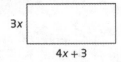

   a) Find a simplified expression for the perimeter.

   b) Find a simplified expression for the area.

   c) Repeat parts a) and b) if both the length and width are doubled.

   d) Has this doubled the perimeter? Justify your answer.

   e) Has this doubled the area? Justify your answer.

13. The formula for the surface area of a rectangular prism is
$SA = 2(lw + hw + lh)$. Apply the distributive property to write this formula in another way.

14. Expand and simplify.

   a) $\dfrac{1}{4}(8x+3) + \dfrac{1}{3}(6x+2)$

   b) $\dfrac{1}{5}(-5a+2b) - \dfrac{3}{4}(4a-b)$

   c) $\dfrac{2}{3}(3m+5) + \dfrac{2}{5}(5m-4)$

   d) $\dfrac{1}{2}(6a-5c) - \dfrac{1}{3}(6a+4c)$

C

15. Expand and simplify.

   a) $3x[x + 4(x+2)]$

   b) $4m[3m - 2(m-5)]$

   c) $2a[3a(a+4)] - a(2a-3)]$

   d) $4[3 - 2(b+1)] + 3[4 - 2(b+1)]$

   e) $-2[4 - (y-4)] - 3[2 + (y-3)]$

   f) $-3[2c + (c+3)] + 2[3c - (c-2)]$

16. Expand and simplify.

   a) $(x+3)(x+4)$

   b) $(a+5)(a+6)$

   c) $(b+7)(b+3)$

   d) $(w+2)(w+8)$

   e) $(d+5)(d-2)$

17. Expand and simplify.

   a) $(z+3)(z-6)$

   b) $(m-4)(m+5)$

   c) $(y-5)(y+3)$

   d) $(h-4)(h-8)$

   e) $(p-3)(p-3)$

18. Expand and simplify.

   a) $(x+2)(x^2 + 3x + 4)$

   b) $(y+3)(y^2 - 4y - 5)$

Chapter 3 Review
Principles of Mathematics 9, pages 174–175

1. Use algebra tiles to build a model for each situation. Write an algebraic expression to represent the model.
   a) Sheila swam 5 km.
   b) Ursula walked an unknown distance, three times.
   c) Tasnia drove 5 km plus an unknown distance.
   d) Susu read a book twice.

2. a) Build a volume model to represent a cube with side length 4 cm. Sketch the model and label the length, width, and height.
   b) What is the volume of the cube? Write this as a power.
   c) Write an expression for the area of one face of the cube as a power. Evaluate the area of one face.
   d) Write an expression for the surface area of the cube. Evaluate the surface area of the cube.

3. Evaluate.
   a) 5^3
   b) $(-2)^6$
   c) $\left(\dfrac{3}{4}\right)^3$
   d) 1.06^5

4. Write as a single power. Then, evaluate the expression.
   a) $3^2 \times 3^3 \times 3$
   b) $5^6 \div 5 \div 5^2$
   c) $4^6 \div 4^5 \times 4^2$
   d) $2^3 \times 2^5 \div 2^4$
   e) $[(-3)^2]^3$
   f) $\dfrac{(5^4)^3}{5^5 \times 5^4}$

5. E. coli is a type of bacteria that can cause dangerous health problems. It doubles every 20 min. The initial population of a sample of E. coli is 400.
   a) Copy and complete this table.

Time (min)	Population of E. coli
0	400
20	800
40	
60	
80	
100	
120	

   b) Construct a graph of population versus time. Use a smooth curve to connect the points. Describe the shape of the graph.
   c) What will the population be after
   • 5 h?   • 8 h?

6. Simplify.
   a) $a^5 b^4 \times a^3 b^2$
   b) $\dfrac{d^6 \times d^5}{d^7}$
   c) $\dfrac{m^{10}}{m^3 \times m^5}$
   d) $\dfrac{(y^6)^3}{(y^5)^2}$

7. Identify the coefficient and variable part of each term.
   a) $6x$
   b) $-5y$
   c) 7
   d) $4a^5 b^3$
   e) dm
   f) $\dfrac{2}{3}x^2 y^3$

8. In a hockey tournament, teams are awarded 4 points for a win and 2 points for an overtime win.

   a) Write an expression that describes the number of points a team has.

   b) Use your expression to find the number of points earned by a team that has five wins and two overtime wins.

9. State the degree of each term.

   a) $5x^4$

   b) $-7m^5$

   c) a^3b^2c

   d) 5

10. State the degree of each polynomial.

   a) $5x + 4$

   b) $3y^4 - 2$

   c) $5m^2 + 3m + 6$

   d) $6a^3 - 5a^2 + 4a - 3$

11. Classify each pair of terms as either like or unlike.

   a) $3x$ and $-7x$

   b) $4y$ and $5z$

   c) $4ab$ and $-2ab$

   d) $3x^2y$ and $4xy^2$

   e) $5xy$ and $3yx$

   f) $5m^2$ and $8m^2$

12. Identify the like terms in each set.

   a) $5a^2, -3b, 2d, 6x^2, 7b^3, -5x^2, 4a, 6c$

   b) $6y^2, 5y^2, -4y^3, 3, -4y^2, -2y^3$

13. Simplify by collecting like terms.

   a) $3x + 5y + 4x + 6y$

   b) $5d + 3m - 4d - 5m$

   c) $2a^2 - 5a + 3 - a^2 + 2a - 6$

   d) $3w^2 + 2wy - y^2 - 2w^2 - 2wy + 4y^2$

   e) $4d - 8e - 6f + 3d + 5e - 10f$

   f) $6a^3 - 4ab + 5b^2 - 3 + 5a^3 - 3ab$

14. Simplify.

   a) $(5x + 3) + (6x - 4)$

   b) $(4y - 3) + (5y - 2)$

   c) $(3p^2 + 5p + 4) + (7p^2 - 4p - 3)$

   d) $(4m^2 - 3mn - 2n^2) - (m^2 + mn - 5n^2)$

   e) $(6a + 8b) + (3a - 4b) - (5a - 3b)$

15. A rectangular cake has dimensions $4x$ by $3x + 2$. Find a simplified expression for its perimeter.

16. Expand.

   a) $5(x + 2)$

   b) $-4(y - 3)$

   c) $2m(3m + 4)$

   d) $-4g(2g - 3)$

17. Expand and simplify.

   a) $4(2x + 3y) + 5(3x + 6y)$

   b) $3(4y - 2w) - 3(2y + 1)$

   c) $4(3a + 2b) + 3(2a - 3b) - (a + 2b)$

   d) $-4[3 - 2(c + 5) - 4c]$

4.1 Solve Simple Equations
Principles of Mathematics 9, pages 186–195

A

1. Solve by inspection.

   a) $x + 4 = 7$

   b) $y - 3 = 5$

   c) $4m = 12$

   d) $\dfrac{c}{3} = 2$

2. Solve using the balance method.

   a) $x + 2 = 6$

   b) $y - 2 = 4$

   c) $3a = 15$

   d) $\dfrac{b}{4} = 5$

3. Solve using opposite operations.

   a) $x + 5 = 8$

   b) $g - 5 = -3$

   c) $2 + h = 9$

   d) $-3 + c = -5$

4. Solve using opposite operations.

   a) $d + 5 = -2$

   b) $k - 4 = -1$

   c) $5u = -20$

   d) $\dfrac{w}{5} = -2$

B

5. Find the root of each equation using paper and pencil. Apply opposite operations. Check each root.

   a) $5x + 3 = 13$

   b) $7w - 3 = 11$

   c) $-2p + 3 = -5$

   d) $-4h - 5 = -1$

6. Use a Computer Algebra System (CAS) to solve. Apply opposite operations. Check each solution.

   a) $q + 3 = 5$

   b) $a - 6 = 7$

   c) $3m + 5 = 11$

   d) $-4b + 3 = -1$

7. Solve using the method of your choice. Check your answers.

   a) $a + 8 = -2$

   b) $c - 4 = 3$

   c) $-6d = -30$

   d) $\dfrac{h}{5} = -3$

8. Solve using the method of your choice. Check your answers.

   a) $5r + 7 = 42$

   b) $-3v + 5 = 8$

   c) $8 + 7g = 15$

   d) $-2j - 8 = 0$

9. At a computer store, packages of DVDs sell for $15 each. One customer buys $120 worth of DVDs.

   a) Write an equation to model the number of packages of DVDs the customer bought.

   b) Solve the equation.

10. Solve each equation. Express fraction answers in lowest terms. Check each solution.

    a) $3h + 4 = 6$

    b) $5k - 3 = -2$

    c) $-7w + 2 = -3$

11. Solve each equation. Express fraction answers in lowest terms. Check each solution.

    a) $-4d - 3 = -1$

    b) $3r + \dfrac{2}{5} = -4$

    c) $5t - 4 = \dfrac{2}{3}$

12. Copy the following solution. Write a short explanation beside each step. The first step has been done for you.

Step	Explanation
$5x - 4 = 6$	
$5x - 4 + 4 = 6 + 4$	Add 4 to both sides.
$5x = 10$	
$\dfrac{5x}{5} = \dfrac{10}{5}$	
$x = 2$	

C

13. The equation $a + b + c = 180°$ describes the sum of the angles in a triangle.

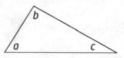

    a) Use this formula to find the values of a, b, and c when $b = 2a$ and $c = 3a$.

    b) Use this formula to find the values of a, b, and c when $b = 3a$ and $c = 5a$.

14. The publicity committee of the organizing committee of a mathematics conference has $2000 to buy T-shirts for the student volunteers. Reflexx Services, a T-shirt supplier, charges $15 per T-shirt plus a $250 logo design fee.

    a) Write an equation that models the number of T-shirts the publicity committee can afford.

    b) Solve the equation. Write a conclusion to the problem.

15. Margaret is buying a new boat. The fuel tank of the boat has a mass of 2000 g. Each litre of gasoline has a mass of 840 g. The total mass of the gasoline plus the tank cannot exceed 10 400 g.

    a) Write an equation that models the number of litres of gasoline that the tank may hold.

    b) Solve the equation to determine the number of litres of gasoline in a full tank.

4.2 Solve Multi-Step Equations
Principles of Mathematics 9, pages 196–203

A

1. Solve using pencil and paper.

   a) $5 + 3x + 4x = 19$

   b) $15y - 6 - 10y = 9$

   c) $32 = 5 - 4a - 5a$

   d) $5m + 3 - 9m + 13 = 0$

2. Solve using pencil and paper.

   a) $6w + 8 = 4w + 18$

   b) $-8k - 5 = 2k + 15$

   c) $3b - 6 = -b - 2$

   d) $5 + 4d = -13 - 2d$

3. Solve using a Computer Algebra System (CAS). Use at least two steps.

   a) $7t + 8 = 3t - 12$

   b) $5c - 3 - 4c = 2c + 2$

   c) $0 = 4x + 3 - x - 9$

   d) $14 - n - 7 = 5n + 1$

4. Find the root of each equation using pencil and paper. Check each solution.

   a) $5(x + 4) = 3x + 14$

   b) $5q - 6 = 2(q + 3)$

   c) $4t + 3(2 - t) = 13$

   d) $u = 3(5 - u) + 1$

5. Find the root of each equation using pencil and paper. Check each solution.

   a) $3(r + 4) + 2(r + 5) = 32$

   b) $5(y - 3) - 3(y - 4) = 12$

   c) $4(v + 3) = 2(v + 6) - 8$

   d) $2(y - 4) = -3(y + 2) + 8$

B

6. Two or more angles are supplementary if their sum is 180°. An angle is four times the value of its supplement. Set up and solve an equation to find the measures of the two angles.

7. Two or more angles are complementary if their sum is 90°. Three angles are complementary. One angle is three times the value of the smallest angle. The largest angle is five times the value of the smallest angle. Find the measures of the three angles.

8. Solve each equation using the method of your choice. Express fraction answers in lowest terms. Check your answers.

   a) $5x - 2 = 2x + 3$

   b) $4 + 5h = h - 2$

   c) $4(m + 3) + 2(m - 3) = 3(m - 2)$

   d) $7 - (4p + 3) = -3(p + 2) - (2p + 3)$

9. An equilateral triangle and a rectangle have the same perimeter. Find the side lengths of the equilateral triangle and the rectangle.

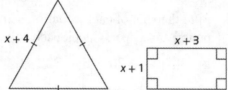

10. A family of isosceles triangles has the property that the two equal angles are each one third the value of the third angle. Find the measures of the angles.

11. The following shows that $x = -3$ is the correct solution to the equation $3(x + 4) + 6 = 9 - (x + 3)$. Copy this check and explain each step. The first step has been done for you.

Step	Explanation
L.S. = $3(x + 4) + 6$	
$\quad = 3[(-3) + 4] + 6$	Substitute the root into the left side.
$\quad = 3(1) + 6$	
$\quad = 3 + 6$	
$\quad = 9$	

R.S. = $9 - (x + 3)$	
$\quad = 9 - [(-3) + 3]$	
$\quad = 9 - (0)$	
$\quad = 9$	

L.S. = R.S.

Therefore, $x = -3$ is correct.

C

12. A family of isosceles triangles has side lengths in the ratio 2:2:3. A triangle belonging to this family has a perimeter of 70 cm.

   a) Find the length of each side.

   b) Explain how you solved this.

13. A family of right triangles has side lengths in the approximate ratio 3:4:5. One right triangle belonging to the family has a perimeter of 180 cm. Find its area.

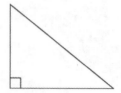

14. Solve each equation. Express fraction answers in lowest terms.

   a) $\dfrac{1}{3}(x + 3) = \dfrac{1}{5}(x - 3)$

   b) $\dfrac{1}{5}k + \dfrac{1}{3} = \dfrac{1}{4}k + \dfrac{1}{2}$

   c) $m(m + 3) + 5m = 3 + m(m - 4)$

   d) $8 - d(d + 4) = 3d - d(d + 2) + 5$

4.3 Solve Equations Involving Fractions
Principles of Mathematics 9, pages 204–210

A

1. Solve using pencil and paper.

   a) $\dfrac{1}{4}(x-3) = -2$

   b) $6 = -\dfrac{3}{5}(a-7)$

   c) $\dfrac{m+7}{5} = 3$

2. Solve using pencil and paper.

   a) $9 = \dfrac{3(k+4)}{2}$

   b) $\dfrac{3k+5}{2} = 10$

   c) $1 = \dfrac{2p-3}{5}$

3. Solve using a Computer Algebra System (CAS). Use at least two steps.

   a) $\dfrac{y-5}{3} = -4$

   b) $\dfrac{1}{3}(p+2) = -5$

   c) $3 = \dfrac{4}{5}(h+2)$

4. Solve using a CAS. Use at least two steps.

   a) $5 = \dfrac{4(n+3)}{2}$

   b) $6 = \dfrac{7-c}{2}$

   c) $\dfrac{3+w}{-2} = 4$

B

5. Find the root of each equation. Check your answers.

   a) $\dfrac{h-4}{5} = \dfrac{h-3}{6}$

   b) $\dfrac{d-2}{4} = \dfrac{d+1}{3}$

   c) $\dfrac{1}{3}(x+4) = \dfrac{1}{5}(x+2)$

6. Find the root of each equation. Check your answers.

   a) $\dfrac{1}{4}(p-7) = \dfrac{1}{6}(p-3)$

   b) $\dfrac{2(k-5)}{3} = \dfrac{4(k+2)}{5}$

   c) $\dfrac{3(s-4)}{4} = \dfrac{2(s-3)}{3}$

7. Find the root of each equation. Use a CAS to check your answers.

   a) $\dfrac{2}{5}(3m+2) = \dfrac{3}{4}(m+5)$

   b) $\dfrac{2}{3}(k+2) = \dfrac{3}{4}(2k-1)$

   c) $\dfrac{4c+5}{3} = \dfrac{2c+4}{5}$

   d) $\dfrac{5-3n}{4} = \dfrac{2-n}{3}$

   e) $\dfrac{2(3w+4)}{5} = \dfrac{2(2w-1)}{3}$

8. A trapezoidal deck has an area of 96 m². The front and back widths are 6 m and 10 m, as shown. What is the length of the deck from front to back?

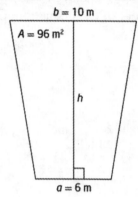

$b = 10$ m

$A = 96$ m²

h

$a = 6$ m

9. Each solution contains an error. Identify the error and describe how to correct it.

a)
$$\frac{x+5}{4} = \frac{x-2}{3}$$
$$4(x+5) = 3(x-2)$$
$$4x + 20 = 3x - 6$$
$$4x + 20 - 3x - 20 = 3x - 6 - 3x - 20$$
$$x = -26$$

b)
$$\frac{1}{5}(2y+4) = \frac{1}{2}(y-3)$$
$$10 \times \frac{1}{5}(2y+4) = 10 \times \frac{1}{2}(y-3)$$
$$2y + 4 = y - 3$$
$$2y + 4 - y - 4 = y - 3 - y - 4$$
$$y = -7$$

10. Find the base of a triangle with height 8 cm and area 72 cm².

C

11. The equation $F = \frac{9}{5}C + 32$ allows you to convert between Fahrenheit and Celsius temperatures. C is the temperature in degrees Celsius (°C) and F is the temperature in degrees Fahrenheit (°F).

a) The temperature at a resort is 30°C. What is this equivalent to in degrees Fahrenheit?

b) The temperature in the living room of a house is 77°F. What is this equivalent to in degrees Celsius?

12. Solve.

a) $\dfrac{2a}{3} + \dfrac{a-4}{5} = \dfrac{1}{2}$

b) $\dfrac{u+1}{2} + \dfrac{2u+3}{3} = \dfrac{u}{4}$

c) $\dfrac{w+3}{4} = \dfrac{w}{3} + \dfrac{2w-1}{5}$

13. The balcony of an apartment is in the shape of a right triangle in which the height is twice the base. The hypotenuse of the triangular area is 4.5 m.

a) Determine the height and base of the triangular area. Round your answers to one decimal place.

b) Approximately how much indoor-outdoor carpet is needed to cover the floor of the balcony?

4.4 Modelling With Formulas
Principles of Mathematics 9, pages 211–219

A

1. Rearrange each formula to isolate the variable indicated using pencil and paper.
    a) $C = \pi d$ for d (circumference of a circle)
    b) $d = vt$ for t (distance)
    c) $A = P + I$ for I (investments)

2. Rearrange each formula to isolate the variable indicated using pencil and paper.
    a) $y = mx + b$ for m (linear relations)
    b) $Ax + By + C = 0$ for y (linear relations)
    c) $F = ma$ for a (motion)
    d) $V = IR$ for R (voltage)

3. Rearrange each formula to isolate the variable indicated.
    a) $V = s^3$ for s (volume of a cube)
    b) $P = I^2 R$ for R (electrical power)
    c) $V = \pi r^2 h$ for h (volume of a cylinder)

4. Rearrange each formula to isolate the variable indicated.
    a) $P = 2l + 2w$ for l (perimeter of a rectangle)
    b) $A = s^2$ for s (area of a square)
    c) $A = \dfrac{1}{2}bh$ for h (area of a triangle)
    d) $c^2 = a^2 + b^2$ for a (Pythagorean theorem)

B

5. You can use the formula $w = 2.2m$ to obtain an approximate value for converting a mass, m, in kilograms, to a weight, w, in pounds.
    a) Use the formula to find the number of pounds in
       • 3 kg
       • 500 g (1 kg = 1000 g)
    b) Rearrange the formula to express m in terms of w.
    c) How many kilograms are in 8 pounds? Round your answer to the nearest tenth of a kilogram.

6. a) Plot a graph of $w = 2.2m$ either by hand or by using technology such as a graphing calculator or graphing software.
    b) Is the graph linear or non-linear? Explain.
    c) Use the graph to find
       • the number of kilograms in 3 pounds
       • the number of pounds in 5 kg
       Round your answers to the nearest tenth, if necessary.

7. The surface area, A, of a cube is related to the length of a side of the cube, s, by the formula $A = 6s^2$.
    a) Rearrange this formula to express s in terms of A.
    b) Find the length of the side of a cube with surface area 800 cm^2. Round your answer to the nearest tenth of a centimetre.

8. Refer to question 7.

a) Solve this problem using a graphing calculator or graphing software, by entering the equation shown.

```
Plot1 Plot2 Plot3
\Y1 = √(X/6)
\Y2 =
\Y3 =
\Y4 =
\Y5 =
\Y6 =
\Y7 =
```

b) Is this a linear or a non-linear relation? Explain how you know.

9. Sometimes the same formula can have many different forms. The formula $I = Prt$ is a useful formula in business.

Variable	Meaning
I	interest
P	principal
r	rate, expressed as a decimal
t	time, in years

Rearrange this formula to isolate each variable. The first one is done for you as an example.

$$I = Prt$$

$$\frac{I}{rt} = \frac{Prt}{rt}$$

$$\frac{I}{rt} = P$$

C

10. The volume, V, of a cube is related to its side length, s, by the formula $V = s^3$.

a) Express s in terms of V.

b) Graph both formulas using a graphing calculator or graphing software.

c) How are the graphs similar?

d) How are the graphs different?

11. The law of universal gravitation states that the force of gravitational attraction is directly proportional to the product of the masses and inversely proportional to the square of the separation distance between their centres:

$$F = \frac{Gm_1m_2}{d^2}$$

In this formula,

- m_1 and m_2 are the masses, in kilograms, of the attracting objects
- d is the separation distance, in metres, as measured from object centre to object centre
- G is the proportionality constant $(6.67 \times 10^{-11}\ \text{N} \cdot \text{m}^2/\text{kg}^2)$

The following steps show how the formula can be rearranged to express d in terms of F, G, m_1, and m_2. Copy these steps into your notebook and write a short explanation beside each one. Some hints are provided for you.

Step	Explanation
$F = \dfrac{Gm_1m_2}{d^2}$	Start with the original formula.
$Fd^2 = Gm_1m_2$	_____ both sides of the equation by _____.
$\dfrac{Fd^2}{F} = \dfrac{Gm_1m_2}{F}$	
$d^2 = \dfrac{Gm_1m_2}{F}$	
$\sqrt{d^2} = \sqrt{\dfrac{Gm_1m_2}{F}}$	Take the _____ _____ of both sides.
$d = \sqrt{\dfrac{Gm_1m_2}{F}}$	

4.5 Modelling With Algebra
Principles of Mathematics 9, pages 220–229

A

1. Write an algebraic expression to represent each description.
   a) quadruple a number
   b) three more than a number
   c) one third a number
   d) four less than triple a number

2. Write an algebraic expression to represent each description.
   a) five times a number
   b) six more than twice a number
   c) two less than a number
   d) three fifths of a number

3. Write an equation to represent each sentence. Explain your choice of variable and what it represents in each case.
   a) five times a number is 85
   b) an area increased by 8 is 177
   c) three more than double a number is 33
   d) the sum of three consecutive integers is 168

4. Solve each equation in question 3 and explain what the answer means.

5. Two friends are collecting pop-can tabs. Natasha has 250 more pop-can tabs than Krysten. Together they have collected 880 pop-can tabs. How many pop-can tabs has each friend collected?

B

6. Justin and Kieran both participated in a walk-a-thon to raise money for a charity. Justin raised $20 more than Kieran. Together they raised $95. How much money did they each raise?

7. Jacinth is 4 years older than her sister Naomi. The sum of their ages is 30. How old are the sisters?

8. Jack is selling used computers. He is paid $15/h plus a 5% commission on sales. What dollar amount of computer sales must Jack make to earn $1000 in a 40-h work week?

9. The sum of three consecutive integers is 120. Find the numbers.

10. Alicia and Wayne are both collecting coins. Alicia has three times as many coins as Wayne. Together they have 712 coins. How many coins does Alicia have and how many coins does Wayne have?

11. Sally, Letitia, and Jessica play together on a basketball team. At the end of the season, Sally had scored 8 more points than Letitia, while Letitia had scored twice as many points as Jessica. The three girls scored a total of 108 points. How many points did each girl score?

12. Ashley works part time, 2 h per day, selling memberships to a video club. She is paid $8.50/h, plus a $2 commission for each video club membership that she sells.

a) Write an algebraic expression that describes Ashley's total earnings.

b) Find the amount that Ashley makes in 10 h when she sells 30 memberships.

c) How many memberships does Ashley have to sell to make $475 in a 10-h workweek?

d) How many hours does Ashley have to work to make $250 if she sells 40 memberships?

13. Anoja, Amani, and Azra are three friends who each have part-time jobs. Last week, Anoja earned twice as much money as Azra, while Amani earned $25 more than Anoja. The total earnings of the three friends last week was $450. How much money did each of them earn last week?

14. The length of the banquet hall where Naomi works is double its width. The area of the banquet hall is 200 m².

a) Find the length and width of the banquet hall.

b) If Naomi walks around the perimeter of the banquet hall, how far does she walk?

c) If Naomi walks diagonally across the banquet hall, how far does she walk? Round your answer to the nearest tenth of a metre.

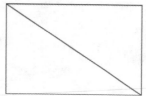

C

15. A reflecting pool is in the shape of a trapezoid. The front width is triple the back width. The pool has an area of 12 m². The distance from the front to the back of the pool is 2 m. Find the front width and the back width of the pool.

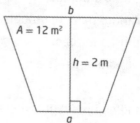

16. An isosceles triangle has been constructed so that its height is one half of its base. Without changing the base length, how should the height of the triangle change to triple the area?

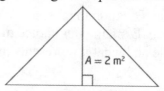

17. Raza works at a flea market selling sunglasses. He is paid $7.50/h plus a 75¢ commission for every pair of sunglasses he sells.

a) Write an equation to model Raza's earnings.

b) Find Raza's earnings if he sells 25 pairs of sunglasses during a 6-h shift.

c) How many pairs of sunglasses must he sell to earn $90 in 8 h?

Chapter 4 Review

Principles of Mathematics 9, pages 230–231

1. Solve using pencil and paper.

    a) $x + 5 = 9$

    b) $f - 7 = 3$

    c) $3h = 15$

    d) $\dfrac{k}{4} = 3$

2. Solve using a Computer Algebra System (CAS).

    a) $2x + 5 = 11$

    b) $3y - 5 = -8$

    c) $10 + 4f = -34$

    d) $-5m - 3 = 12$

3. Find the root of each equation using any method. Express fraction answers in lowest terms. Check each answer.

    a) $5x + 2 = 12$

    b) $3p + 8 = 5$

    c) $4 + 6w = 2$

    d) $-6 + 4u = -3$

4. John has $23.65 to spend on a book and magazines. The book costs $5.95. The magazines cost $2.95 each.

    a) Write an equation that models the number of magazines that John can afford.

    b) Solve the equation.

5. Solve using pencil and paper.

    a) $5x + 4 = 2x + 13$

    b) $4c - 3 = 2c + 5$

    c) $-3r + 7 = -5r - 3$

    d) $-6g - 4 = -3g + 2$

6. Solve using a CAS.

    a) $2a + 5 = 6a + 9$

    b) $3b - 7 = b + 5$

    c) $5n + 8 = 8n - 10$

    d) $-7d + 3 = -3d + 11$

7. A triangle has angle measures that are related as follows:

    • The largest angle is 12 times the smallest angle

    • The middle angle is 5 times the smallest angle.

    Find the measures of the angles.

8. Find the root of each equation using pencil and paper. Check each root.

    a) $\dfrac{1}{2}(x + 3) = 5$

    b) $\dfrac{b - 5}{7} = 3$

    c) $6 = \dfrac{2}{3}m - 1$

    d) $-5 = \dfrac{3d + 4}{3}$

9. Find the root of each equation using a CAS. Check each root.

a) $4 = \dfrac{5r + 7}{3}$

b) $\dfrac{1}{3}(p + 5) = 2p - 3$

c) $3q + 15 = \dfrac{1}{2}(q - 5)$

d) $\dfrac{2b + 5}{4} = 3$

10. Find the solution to each equation.

a) $\dfrac{x - 5}{3} = \dfrac{x + 4}{4}$

b) $\dfrac{3}{4}(y - 2) = \dfrac{2}{3}(y + 1)$

c) $\dfrac{b + 5}{3} = \dfrac{b - 3}{5}$

d) $\dfrac{3}{5}(v + 2) = \dfrac{1}{2}(v - 3)$

11. Rearrange each formula to isolate the variable indicated.

a) $F = ma$ for m (motion)

b) $V = IR$ for I (voltage)

c) $A = \pi r^2$ for r (area of a circle)

d) $P = 2l + 2w$ for w (perimeter of a rectangle)

e) $y = mx + b$ for x (linear relations)

12. The power, P, in an electric circuit is related to the voltage, V, and resistance, R, by the formula $P = \dfrac{V^2}{R}$.

a) Find the power, in watts (W), when the voltage is 100 V (volts) and the resistance is 50 Ω (ohms).

b) What is the resistance of a circuit that uses 100 W of power with a voltage of 20 V?

c) The resistance of a circuit is 15 Ω. The same circuit uses 60 W of power. Find the voltage in the circuit.

13. The total of three cousins' ages is 48. Suresh is half as old as Hakima and 4 years older than Saad. How old are the cousins?

14. Adila sells T-shirts at a rock concert. She earns $8.00/h, plus $0.50 for each T-shirt she sells.

a) How much will Adila earn in a 4-h shift if she sells 35 T-shirts?

b) How many T-shirts must Adila sell to earn $80 in a 6-h shift?

15. Ramesh sells hot dogs at a ball game. He earns $8.50/h, plus $0.35 for each hotdog he sells.

a) How much will Ramesh earn in a 4-h shift if he sells 52 hot dogs?

b) How many hot dogs must Ramesh sell to earn $103 in an 8-h shift?

c) How many hot dogs must Ramesh sell to earn $79 in a 6-h shift?

5.1 Direct Variation
Principles of Mathematics 9, pages 238–245

A

1. Determine the constant of variation for each direct variation.

   a) The distance travelled by a car varies directly with time. The car travels 270 km in 3 h.

   b) The distance travelled on a trip varies directly with the amount of gas used. A car travelled 375 km and used 25 litres of gas.

   c) The money earned by an employee varies directly with time. The employee earned $320 in 40 h.

2. The cost, C, in dollars, of building a patio varies directly with its width, w, in metres.

   a) Find an equation relating C and w if the cost of building a patio with a width of 4 m is $300.

   b) What does the constant of variation represent?

   c) Use the equation to determine the cost of a patio with a width of 7 m.

3. The total cost of potatoes varies directly with the mass, in kilograms, bought. Potatoes cost $2.18/kg.

   a) Choose appropriate letters for variables. Make a table of values showing the cost of 0 kg, 1 kg, 2 kg, 3 kg, 4 kg, and 5 kg of potatoes.

   b) Graph the relationship.

   c) Write an equation for the relationship in the form $y = kx$.

B

4. A marina charges $9.50 per hour to rent a boat.

   a) Describe the relationship between the cost of the boat rental and the time, in hours, the boat is rented for.

   b) Illustrate the relationship graphically and represent it with an equation.

   c) Use your graph to estimate the cost of renting the boat for 12 h.

   d) Use your equation to determine the exact cost of renting the boat for 12 h.

5. A rental agency charges $8 per hour to rent a canoe.

   a) Describe the relationship between the cost of the canoe rental and the time, in hours, the canoe is rented for.

   b) Illustrate the relationship graphically and represent it with an equation.

   c) Use your graph to estimate the cost of renting the canoe for 8 h.

   d) Use your equation to determine the exact cost of renting the canoe for 8 h.

6. A parking lot charges $14.50 per day for long-term parking at the airport.

   a) Describe the relationship between the cost of the long-term parking and the time, in days, the car is parked for.

   b) Illustrate the relationship graphically and represent it with an equation.

   c) Use your graph to estimate the cost of parking the car for 6 days.

   d) Use your equation to determine the exact cost of parking the car for 6 days.

7. The cost of a certain type of cookies varies directly with the number of packages of cookies that are purchased. The cookies cost $3.50/package.

a) Choose appropriate letters for variables. Make a table of values showing the cost of 0 packages, 1 package, 2 packages, 3 packages, and 4 packages.

b) Graph the relationship.

c) Write an equation for the relationship in the form $y = kx$.

8. Alison has a part-time job as a lifeguard. Alison's pay varies directly with the time, in hours, she works. She earns $9.75/h.

a) Explain why this relationship is considered a direct variation.

b) Write an equation representing Alison's regular pay.

c) Graph this relationship, using pencil and paper or technology.

9. Describe a situation that could be illustrated by the graph below.

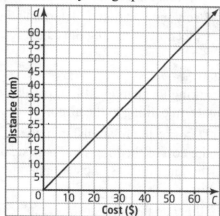

C

10. To raise money for a local charity, students organized a walk-a-thon. For the walk-a-thon, the amount of money raised by each student varied directly with the number of kilometres walked. Dieter raised $320 by walking 20 km.

a) Graph this direct variation for distances from 0 km to 20 km, using pencil and paper or technology.

b) Write an equation relating the money Dieter raised and the distance, in kilometres, that he walked.

c) How much would he have raised by walking 25 km?

11. The volume of water in a water tank varies with time. The tank contains 200 L of water after 2 min.

a) Write an equation relating the volume of water and time. What does the constant of variation represent?

b) Graph this relationship using pencil and paper or technology.

c) What volume of water is in the tank after 30 min?

d) How long will it take to fill a water tank that can hold 100 000 L of water?

12. To convert from Canadian (= British Imperial) gallons to litres, multiply by 4.546. Write an equation to convert litres to Canadian gallons. Round the constant of variation to the nearest thousandth.

5.2 Partial Variation

Principles of Mathematics 9, pages 246–253

A

1. Identify each relation as a direct variation, a partial variation, or neither. Justify your answer.

   a) $y = 10x$

   b) $C = 4t + 3$

   c) $y = 3x + 2$

   d) $d = 3t$

2. a) Copy and complete the table of values given that y varies partially with x.

x	y
0	4
1	7
2	
3	13
4	
	25

   b) Identify the initial value of y and the constant of variation from the table.

   c) Write an equation relating y and x in the form $y = mx + b$.

   d) Graph the relation.

   e) Describe the graph.

3. a) Copy and complete the table of values given that y varies partially with x.

x	y
0	-3
1	1
2	
3	9
4	
	29

   b) Identify the initial value of y and the constant of variation from the table.

   c) Write an equation relating y and x in the form $y = mx + b$.

   d) Graph the relation.

   e) Describe the graph.

B

4. A charitable organization is planning to rent a hall for a fundraiser. The cost of renting the hall is $200. There is an additional cost of $3 for each person attending the fundraiser for the entrance fee.

   a) Identify the fixed cost and the variable cost of this partial variation.

   b) Write an equation relating the cost, C, in dollars, and the number of people, n.

   c) Use your equation to determine the total cost if 100 people attend the fundraiser.

5. A cellular phone company offers two types of monthly plans:
   • Plan A: 10¢ per minute
   • Plan B: a monthly fee of $10 plus 7.5¢ per minute

   a) Graph both relations for 0 to 100 min in 1 month.

   b) Classify each relation as a direct variation or a partial variation.

   c) Write an equation relating the cost and the number of minutes for each plan.

   d) Compare the monthly cell phone plan costs. When is Plan A cheaper than Plan B? When is Plan B cheaper than Plan A?

6. This table shows the amount a printing company charges to print a newsletter.

Number of Newsletters, n	Cost, C ($)
0	50
200	450
400	850
600	1250
800	1650
1000	2050

a) Identify the fixed cost this company charges to print the newsletter. What do you think this amount might represent?

b) Determine the variable cost of printing one newsletter. Explain how you found this.

c) Write an equation representing the price to print the newsletters.

d) What is the cost to print 1200 newsletters?

e) How many newsletters can be printed for $300?

7. Describe a situation that might lead to this graph.

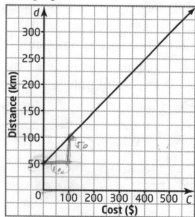

C

8. The prom committee of a school is planning the school prom. The cost of renting the hall for the prom and hiring the serving staff is $825. There is an additional cost of $15 per person for the meal.

a) Identify the fixed cost and the variable cost of this partial variation.

b) Write an equation to represent this relationship.

c) Use your equation to determine the total cost if 150 people attend the prom.

d) How many people can attend the prom for $3450?

9. A health club offers two types of monthly memberships:

• Membership A: $3 per visit
• Membership B: a flat fee of $8 and $2 per visit

a) Graph both relations for 0 to 10 visits.

b) Classify each relation as a direct variation or a partial variation.

c) Write an equation relating the cost and the number of visits for each membership.

d) Compare the monthly membership costs. When is Membership A cheaper than Membership B? When is Membership B cheaper than Membership A?

5.3 Slope

Principles of Mathematics 9, pages 254–263

A

1. Determine the slope of the sail on the toy sailboat.

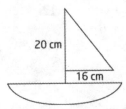

2. A set of stairs is to be built so that each step has a vertical rise of 20 cm over a horizontal run of 27.5 cm. Find the slope, to the nearest hundredth.

3. Calculate the slope of each line segment, where possible.

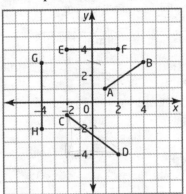

   a) AB

   b) CD

   c) EF

   d) GH

B

4. a) A line segment has one endpoint of A(2, 5) and a slope of $\frac{2}{3}$. Find the coordinates of another possible endpoint B.

   b) A line segment has one endpoint of A(−3, 2) and a slope of $-\frac{3}{5}$. Find the coordinates of another possible endpoint B.

   c) A line segment has one endpoint of A(4, −1) and a slope of 0. Find the coordinates of another possible endpoint B.

   d) A line segment has one endpoint of A(−5, −3) and an undefined slope. Find the coordinates of another possible endpoint B.

5. Two ramps are being built with the same slope. The first ramp is three times the height of the second ramp. Does the first ramp have to be three times as long as the second ramp? Explain.

6. A steel wire goes between the tops of two walls that are 15 m apart. One wall is 8 m high. The other is 5 m high. What is the slope of the steel wire?

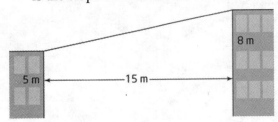

7. A wheelchair ramp is built so that the height of the ramp is 1 m and the length of the base of the ramp is 7 m. What is the slope of the wheelchair ramp, to the nearest thousandth?

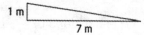
1 m
7 m

C

8. A square-based pyramid has a height of 155 m and a base width of 238 m. Find the slope of the pyramid, to the nearest tenth.

9. A ladder is leaning up against a wall of a building so that it reaches 10 m up the wall. The bottom of the ladder is 1.25 m from the base of the wall.

a) What is the slope of the ladder?

b) Has the ladder been placed according the safety standards, which state that the ladder should have a slope of between 6.3 and 9.5 when it is placed up against a building?

10. Use the classifications below to determine the pitch of each of the following roofs.

Shallow: $m \leq \dfrac{3}{12}$

Medium: $\dfrac{3}{12} < m \leq \dfrac{6}{12}$

Steep: $m > \dfrac{6}{12}$

a)

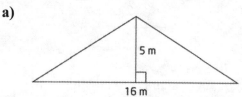
5 m
16 m

b)

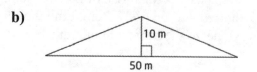
10 m
50 m

c)

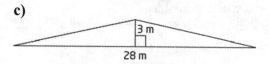
3 m
28 m

5.4 Slope as a Rate of Change
Principles of Mathematics 9, pages 264–271

A

1. A heron can travel an average of 400 km in 10 h. What is the rate of change of distance?

2. A small bird can flap its wings 120 times in 30 s. What is the rate of change of wing flaps?

3. The average resting adult heart beats 720 times in 10 min. What is the rate of change of heart beats?

4. This graph shows the height above ground of a skier over time.

    a) Calculate the slope of the graph.

    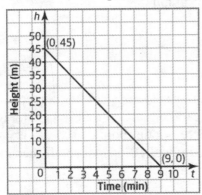

    b) Interpret the slope as a rate of change.

5. This graph shows the relationship between atmospheric pressure and altitude.

    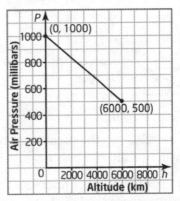

    a) Calculate the slope of the graph.

    b) Interpret the slope as a rate of change.

B

6. The price of a litre of milk increased from $1.25 in 2004 to $1.35 in 2006. What is the average price increase per year?

7. This graph shows the height of a tree over a 5-year growing period. Calculate the rate of change of height per year.

    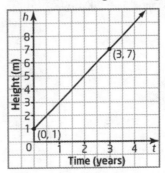

8. This distance-time graph shows two cyclists that are travelling at the same time.

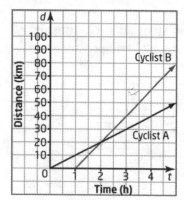

a) Which cyclist has the greater speed, and by how much?

b) What does the point of intersection of the two lines represent?

9. This table shows the average undergraduate tuition fees for full-time students in Ontario in engineering by year. Is the rate of change constant over the 5-year period?

| Average Undergraduate Tuition Fees for Full-Time Students in Ontario in Engineering ||
Year	Tuition ($)
1999–2000	4456
2000–2001	4742
2001–2002	5011
2002–2003	5302
2003–2004	5968

Source: Statistics Canada, Centre for Education Statistics. Last modified: 2004-09-01.

10. A water tank is being filled with water at a constant rate. After 20 s, the tank contains 200 L of water.

a) Graph this relation.

b) The water tank will overflow if it contains more than 300 L of water. How long will it take to fill the water tank? Mark this point on your graph.

11. Selam is on the track team at school. He runs every day after school. One day he ran 6 km in 30 min.

a) Calculate the rate of change of Selam's distance from his starting point.

b) Graph Selam's distance as it relates to time.

c) Explain the meaning of the rate of change and how it relates to the graph.

C

12. A music store is holding a special clearance sale on a $1500 piano. Initially there is a discount of 10%, Every 4 h, an additional 10% is taken off the latest price.

a) Make a table showing the price over the 12 h the sale is in effect.

b) Graph the price over the 12 h of the sale.

c) Explain the shape of the graph.

13. A health club membership costs $600 for 1 year. The health club is holding a membership drive and is reducing the price of club memberships over the next 8 h. Initially there is a discount of 5%. Every 2 h the discount is increased by 5%.

a) Make a table showing the cost of a health club membership over the next 8 h.

b) Graph the price over the 8 h of the membership drive.

c) Explain the shape of the graph.

14. A liquid is being poured slowly onto a level surface, making a circular pattern.

a) Find the circumference of the circular pattern when the radius is 20 cm.

b) Write an equation relating the circumference, C, of the circular pattern to the radius, r.

c) Find the rate of change of circumference with respect to radius of the relation.

5.5 First Differences

Principles of Mathematics 9, pages 272–278

A

1. Look at each equation. Predict whether it represents a linear relation or a non-linear relation. Use a graphing calculator to confirm your answers.

   a) $y = 3x - 8$

   b) $y = -4x + 2$

   c) $y = 3x^2 - 2$

   d) $y = 3^x$

   e) $y = -\dfrac{2}{3}x + 5$

   f) $y = \dfrac{5}{x}$

2. Copy each table and include a third column to record first differences. Classify each relation as linear or non-linear.

   a)

x	y
0	2
1	6
2	10
3	14

   b)

x	y
−3	−4
−1	−1
1	1
3	4

3. These tables show the distance travelled by a canoeist. Without graphing, determine if each relation is linear or non-linear.

   a) In still water:

Time (s)	Distance (m)
0	0
1	1
2	2
3	3
4	4
5	5

   b) With the current:

Time (s)	Distance (m)
0	0
1	1
2	3
3	6
4	10
5	15

B

4. The triangle's base is one-half its height. The triangle is painted from the bottom up.

   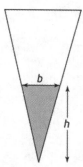

   a) Create a table comparing the height of the painted portion to its area as the height increases.

   b) Use first differences to determine whether the relation is linear.

5. Use first differences to determine which relations are linear and which are non-linear. Write an equation representing each linear relation. Extrapolate the relation to predict the outcome for the seventh step.

a)

Number of Pentagons	Number of Segments
1	
2	
3	
4	

b)

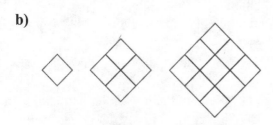

Base Side Length	Total Number of Tiles
1	
2	
3	
4	

6. Use first differences to predict which relationships are linear and which are non-linear for the following pattern. Write an equation representing each linear relation. Extrapolate the relation to predict the outcome for the seventh step.

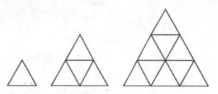

a)

Base Side Length	Number of Triangles
1	
2	
3	
4	

b)

Base Side Length	Number of Segments
1	
2	
3	
4	

c)

Base Side Length	Number of Horizontal Lines in Shape
1	
2	
3	
4	

C

7. A triangular piece of cardboard is 10 cm wide. Its base is half its height. It is dipped in water and is wet from the bottom up.

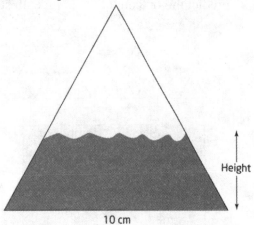

Height

10 cm

a) Create a table comparing the height of the wet cardboard to its area as the height increases from 0 cm to 5 cm.

b) Use first differences to determine whether the relation is linear.

c) What is the area of the wet cardboard if the height is 16 cm?

8. The first few figures in a pattern are shown.

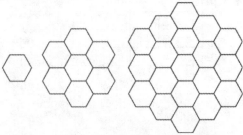

a) Copy and complete the table.

Figure Number	Number of Hexagons in Pattern
1	
2	
3	
4	

b) Use first differences to predict if the relationship is linear or non-linear.

5.6 Connecting Variation, Slope, and First Differences

Principles of Mathematics 9, pages 279–287

A

1. **a)** Determine the slope.

    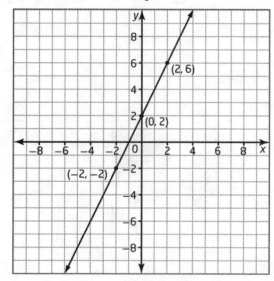

    b) Determine the vertical intercept.

    c) Write an equation for the relation.

2. **a)** Determine the slope. $= 0.5$

    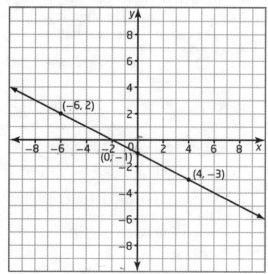

    b) Determine the vertical intercept.

    c) Write an equation for the relation.

    $y = (-0.5x + 1)$

3. Make a table of values and graph each relation. Draw a right triangle on your graph to find the slope.

    a) $y = 3x - 2$

    b) $y = -2x + 1$

    c) $y = \dfrac{1}{2}x$

    d) $y = -0.5x - 1$

B

4. Use the rule of four to represent this relation in three other ways.

x	y
0	1
1	3
2	5
3	7
4	9

    a) Use a graph.

    b) Use words.

    c) Use an equation.

5. Use the rule of four to represent this relation in three other ways.

x	y
0	3
1	1
2	-1
3	-3
4	-5

    a) Use a graph.

    b) Use words.

    c) Use an equation.

6. A cleaning service charges $50 plus $10 per room to clean an apartment. Represent the relation using numbers, a graph, and an equation.

7. The cost of renting a bicycle is $20.00 plus $2.00/h.

   a) Graph this relation.

   b) Identify the slope and the vertical intercept of the line. What do they represent?

   c) Is this a direct or a partial variation? Explain.

   d) Write an equation relating the cost and the rental hours.

8. d varies directly with t. When $t = 5$, $d = 11$.

   a) Find the slope and the vertical intercept of the line.

   b) Write an equation for this relation.

   c) Graph this relation.

9. Complete the rule of four for this relation by representing it numerically, in words, and with an equation.

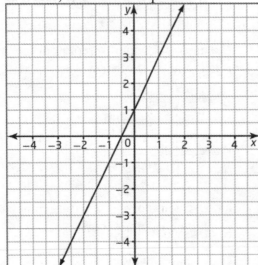

C

10. Complete the rule of four for this relation by representing it numerically, in words, and with an equation.

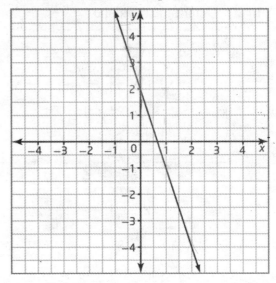

11. Complete the rule of four for the relation $y = 3x + 2$ by representing it numerically, graphically, and in words.

12. A water tank is being filled. The table shows the volume, in kilolitres, of water for the elapsed time, in minutes.

Time (min)	0	20	40	60	80
Volume of Water (kL)	20	50	80	110	140

   a) Confirm that this relation is linear.

   b) Graph this relation.

   c) Find the slope of the graph as both a fraction and a decimal. Is the slope constant? What does the slope represent?

   d) Write an equation for the volume of water in terms of the time.

   e) Use your graph or equation to find the volume of water after 30 min.

1. Semir works during the weekends at a restaurant. He earns $10.50/h. His pay varies directly with the time, in hours.

   a) Choose appropriate letters for variables. Make a table of values showing Semir's pay for 0 h, 1 h, 2 h, 3 h, and 4 h.

   b) Graph the relationship.

   c) Write an equation in the form $y = kx$.

2. Matthew cycles 50 km to a friend's home. The distance, d, in kilometres, varies directly with the time, t, in hours.

   a) Find an equation relating d and t if $d = 24$ when $t = 1.5$. What does the constant of variation represent?

   b) Use the equation to determine how long it will take Matthew to reach his destination.

3. The volume of juice varies directly with the volume of water used to prepare it. Tommy used 2 L of water to make 2.5 L of juice.

   a) Explain why this relation is a direct variation.

   b) Graph this relation.

4. Identify each relation as a direct variation, a partial variation, or neither. Justify your answer.

   a) $y = 5x + 2$

   b) $C = \pi d$

   c) $y = x^2 - 1$

5. Identify each relation as a direct variation, a partial variation, or neither. Justify your answer.

   a) $y = -2x - 3$

   b) $F = 2.5a$

   c) $y = -x^2 + 2$

6. a) Copy and complete the table of values given that y varies partially with x.

x	y
0	5
1	9
2	
3	17
4	
	37

   b) Identify the initial value of y and the constant of variation from the table.

   c) Write an equation relating y and x in the form $y = mx + b$.

   d) Graph the relation. Describe the graph.

7. A company is having business cards printed. The cost to design the business card is $25. There is an additional charge of $0.02 per business card printed.

   a) Identify the fixed cost and the variable cost for this partial variation.

   b) Write an equation representing this relationship.

   c) Use your equation to determine the total cost of 500 business cards.

8. Determine the slope of each object.

a)

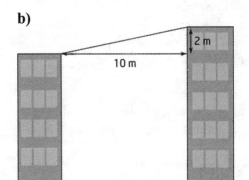

1.5 m
4 m

b)

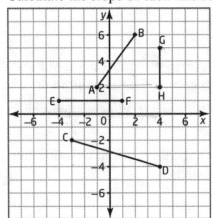

2 m
10 m

9. Calculate the slope of each line segment.

a) AB

b) CD

c) EF

d) GH

10. A plant is growing at a constant rate. The plant was 4 cm tall after 1 month. The plant was 32 cm tall after 9 months. If you graphed the growth of the plant with respect to time, what would the slope of the graph be? Express it as a rate of change.

11. For safety reasons, an extension ladder should have a slope of between 6.3 and 9.5 when it is placed against a wall. Determine if each of the following ladders has been placed within the safe range.

a) A ladder reaches 4 m up the wall. The foot of the ladder is 0.5 m from the wall.

b) A ladder reaches 3 m up the wall. The foot of the ladder is 0.6 m from the wall.

12. Use first differences to determine whether each relation is linear or non-linear.

a)

x	y
0	5
1	11
2	17
3	23
4	29

b)

x	y
0	14
1	8
2	3
3	−1
4	−4

13. a) Confirm that this relation is linear.

x	y
0	−4
1	1
2	6
3	11
4	16

b) Calculate the slope.

c) Write an equation for the relation.

d) Graph the relation.

6.1 The Equation of a Line in Slope *y*-Intercept Form: y = *mx* + *b*

Principles of Mathematics 9, pages 296–307

A

1. Identify the slope and the *y*-intercept of each line.

  a) $y = 3x - 2$

  b) $y = -2x + 4$

  c) $y = \dfrac{3}{4}x - 5$

  d) $y = -\dfrac{2}{5}x$

  e) $y = 2x - \dfrac{1}{3}$

  f) $y = 5$

2. Find the slope and *y*-intercept of each line.

  a)

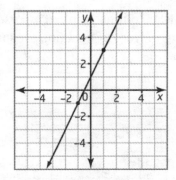

  b)

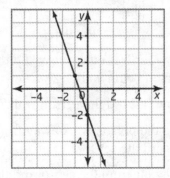

3. Write the equation of each line in question 2.

4. Find the slope and *y*-intercept of each line.

  a)

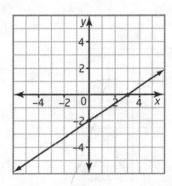

  b)

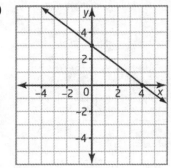

5. Write the equation of each line in question 4.

B

6. Identify the slope and *y*-intercept of each line, if they exist.

  a) $y = 2$

  b) $x = 3$

  c) $y = -4$

  d) $x = -1$

7. Find the slope and the *y*-intercept of each line.

a)

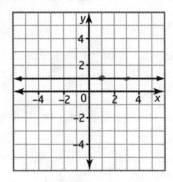

b)

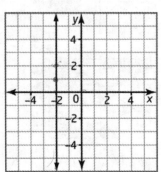

c)

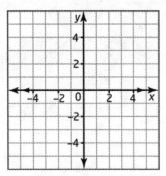

d)

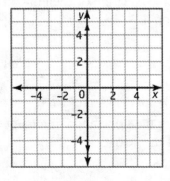

8. Write the equation of each line in question 7.

9. a) The line in question 5 part c) has a special name. What is it?

b) The line in question 5 part d) has a special name. What is it?

10. The slope and the *y*-intercept are given. Write the equation and graph each line.

a) slope $= \dfrac{2}{5}$, *y*-intercept $= -1$

b) slope $= -\dfrac{2}{3}$, *y*-intercept $= 2$

c) slope $= 0$, *y*-intercept $= -2$

d) slope $=$ undefined,

y-intercept $=$ none, *x*-intercept $= 3$

11. This distance-time graph of a person walking in front of a motion sensor is shown.

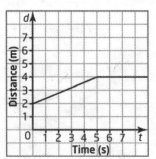

a) How far from the sensor did the person begin walking?

b) How fast did the person walk?

c) Did the person walk away from or toward the sensor? Explain.

d) How far from the sensor did the person stop walking?

12. Sketch a distance-time graph for each walker for the first 4 s.

a) Kurtis started at a distance of 2 m and walked away from the sensor at a constant speed of 0.5 m/s.

b) Nicole began walking toward the sensor at a constant speed of 0.5 m/s from an initial distance of 4 m.

c) Julianne stood at a distance of 3.5 m from the sensor and did not move.

d) Benjamin started at 4 m from the sensor and walked towards it at a constant speed of 1m/s for 2 s. Then, he turned around and walked, at the same speed, away from the sensor for 2 s.

13. Identify the slope and the vertical intercept of each linear relation and explain what they represent. Write an equation to describe the relationship.

a)

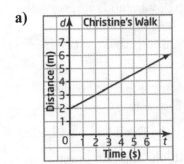

b)

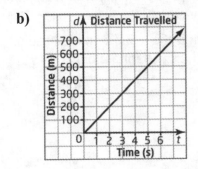

14. The y-intercept is the y-coordinate of the point where a graph crosses the y-axis. The value of the x-coordinate for any y-intercept is 0. The x-intercept is the x-coordinate of the point where a graph crosses the x-axis. The value of the y-coordinate for any intercept is 0. Find the x-intercept and the y-intercept of each line.

a) $y = 2x - 6$

b) $y = \dfrac{2}{5}x + 4$

6.2 The Equation of a Line in Standard Form: $Ax + By + C = 0$
Principles of Mathematics 9, pages 308–314

A

1. Express each equation in the form $y = mx + b$.

   a) $x + y - 4 = 0$

   b) $x - y + 2 = 0$

   c) $x + 4y + 3 = 0$

   d) $x - 3y - 8 = 0$

   e) $2x + 5y + 10 = 0$

   f) $3x - 2y + 6 = 0$

2. For each linear relation in question 1,

   • identify the slope and the y-intercept

   • use this information to graph the line

3. The Gala Restaurant uses the equation $30n - C + 200 = 0$ to determine the cost for a room rental, where C represents the cost, in dollars, which depends on n, the number of people attending.

   a) Express the equation in slope y-intercept form: $C = mn + b$.

   b) Identify the fixed and variable costs.

   c) Illustrate the relation graphically using pencil and paper or a graphing calculator.

   d) What is the rental cost if 100 people attend a hockey banquet?

B

4. The Everything for Events Rental Company charges according to the equation $25n - C + 100 = 0$ to rent tables for events, where C represents the cost, in dollars, which depends on n, the number of tables that are rented.

   a) Express the equation in slope y-intercept form: $C = mn + b$.

   b) Identify the fixed and variable costs.

   c) Illustrate the relation graphically using pencil and paper or a graphing calculator.

   d) What is the rental cost if 200 tables are rented for a charity event?

5. The Home Medical Supplies Rental Company charges according to the equation $60m - C + 75 = 0$ to rent hospital beds, where C represents the cost, in dollars, which depends on m, the number of months that the bed is rented for.

   a) Express the equation in slope y-intercept form: $C = mn + b$.

   b) Identify the fixed and variable costs.

   c) Illustrate the relation graphically using pencil and paper or a graphing calculator.

   d) What is the rental cost if a hospital bed is rented for 5 months?

6. The Tent-All Company charges according to the equation $10d - C + 50 = 0$ to rent tents for camping, where C represents the cost, in dollars, which depends on d, the days that the tent is rented for.

   a) Express the equation in slope y-intercept form: $C = mn + b$.

   b) Identify the fixed and variable costs.

   c) Illustrate the relation graphically.

   d) What is the rental cost if a tent is rented for 7 days.

7. The steps show how to convert an equation in standard form to slope y-intercept form. Explain each step.

Step	Explanation
$2x + 3y - 6 = 0$	Start with the equation in standard form.
$3y = -2x + 6$	
$\dfrac{3y}{3} = \dfrac{-2x + 6}{3}$	
$y = -\dfrac{2}{3}x + 2$	

8. The steps show how to convert an equation in standard form to slope y-intercept form. Explain each step.

Step	Explanation
$3x + 2y + 5 = 0$	Start with the equation in standard form.
$2y = -3x - 5$	
$\dfrac{2y}{2} = \dfrac{-3x - 5}{2}$	
$y = -\dfrac{3}{2}x - \dfrac{5}{2}$	

C

9. The steps show how to convert an equation in slope y-intercept form to standard form. Explain each step.

Step	Explanation
$y = -\dfrac{3}{4}x + 2$	Start with the equation in slope y-intercept form.
$4 \times y = 4 \times \left(-\dfrac{3}{4}x + 2\right)$	
$4y = -3x + 8$	
$3x + 4y - 8 = 0$	

10. Express each equation in standard form using pencil and paper or a CAS.

   a) $y = x - 5$

   b) $y = -x + 3$

   c) $y = 2x + 5$

   d) $y = -3x + 4$

   e) $y = \dfrac{2}{5}x + 4$

   f) $y = -\dfrac{2}{3}x - \dfrac{3}{4}$

6.3 Graph a Line Using Intercepts

Principles of Mathematics 9, pages 315–322

A

1. Identify the *x*- and *y*-intercepts of each graph.

a)
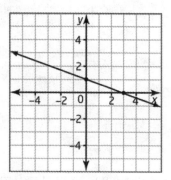

b)
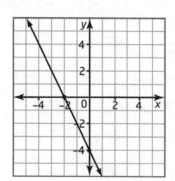

c)
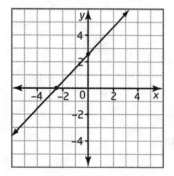

2. Identify the *x*- and *y*-intercepts of each graph, if they exist.

a)
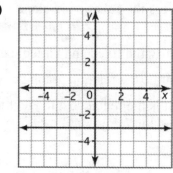

b)
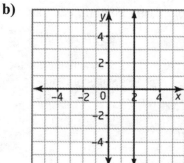

c)
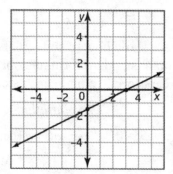

B

3. For each part, plot the intercepts and graph the line.

	x-intercept	*y*-intercept
a)	2	3
b)	−4	1
c)	2.5	−3.5
d)	none	4
e)	−3	none

4. Determine the *x*- and *y*-intercepts and use them to graph each line.

   a) $3x + 4y = 12$

   b) $2x + y = 8$

   c) $x - 3y = 6$

   d) $-2x + 3y = 6$

   e) $3x = 9$

   f) $4y = 8$

5. Draw a graph and determine the slope of each line using the rise and run from the graph.

	x-intercept	*y*-intercept
a)	−3	3
b)	−2	−4
c)	0.5	2.5
d)	none	2
e)	−1	none
f)	−4	−3
g)	−1.5	1.5
h)	2	1
i)	none	−3
j)	3	none

6. Find the slope of each line given the *x*- and *y*-intercepts, using the slope formula.

	x-intercept	*y*-intercept
a)	5	4
b)	2	−5
c)	−3	6
d)	none	7
e)	−2	none

7. An ice sculpture in the form of a tower is melting at a constant rate of 4 cm/h. The ice sculpture is 40 cm high when it first starts to melt.

   a) Set up a graph of height, *h*, in centimetres, versus time, *t*, in hours, and plot the *h*-intercept.

   b) Should the slope of this linear relation be positive or negative? Explain.

   c) Graph the line.

   d) What is the height of the ice sculpture after

   - 4 hours
   - 5.5 hours?

   e) Identify the *t*-intercept and explain what it means.

   f) Explain why this graph has no meaning below the *t*-axis.

8. When you buy a car, its value depreciates (becomes less) over time. The graph illustrates the value of a car from the time it was bought.

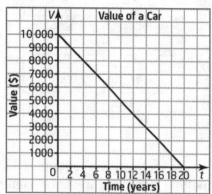

a) How much did the car originally cost?

b) After what period of time does the car no longer have any value?

c) What is the slope of this graph and what does it mean?

C

9. Refer to question 8. Suppose that each year, the car's value becomes 75% of its previous year's value.

a) Construct a table of values of the computer's value versus time for the first 5 years after the date of purchase.

b) Graph this relation. Is it linear or non-linear? Explain.

c) After how many years will the car be worth
   • Less that 30% of its original value?
   • 0

d) Does the *t*-intercept exist? If yes, what is it? If no, why not?

e) Compare this graph with the one in question 7. Under which system does the car's value depreciate faster? Explain.

10. a) Is the relationship in the graph linear or non-linear. Explain.

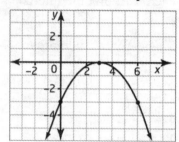

b) How many *x*-intercepts does the graph have? What are they?

c) How many *y*-intercepts does the graph have? What are they?

d) Sketch the graph of a relation that has the same shape as the given relation with one *x*-intercept and one *y*-intercept.

e) Sketch the graph of a relation that has the same shape as the given relation with no *x*-intercept and one *y*-intercept.

6.4 Parallel and Perpendicular Lines

Principles of Mathematics 9, pages 326–329

A

1. Graph each pair of lines on the same coordinate grid using pencil and paper or technology. Find their slopes and conclude whether the lines are parallel, perpendicular, or neither.

   a) $y = 2x + 3$ $\qquad$ $y = 2x - 1$

   b) $y = 4x + 2$ $\qquad$ $y = -\dfrac{1}{4}x + 1$

   c) $y = 3x + 1$ $\qquad$ $y = \dfrac{1}{3}x + 1$

   d) $y = \dfrac{1}{2}x + 1$ $\qquad$ $y = \dfrac{1}{2}x - 1$

   e) $y = x + 1$ $\qquad$ $y = -x + 1$

   f) $y = 3x - 2$ $\qquad$ $y = 2x - 3$

2. Graph each pair of lines on the same coordinate grid using pencil and paper or technology. Find their slopes and conclude whether the lines are parallel, perpendicular, or neither.

   a) $y = 3$ $\qquad$ $y = -2$

   b) $y = 1$ $\qquad$ $x = -1$

   c) $y = 2$ $\qquad$ $y = x$

   d) $x = 3$ $\qquad$ $x = 0$

   e) $y = x + 2$ $\qquad$ $y = -x$

   f) $x = 4$ $\qquad$ $y = -x + 4$

3. Graph each pair of lines on the same coordinate grid using pencil and paper or technology. Find their slopes and conclude whether the lines are parallel, perpendicular, or neither.

   a) $x + y = 3$ $\qquad$ $x + y = 2$

   b) $3x + 2y - 6 = 0$ $\qquad$ $2x - 3y + 6 = 0$

   c) $2x + y - 1 = 0$ $\qquad$ $\dfrac{1}{2}x + y - 2 = 0$

   d) $x + y - 2 = 0$ $\qquad$ $x - y - 2 = 0$

4. The slopes of two lines are given. Conclude whether the lies are parallel, perpendicular, or neither, Justify your answers.

   a) $m = \dfrac{3}{4},\ m = \dfrac{6}{8}$

   b) $m = 3,\ m = -\dfrac{1}{3}$

   c) $m = 5,\ m = -5$

   d) $m = 0.4,\ m = \dfrac{2}{5}$

   e) $m = 2\dfrac{1}{2},\ m = -\dfrac{2}{5}$

   f) $m = -\dfrac{1}{2},\ m = \dfrac{1}{2}$

   g) $m = 0,\ m = \text{undefined}$

5. What is the slope of a line that is parallel to each line?

a) $y = 3x + 5$

b) $y = -2x + 3$

c) $y = \frac{2}{3}x + 4$

d) $y = -\frac{2}{5}x - 7$

e) $2x + 3y = 12$

f) $5x - 3y - 15 = 0$

g) $x = 3$

h) $y = -4$

6. For each line in question 5, give the slope of a perpendicular line.

7. Copy and complete the following table.

Slope of a Line	Slope of a Parallel Line	Slope of a Perpendicular Line
4		
−3		
$\frac{2}{3}$		
0		
undefined		

8. a) Write the line $3x + 2y - 7 = 0$ in the form $y = mx + b$.

b) State the slope of the line $3x + 2y - 7 = 0$.

c) State the slope of a line parallel to the line $3x + 2y - 7 = 0$.

d) Write the equations of two lines that are parallel to the line $3x + 2y - 7 = 0$.

C

9. a) Write the line $5x - 2y + 4 = 0$ in the form $y = mx + b$.

b) State the slope of the line $5x - 2y + 4 = 0$.

c) State the slope of a line that is perpendicular to the line $5x - 2y + 4 = 0$.

d) Write the equations of two lines that are perpendicular to the line $5x - 2y + 4 = 0$.

10. The lines in the following table are parallel to the line $2x + 3y = 18$.

a) Determine the x- and y-intercepts of the line $2x + 3y = 18$.

b) Complete the following table.

Line Equation	x-intercept	y-intercept
$2x + 3y = 12$		
$2x + 3y = 6$		
$2x + 3y = -6$		
$2x + 3y = -12$		
$2x + 3y = -18$		

c) Describe how you can use intercepts to find a line that is parallel to a given line.

11. Determine whether or not the following sets of points form right triangles. Justify your answers with mathematical reasoning.

a) A(1, 3), B(5, 1), C(6, 3)

b) D(−2, 5), E(2, 3), F(3, −2)

c) M(−4, 2), N(−1, 4), O(1, 1)

12. ΔLMN has vertices L(−1, 2) and M(−4, −1).

a) Find the coordinates of N such that ΔLMN is a right triangle.

b) Is there more than one solution? Explain.

6.5 Find an Equation for a Line Given the Slope and a Point

Principles of Mathematics 9, pages 330–337

A

1. Find the equation of a line with the given slope and passing through the given point.

   a) $m = 2$, P(4, 5)

   b) $m = -4$, P(-3, -2)

   c) $m = \dfrac{3}{5}$, P(5, -1)

   d) $m = -\dfrac{1}{4}$, P(2, 6)

2. Find the equation of a line with the given slope and passing through the given point.

   a) $m = 0$, P(5, -4)

   b) $m = 3$, P$\left(\dfrac{2}{3}, \dfrac{1}{4}\right)$

   c) $m = \dfrac{2}{3}$, P(0, 0)

   d) $m = \dfrac{1}{2}$, P(-3, -4)

3. Find the equation of a line

   a) with a slope of 5, passing through (2, 3)

   b) with a slope of -4, passing through (-3, 5)

   c) parallel to $y = 2x + 5$, passing through (3, 2)

   d) perpendicular to $y = 3x - 4$, passing through (5, -3)

   e) parallel to $y = 4$, passing through (2, 3)

   f) perpendicular to $y = -2$, passing through (-3, 1)

4. Find the equation of a line.

   a) parallel to $y = \dfrac{1}{2}x + 3$, passing through the origin

   b) perpendicular to $y = -\dfrac{5}{2}x + 3$, passing through (-2, -3)

   c) parallel to $y = -2x + 3$, passing through (0, 0)

   d) perpendicular to $y = 3x + 4$, passing through (0, 0)

B

5. Find an equation for the line parallel to $3x + 5y - 4 = 0$, with the same x-intercept as $2x - 3y - 6 = 0$.

6. Find an equation for the line perpendicular to $2x + 5y - 3 = 0$, with the same y-intercept as $2x + 3y + 6 = 0$.

7. In Ottawa, you can ride on a tour bus for a fixed price plus a variable amount that depends on the length of the trip. The variable cost is \$2/km and a 20-km trip costs \$55.

   a) Determine the equation relating cost, C, in dollars, and distance, d, in kilometres.

   b) Use your equation to find the cost of a 15-km tour.

   c) Graph the relation.

   d) Use the graph to find the cost of a 15-km tour.

8. Refer to question 7.

    a) Copy and complete the table to solve the problem using a third method. Explain this method.

Distance (km)	Cost ($)	First Differences
2	19	
3	21	2
4		
5		
6		

    b) Use all three methods (equation, graph, and table) to determine how far you could travel on the tour bus for $105.

    c) Use each method to determine the cost of a 10.5 km tour.

    d) Describe at least one advantage and one disadvantage to each method of solution.

9. **Use Technology** A city taxi charges $3/km and a fixed cost. A 5-km taxi ride costs $21. Use *The Geometer's Sketchpad*® to find

    a) the fixed cost

    b) the equation relating cost, C, in dollars, and distance, d, in kilometres

    c) the equation using another method to check your results.

C

10. Ahmed has been running at an average speed of 15 km/h towards the finish line of a 45 km race for 2 h, when he sees a checkpoint sign shown.

Finish Line 15 km

    a) What does the ordered pair (2, 15) mean?

    b) The slope is $m = -15$. What does this value represent? Why is it negative?

    c) Determine the value of b.

    d) Write an equation relating distance and time.

    e) Graph the relation. What is the meaning of the d-intercept?

    f) How long will the race take, in total?

    g) Has Ahmed reached the halfway point of his race yet? Explain.

11. Emeline has been driving at an average speed of 100 km/h towards Hamilton for 2 h, when she sees the sign shown.

Hamilton 300 km

    a) What does the ordered pair (2, 300) mean?

    b) The slope is $m = -100$. What does this value represent? Why is it negative?

    c) Determine the value of b.

    d) Write an equation relating distance and time.

    e) Graph the relation. What is the meaning of the d-intercept?

    f) How long will the car drive take, in total?

    g) Has Emeline reached the halfway point of her trip yet? Explain.

6.6 Find an Equation for a Line Given Two Points

Principles of Mathematics 9, pages 338–343

A

1. Find an equation for each line.

a)

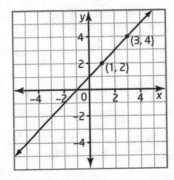

b)

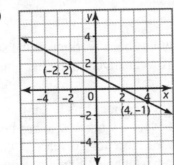

c)

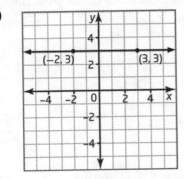

d)

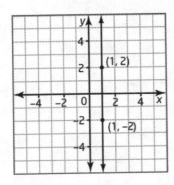

2. Find an equation for the line passing through each pair of points.

    a) A(3, 4) and B(6, 10)

    b) D(1, 5) and E(3, −3)

    c) M(−3, 6) and N(1, −4)

    d) P(−4, 7) and Q(2, −3)

B

3. a) Find an equation for a line with an *x*-intercept of −3 and a *y*-intercept of 5.

    b) Find an equation for a line with an *x*-intercept of 4 and a *y*-intercept of −2.

4. a) Find an equation for a line with the same *x*-intercept as the line $2x + 5y - 4 = 0$ and the same *y*-intercept as the line $3x - 2y + 8 = 0$.

    b) Find an equation for a line with the same *x*-intercept as the line $3x - 4y + 6 = 0$ and the same *y*-intercept as the line $4x - 5y - 10 = 0$.

5. Dajanth is walking at a constant speed in front of a motion sensor. Dajanth starts at a distance of 2.5 m from the sensor. 2 s later, he is 7.5 m from the sensor.

a) Is Dajanth moving toward or away from the sensor? Explain how you know.

b) How fast is Dajanth walking?

c) Find the equation that describes Dajanth's motion in the form $d = mt + b$.

d) What is the d-intercept? What does it mean?

6. Helen is walking at a constant speed in front of a motion sensor. Helen starts at a distance of 8 m from the sensor. 4 s later, she is 4 m from the sensor.

a) Is Helen moving toward or away from the sensor? Explain how you know.

b) How fast is Helen walking?

c) Find the equation that describes Helen's motion in the form $d = mt + b$.

d) What is the d-intercept? What does it mean?

7. Employees of a Department Store get the same raise each year. Patti, who has been working at the store for 2 years, earns \$16.75/h. Susan, who has been working at the store for 5 years, earns \$22.75/h. The equation relating salary and number of years worked is of the form $s = mn + b$, where s is the hourly wage and n is the number of years worked.

a) (2, 16.75) and (5, 22.75) are two points on the line. Explain why.

b) Find the slope and the s-intercept of this line, and explain what they mean.

c) Write the equation of the line.

d) Carol has been working at the store for 10 years. Determine her hourly wage.

e) What wage does this linear model predict for a worker who has been with the store for 20 years? Does this seem reasonable? Explain. How might the store modify the raise policy?

C

8. Two students are walking at constant speeds in front of two motion sensors.
   - Susu starts at a distance of 6 m and, after 4 s, she is 14 m away from the sensor.
   - Meisrain starts at a distance of 12 m and, after 4 s, she is 8 m from the sensor.

   a) Find a distance-time equation for each walker.

   b) At what time were they at the same distance from their sensors?

   c) At what distance did this occur?

   d) Explain how you solved parts b) and c).

9. Refer to question 8.

   a) Graph both linear relations on the same grid.

   b) Identify the point where the two lines cross. This is called the point of intersection. What are the coordinates of this point?

   c) Compare this point to your answers to question 9 parts b) and c). Explain what you notice.

10. Find an equation for the line passing through each pair of points.

    a) $G\left(\dfrac{2}{3}, 3\right)$ and $H\left(3, \dfrac{1}{4}\right)$

    b) $J\left(\dfrac{1}{2}, -\dfrac{3}{4}\right)$ and $K\left(-\dfrac{3}{5}, -\dfrac{1}{3}\right)$

6.7 Linear Systems
Principles of Mathematics 9, pages 344–351

A

1. Give coordinates of the point of intersection of each linear system.

   a)
   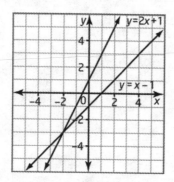

   b)
   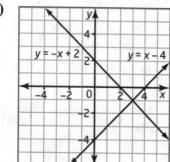

   c)
   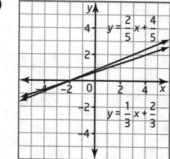

   d)
   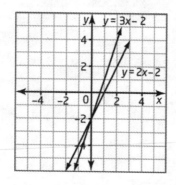

2. Which ordered pair is a solution to the given system of linear equations?

   a) $x + y = 6$ $(-2, 4)$ or $(2, 4)$
   $2x - y = 0$

   b) $4x + 3y = 7$ $(1, 1)$ or $(2, 1)$
   $2x - 5y = -3$

   c) $x - 4y = -6$ $(-2, 2)$ or $(-2, 1)$
   $2x - 3y = -7$

   d) $-4x + y = 5$ $(-3, -7)$ or $(7, -3)$
   $x - 3y = 18$

B

3. Solve each linear system using pencil and paper or technology. Verify each solution by substituting the coordinates of your solution into both equations.

   a) $y = x + 1$ and $y = 2x + 3$

   b) $x + y = 3$ and $x + 2y = 5$

   c) $x - 3y - 4 = 0$ and $2x + y + 6 = 0$

   d) $y = 3x - 5$ and $2x - 4y = 10$

   e) $3x - y = 4$ and $2x - 4y = 6$

   f) $x + 2y - 8 = 0$ and $2x - 4y + 16 = 0$

   g) $3x + 4y = 4$ and $4x - 5y = 3$

   h) $-x + 5y = 7$ and $3x - 2y = -6$

4. The cost of operating a gas-powered car is $0.90/km. The cost of operating an electric car is $0.30/km plus a fixed cost of $2400. The costs can be compared with the following equations.

Gas powered car: $C = 0.90d$

Electric car: $C = 0.30d + 2400$

a) What does each variable represent?

b) Solve the system of equations.

c) What does the point of intersection represent?

d) Which type of car is more economical for driving 3000 km?

5. A printer has two presses. The cost to print a book on printer A includes a set-up cost of $225 plus $6 per page. The cost to print the same book on printer B includes a set-up cost of $375 plus $5.50 per page.

a) Write an equation to model each cost, C, in dollars, as it relates to the number of pages, p.

b) Solve the system of equations using a graphing calculator.

c) How many pages must a book contain for the total cost to be the same on both printers?

d) For what number of pages is it more economical to use printer A? printer B?

6. First Choice Taxi charges $2.50, plus 40 cents for each kilometre. G.T.A. Taxi charges $3.25 plus 25 cents for each kilometre.

a) Write an equation to model each cost, C, in dollars, as it relates to the distance, d, in kilometres.

b) Solve the system of equations using a graphing calculator.

c) For what number of kilometres is it more economical to use First Choice Taxi? G.T.A. Taxi?

7. If $(1, 3)$ and $(-1, -3)$ are both solutions to the equations $3x - y = 0$ and $6x - 2y = 0$, what can you conclude about the equations? Explain.

C

8. Find the equation of the line that passes through the point of intersection of $4x + y = -13$ and $3x - 4y = 14$ and is parallel to the line $5x + 3y - 4 = 0$.

9. The sides of a triangle lie on the following three lines.

$5x - 3y = 19$ (1)
$x + 6y = 17$ (2)
$2x + y = 1$ (3)

a) Solve equations (1) and (2) to find the coordinates of one vertex.

b) Solve equations (2) and (3) to find the coordinates of another vertex.

c) Solve equations (1) and (3) to find the coordinates of the third vertex.

10. Linear equations in three variables also exist. The solution to a system of three linear equations in three variables is an ordered triple, such as P(x, y, z). Solve the following system of equations. Write your solution as an ordered triple, (x, y, z).

$x + y + z = 3$
$y = 4x$
$z = -2x$

11. If two lines are parallel to each other, would they have a point of intersection? Graph the equations $y = 2x + 1$ and $y = 2x - 1$ to help you explain.

12. If two lines represent the same line, or are coincidental, how many points of intersection, if any, would they have? Graph the equations $y = x + 2$ and $2y = 2x + 4$ to help you explain.

1. Identify the slope and *y*-intercept of each line.

   a)
   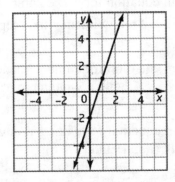

   b)
   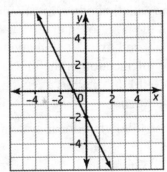

   c)
   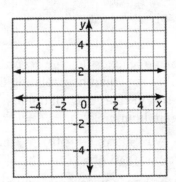

   d)
   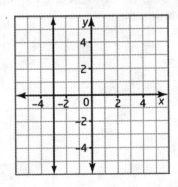

2. Identify the slope and the *y*-intercept of each line.

   a) $y = 4x + 2$

   b) $y = -\dfrac{5}{6}x + 4$

   c) $y = 5$

   d) $x = -2$

3. Write the equation of a line with the given slope and *y*-intercept. Then, graph the line.

   a) $m = 2, b = -3$

   b) $m = -\dfrac{2}{3}, b = 1$

   c) $m = 0, b = 3$

   d) m = undefined, b = none, *x*-intercept 2

4. The distance-time graph illustrates a person's movements in front of a motion sensor.

   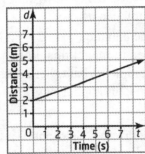

   a) Identify the slope and the *d*-intercept. Explain what they mean.

   b) Write an equation in the form $d = mt + b$ that describes the walker's motion.

5. Rewrite each equation in the form $y = mx + b$.

   a) $3x + y - 4 = 0$

   b) $2x - 3y + 4 = 0$

6. An electrician charges according the equation $35n - C + 50 = 0$, where C is the total charge, in dollars, for a house call, and n is the time, in hours, the job takes.

   a) Rearrange the equation to express it in the form $C = mn + b$.

   b) Identify the slope and the C-intercept and explain what they mean.

   c) Graph the relation.

   d) What would a 4-h house call cost?

7. Determine the x- and y-intercepts of each line. Then, graph the line.

   a) $4x + 5y = 20$ **b)** $2x - 3y = 6$

8. Christopher is at a movie with his younger sister, Cindy. He has $24 to spend on popcorn and pop. Popcorn costs $4 per bag and pop cost $2 each.

   a) If Christopher buys only popcorn, how many bags can he buy?

   b) If Christopher buys only pop, how many can he buy?

   c) The equation $4x + 2y = 24$ can be used to model this problem. Graph this line. What other combinations can Christopher buy?

9. a) Determine the x- and y-intercept of the line $5x + 2y = 10$.

   b) The lines in the table are perpendicular to the line $5x + 2y = 10$. Complete the table.

Line Equation	x-intercept	y-intercept
$2x - 5y = 20$		
$2x - 5y = 10$		
$2x - 5y = -10$		
$2x - 5y = -20$		
$2x - 5y = -30$		

   c) Describe how you can use intercepts to find a line that is perpendicular to a given line.

10. Find an equation for a line with a slope of $\dfrac{3}{5}$, passing through $(2, -4)$.

11. Find an equation for a line parallel to $4x + 5y + 2 = 0$, with an x-intercept of 3.

12. Find an equation for a line perpendicular to $y = 3x - 5$, with a y-intercept of -2.

13. Find an equation for a line passing through $(-3, 4)$ and $(2, -6)$.

14. Find the equation of the line that passes through the point of intersection of $x + 2y = 9$ and $4x - 2y = -4$ and the point of intersection of the lines $3x - 4y = 14$ and $3x + 7y = -8$.

15. Solve the following linear system:

$$y = -\frac{1}{2}x + 2$$

$$y = 3x - 5$$

16. Two piano teachers charge according to the following equations, relating the piano lesson charge, C, in dollars, to the time, t, in hours:

   • Mr. Sharp: $C = 30t$

   • Mr. Flat: $C = 20t + 10$

Solve the linear system and explain what the solution means.

7.1 Angle Relationships in Triangles

Principles of Mathematics 9, pages 364–373

A

1. Find the measure of each exterior angle.

a)
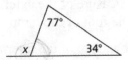

b)
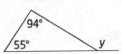

c)
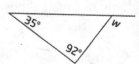

d)
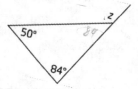

2. Find the measure of each unknown exterior angle.

a)
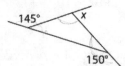

b)
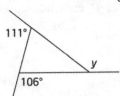

c)
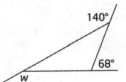

d)
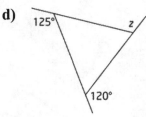

B

3. The measures of two of the exterior angles of a triangle are given. Find the measure of the third exterior angle.

a) 80° and 110°

b) 60° and 105°

c) 65° and 140°

d) 80° and 130°

4. Find the measure of the exterior angle labelled *x* for each isosceles triangle.

a)
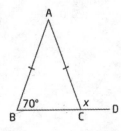

b)
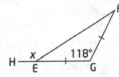

c)
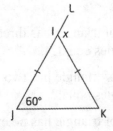

d)
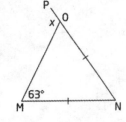

5. Find the measure of each unknown angle.

a)

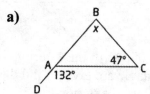

b)

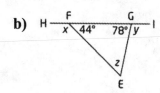

c)

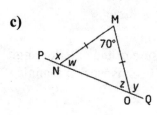

d)

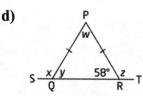

e)

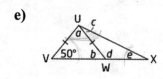

6. a) What type of triangle has three exterior angles equal?

b) What type of triangle has two exterior angles equal?

c) What type of triangle has no exterior angles equal?

7. A boat ramp is shown in the diagram.

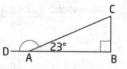

a) Find the measure of the exterior angle at the foot of the ramp.

b) Find the measure of the interior and exterior angles at the top of the ramp.

C

8. Find the measure of each unknown angle.

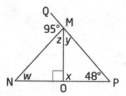

9. Find the angles in a triangle if the measures of the angles are

a) x, $2x$, and $3x$

b) $x - 10$, x, and $x + 10$

10. Do an Internet search for *pentaflexagon*. Then, construct a pentaflexagon using the information you find.

7.2 Angle Relationships in Quadrilaterals

Principles of Mathematics 9, pages 374–383

A

1. Find the angle measures *a*, *b*, *c*, *d*, *e*, and *f*.

   a)

   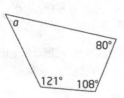

   b)

   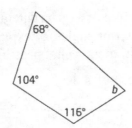

   c)

   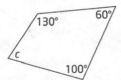

   d)

   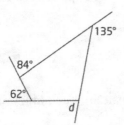

   e)

   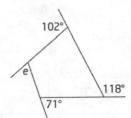

   f)

   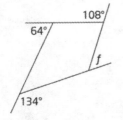

B

2. The measures of three of the interior angles of a quadrilateral are given. Find the measure of the fourth interior angle.

   a) 42°, 91°, and 115°

   b) 50°, 87°, and 108°

   c) 103°, 92°, and 78°

   d) 100°, 72°, and 67°

3. The measures of exterior angles at three vertices of a quadrilateral are given. Find the measure of the exterior angle at the fourth vertex.

   a) 104°, 95°, and 73°

   b) 93°, 78°, and 85°

   c) 92°, 79°, and 113°

   d) 114°, 85°, and 68°

4. Each row of this table lists measures of three interior angles in a quadrilateral. Find the measure of the fourth interior angle in each quadrilateral.

	∠A	∠B	∠C	∠D
a)	102°	77°	48°	unknown
b)	54°	68°	unknown	107°
c)	72°	unknown	82°	101°
d)	unknown	90°	85°	104°

5. Each row of this table lists measures of three exterior angles at three vertices of a quadrilateral. Find the measure of the fourth exterior angle at the fourth vertex in each quadrilateral.

	∠A	∠B	∠C	∠D
a)	100°	80°	63°	unknown
b)	74°	76°	unknown	110°
c)	91°	unknown	78°	103°
d)	unknown	75°	108°	86°

6. Find the measure of each unknown angle.

a)

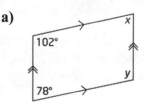

b)

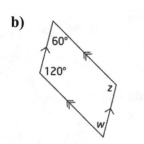

c)

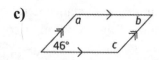

7. Find the measure of each unknown angle.

a)

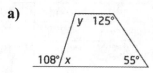

b)

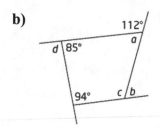

8. Draw an example of a quadrilateral with each set of interior angles, or explain why the quadrilateral is not possible.

a) ∠A = 104°, ∠B = 85°, and ∠C = 93°

b) ∠D = 99°, ∠E = 84°, and ∠F = 102°

c) ∠G = 150°, ∠H = 130°, and ∠I = 84°

9. Draw an example of a quadrilateral with each set of interior angles, or explain why the quadrilateral is not possible.

a) four acute angles

b) exactly two acute angles

c) one right angle and two obtuse angles

10. Calculate the mean measure for the exterior angles of a quadrilateral.

C

11. Find the measure of each unknown angle.

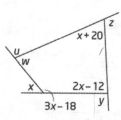

12. Draw a square EFGH and a rectangle JKLM. Construct diagonals EG and JL. Investigate the properties of the two quadrilaterals to answer parts a) to c). Describe how you determined the answer to each question.

a) Does the diagonal divide the square into two congruent triangles?

b) Does the diagonal divide the rectangle into two congruent triangles?

c) Is the diagonal a line of symmetry in the square?

d) Is the diagonal a line of symmetry in the rectangle?

e) Does the diagonal bisect any angles in the square?

f) Does the diagonal bisect any angles in the rectangle?

13. Find the measures of the interior angles of a quadrilateral so that the measures have each ratio.

a) 2:2:3:3

b) 3:3:5:5

7.3 Angle Relationships in Polygons
Principles of Mathematics 9, pages 384–393

A

1. Find the sum of the interior angles of a polygon with

   a) 12 sides

   b) 17 sides

   c) 22 sides

   d) 24 sides

2. Find the measure of each interior angle of a regular polygon with

   a) 8 sides

   b) 10 sides

   c) 14 sides

   d) 24 sides

3. How many sides does a polygon have if the sum of its interior angles is

   a) 1440°?

   b) 720°?

   c) 1980°?

   d) 2340°?

4. How many sides does a polygon have if each of its interior angles measures

   a) 120°?

   b) 144°?

   c) 135°?

B

5. a) The polygon shown has three equal sides and three equal angles. Write the name of a regular polygon with three sides.

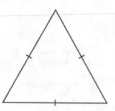

   b) The polygon shown has four equal sides and four equal angles. Write the name of a regular polygon with four sides.

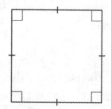

6. Copy this table and fill in the missing entries. To find the number of triangles in the polygon, draw diagonals from one vertex.

Polygon	Number of Sides	Number of Diagonals From One Vertex	Number of Triangles in the Polygon	Sum of Interior Angles
pentagon	5	2	3	540°
hexagon				
octagon	8			
dodecagon	12			

7. **a)** Use the formula for the sum of the interior angles of a polygon to show that each interior angle of an equilateral triangle measures 60°.

   b) Use the formula for the sum of the interior angles of a polygon to show that each interior angle of a rectangle measures 90°.

8. Ron who is a furniture-maker is designing an octagonal wooden container.

   a) At what angle will the adjacent sides of the wooden container meet if its shape is a regular octagon?

   b) Do you think the angles between the adjacent sides of the wooden container will all be equal if one pair of opposite sides are twice as long as the other sides?

   c) Check your answer to part b) by making a drawing and measuring the angles.

9. **a)** Draw a ten-sided polygon.

   b) Calculate how many diagonals you can draw from any one vertex of this polygon. Check your answer by drawing all possible diagonals from one of the vertices.

   c) Calculate the sum of the interior angles of the polygon. Check you answer by measuring the angles on your drawing.

10. **a)** Find the measure of each interior angle of a regular 9-sided polygon. Use a second method to check your answer.

    b) Find the measure of each interior angle of a regular 15-sided polygon. Use a second method to check your answer.

    c) Find the measure of each interior angle of a regular 24-sided polygon. Use a second method to check your answer.

    d) Write an expression for the measure of each interior angle of a regular polygon with n sides.

C

11. The sides of a gazebo form a regular 15-sided polygon.

    a) Calculate the angle between adjacent sides of the gazebo.

    b) Calculate the angle between the 15 adjacent roof supports in the gazebo.

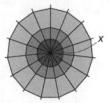

    c) Draw a plan of the gazebo.

    d) Calculate the angle between adjacent sides in a gazebo with 10 sides.

    e) Calculate the angle between the 10 adjacent roof supports in a gazebo with 10 sides.

12. A table is to be constructed from wood and used on the patio of a house.

a) At what angle will the adjacent sides of the table meet if its shape is a regular 12-sided polygon?

b) Do you think the angles between the adjacent sides of the table will all be equal if one pair of opposite sides are twice as long as the other sides?

c) Check you answer to part b) by making a drawing and measuring the angles.

13. Find the measure of $\angle$ BCA in the diagram shown.

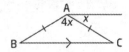

7.4 Midpoints and Medians in Triangles
Principles of Mathematics 9, pages 394–400

A

1. Calculate the length of line segment XY in each triangle.

a)

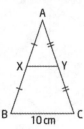

b)

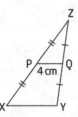

c)

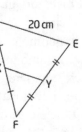

d)

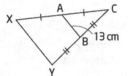

2. The area of $\triangle ABC$ is 20 cm^2.

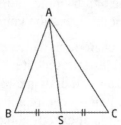

a) Calculate the area of $\triangle ABS$.

b) Calculate the area of $\triangle ACS$.

B

3. The area of $\triangle DEF$ is 26 cm^2.

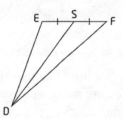

a) Calculate the area of $\triangle DES$.

b) Calculate the area of $\triangle DFS$.

4. The area of $\triangle XYZ$ is 15 cm^2.

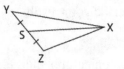

a) Calculate the area of $\triangle XYS$

b) Calculate the area of $\triangle XZS$

5. Calculate the length of the cross-brace PQ in this bridge support.

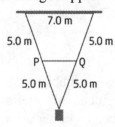

6. a) Make a conjecture about whether the medians in an equilateral triangle bisect each angle at the vertex.

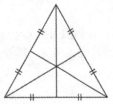

b) Describe how you can see if your conjecture is correct by folding a diagram of an equilateral triangle.

c) Describe how you could use geometry software to see if your conjecture is correct.

d) Use one of the two methods you described to test your conjecture. Describe your results.

7. Virginia conjectures that ∠ AXZ in this diagram will be obtuse when point A is located anywhere on the side YZ. Use a counter-example to show that this conjecture is false.

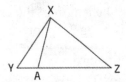

8. Here are two conjectures about isosceles triangles with an 80° interior angle. For each conjecture, either draw a counter-example or explain why you think the conjecture is true.

a) The 80° angle is always opposite one of the two equal sides.

b) The 80° angle is always opposite the unequal side.

9. Carey constructed △ DEF with DE = EF = DF. He then constructed the midpoint of DE at A and drew a perpendicular line through DE at A. Will this right bisector pass through the vertex F? Justify your answer.

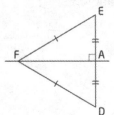

C

10. Determine whether the right bisectors of the sides of a triangle intersect at a single point.

- If you are using pencil and paper, draw the right bisectors in at least one example of each type of triangle.
- If you are using geometry software, construct a triangle and the right bisector of each side. Drag each vertex to various new locations. Does changing the shape of the triangle affect how the right bisectors intersect?

Do you think that the right bisectors intersect at a single point in all triangles? Explain your reasoning.

11. a) Investigate whether the three medians of a triangle intersect at a single point. Describe your findings.

b) Draw a triangle in which the medians of the sides intersect at a single point. Can you draw a circle that has this point as its centre and intersects the triangle at exactly three points? If so, describe the properties of the circle.

7.5 Midpoints and Diagonals in Quadrilaterals
Principles of Mathematics 9, pages 401–407

A

1. Which line segments in the following diagrams are parallel?

   a)
   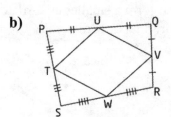

   b)
   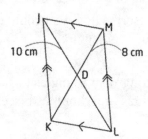

2. Calculate the lengths of KD, LD, KM and LJ.

   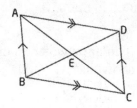

3. Calculate the lengths of AE and BE given that AC measures 22 cm and BD measures 20 cm.

   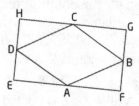

4. Shankar is using a scissor lift trolley to move equipment in a hospital. How high will the platform be when the point C is 60 cm above the base?

   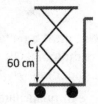

5. Sam is using a scissor jack to change a tire on his car. How high will the top of the jack be when the shaft is 30 cm from the base?

   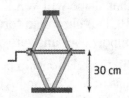

6. Construct parallelogram EFGH. Let A be the midpoint of EF, B be the midpoint of FG, C be the midpoint of GH, and D be the midpoint of HE. Connect AB, BC, CD and DA to form a new parallelogram ABCD. Under what conditions is ABCD a rhombus?

7. For each statement, either explain why it is true or draw a counter-example to show that it is false.

   a) Any diagonal of a trapezoid bisects its area.

   b) Any line segment joining the midpoints of opposite sides of a rectangle bisects its area.

8. On grid paper, draw a rectangle ABCD and mark the midpoints of the four sides. Label these midpoints W, X, Y, and Z.

   a) What type of quadrilateral is WXYZ?

   b) How is the area of WXYZ related to the area of ABCD? Explain your reasoning.

   c) What shape will WXYZ become if ABCD is shrunk to form a square? Support your answer with a drawing.

   d) Will the relationship between the areas of WXYZ and ABCD change when ABCD is shrunk into a square. Explain.

9. a) Draw a quadrilateral STUV with ST = SV and UT = UV.

   b) At what angle do the diagonals of the quadrilateral intersect?

   c) Join the midpoints of the sides of the quadrilateral to form a smaller quadrilateral WXYZ. What type of quadrilateral is WXYZ?

   d) Make a conjecture about how the area of WXYZ is related to the area of STUV.

   e) Describe how you can use geometry software to test your conjecture.

10. **Use Technology**

   a) Construct $\angle$ DEF with ED = EF. Construct a line perpendicular to DE at point D and a line perpendicular to EF at F. Label the intersection of these lines G.

   b) Show that DG = FG.

   c) Show that EG bisects $\angle$ DEF.

C

11. In this diagram, line segments joining the midpoints of the four sides of a quadrilateral form a smaller quadrilateral inside the original quadrilateral.

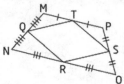

   a) How do you think the area of the smaller quadrilateral compares to the area of the original quadrilateral?

   b) Describe how you could confirm your conjecture.

12. Use congruent triangles to show that the diagonals of a rhombus bisect each other.

13. a) Draw a quadrilateral EFGH with EF = GH and EH = GF.

   b) Show that this quadrilateral must be a parallelogram.

14. For the regular pentagon in the diagram shown, show that AC = AD.

Chapter 7 Review

Principles of Mathematics 9, pages 408–409

1. Find the measure of each unknown angle.

   a)

   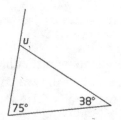

   b)

   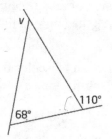

   c)

   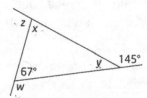

   d)

   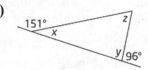

2. Explain why the angle relationships shown are not possible.

   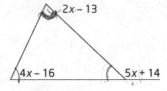

3. For each description , draw an example of the triangle or explain why it cannot exist.

   a) a triangle with an obtuse exterior angle

   b) a triangle with three acute exterior angles

4. Calculate the measure of each unknown angle.

   a)

   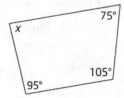

   b)

   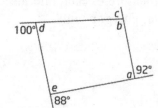

   c)

   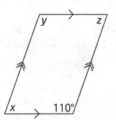

   d)

   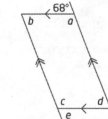

5. For each description, draw an example of the quadrilateral or explain why it cannot exist.

   a) a quadrilateral with three acute interior angles

   b) a quadrilateral with four acute interior angles

6. Find the sum of the interior angles of each polygon.

   a) pentagon

   b) heptagon (7-sided figure)

   c) pentadecagon (15-sided figure)

   d) undecagon (11-sided figure)

   e) octagon

7. Find the measure of each interior angle of a regular polygon with

   a) 6 sides

   b) 7 sides

   c) 12 sides

   d) 15 sides

8. How many sides does a polygon have if the sum of its interior angles is

   a) 1080°?

   b) 1260°?

9. **a)** Construct a regular hexagon.

   b) Describe the method you used.

10. Show that the area of $\triangle$DGH is one quarter of the area of $\triangle$DEF.

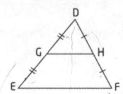

11. For each of these statements, either explain why it is true or draw a counter-example to show that it is false.

   a) The median to the vertex opposite the unequal side of an isosceles triangle bisects the angle at the vertex.

   b) The medians of an isosceles triangle are equal in length.

12. For each of these statements, either use a diagram to help explain why the statement is true, or draw a counter-example and explain why the statement is false.

   a) A line segment joining the midpoints of opposite sides of a rhombus bisects its area.

   b) A line segment joining the midpoints of two sides of a parallelogram bisects the area of the parallelogram.

   c) A line segment joining the midpoints of the parallel sides of a trapezoid bisects its area.

   d) The diagonal of a trapezoid bisects the area.

13. Describe how you can use geometry software to determine the types of quadrilaterals in which the diagonals bisect the area of the quadrilateral.

8.1 Apply the Pythagorean Theorem
Principles of Mathematics 9, pages 418–425

A

1. Calculate the length of the hypotenuse in each triangle. Round your answers to the nearest tenth of a unit, when necessary.

   a)

   4 cm, c, 3 cm

   b)

   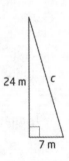

   24 m, c, 7 m

   c)

   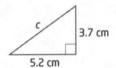

   c, 3.7 cm, 5.2 cm

   d)

   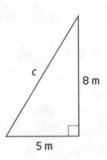

   c, 8 m, 5 m

2. Calculate the length of the unknown side in each triangle. Round your answers to the nearest tenth of a unit, when necessary.

   a)

   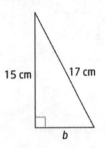

   15 cm, 17 cm, b

   b)

   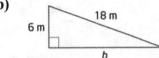

   18 m, 6 m, b

   c)

   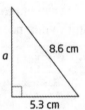

   a, 8.6 cm, 5.3 cm

   d)

   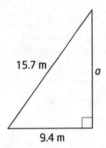

   15.7 m, a, 9.4 m

B

3. Determine the area of each right triangle. Round your answers to the nearest square unit, when necessary.

   a)

   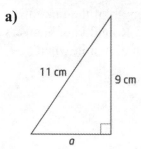

   b)

   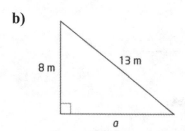

4. Calculate the length of each line segment. Round your answers to the nearest tenth of a unit, when necessary.

   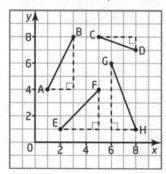

   a) AB

   b) CD

   c) EF

   d) GH

5. What is the length of the diagonal of a plasma TV screen that measures 127 cm by 107 cm? Round your answer to the nearest centimetre.

6. In a major league baseball game, a baseball diamond is a square with sides that measure about 27 m. How far does the first base player have to throw the ball to get a runner out a third base? Round your answer to the nearest metre.

7. a) What length of fencing is needed to surround this triangular section of land, to the nearest metre?

   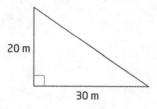

   b) What is the area of the triangular section of land?

   c) Explain the steps you took to solve this problem.

C

8. A cardboard box measures 50 cm by 50 cm by 40 cm. Calculate the length of the space diagonal, to the nearest centimetre.

   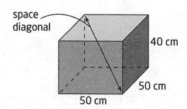

9. A spiral is formed with right triangles as shown in the diagram.

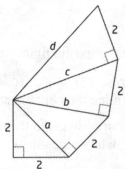

a) Calculate the length of the hypotenuse of each triangle, leaving your answers in square root form. Describe the pattern that results.

b) Write an expression for the total area of the spiral shown.

c) Describe how the expression for the total area would change if the pattern continued.

10. a) Complete the following chart of Pythagorean Triples.

Length Side, a	Length Side, b	Hypotenuse
3	4	5
5	12	
7		25
9		

b) Describe any patterns that you can find in the table.

8.2 Perimeter and Area of Composite Figures

Principles of Mathematics 9, pages 426–435

A

1. For each composite figure,

   • solve for any unknown lengths
   • determine the perimeter

   Round your answers to the nearest tenth of a unit, when necessary.

   a)

   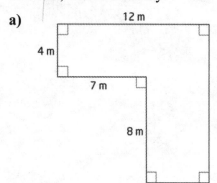

   b)

   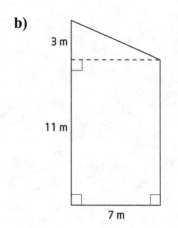

   c)

   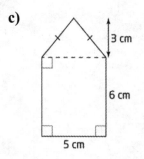

2. For each composite figure,

   • solve for any unknown lengths
   • determine the perimeter

   Round your answers to the nearest tenth of a unit, when necessary.

   a)

   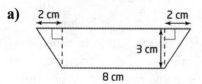

   b)

   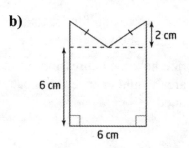

   c)

   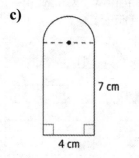

B

3. Calculate the area of each composite figure. Round your answers to the nearest square unit, when necessary.

a)

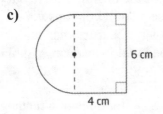

b)

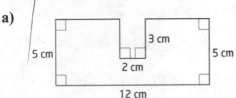

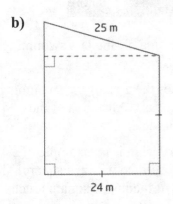

c)

d)

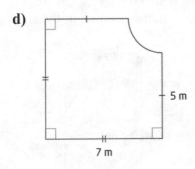

4. a) What length of moulding is needed to surround this window, to the nearest metre?

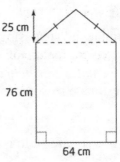

b) What is the area of the window?

c) Explain the steps you took to solve this problem.

5. Michael is designing a garden railway for his parents' back yard.

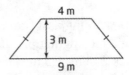

a) What length of fencing is needed to surround the garden railway, to the nearest tenth of a metre?

b) What is the area of the garden railway?

6. Stella has designed a number for her art project. Use a ruler to make the appropriate measurements and calculate the area of the number, to the nearest hundred square millimetres.

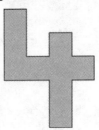

7. Use Technology Use *The Geometer's Sketchpad*® to create a composite figure made up of at least four different shapes.

   a) Estimate the perimeter and area of the figure you created.

   b) Determine the area using the measurement feature of *The Geometer's Sketchpad*®. Was your estimate reasonable?

8. The area of a square patio is 8 m².

   a) Find the length of one of its sides, to the nearest tenth of a metre.

   b) Find the perimeter of the patio, to the nearest metre.

C

9. Junjie is working as a framer. He is framing a rectangular picture that measures 2 m by 1.5 m. The frame is 5 cm wide and is made up of four trapezoids. Find the total area of the frame, in square centimetres.

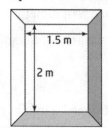

1.5 m

2 m

10. Sheila is designing a square swimming pool to fit inside a square yard with side length 8 m so that there is a triangular deck at each corner.

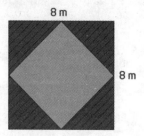

8 m

8 m

   a) Find the area of Sheila's swimming pool.

   b) How does the area of the swimming pool compare to the area of the triangular deck areas?

   c) Sheila's design is an example of a square inscribed within a square. The vertices of the inside square touch the sides of the outside square but do not intersect. Will your answer in part b) always be true when a square is inscribed within a square? Explain.

11. The midpoints of the sides of a rectangle that measures 15 cm by 10 cm are joined. Determine the area of the shaded region.

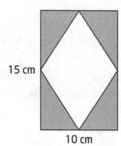

15 cm

10 cm

8.3 Surface Area and Volume of Prisms and Pyramids

Principles of Mathematics 9, pages 436–443

A

1. Determine the surface area of each object. Round to the nearest tenth of a square unit, when necessary.

a)

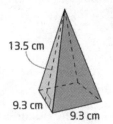

b)

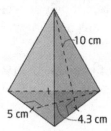

2. Determine the volume of each object. Round to the nearest cubic unit, when necessary.

a)

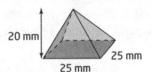

b)

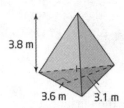

B

3. Determine the surface area of each object.

a)

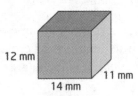

b)

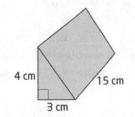

4. Determine the volume of each object. Round to the nearest cubic unit, when necessary.

a)

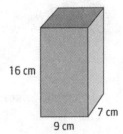

b)

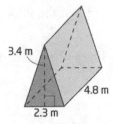

5. A rectangular prism has length 4 m, width 3 m, and height 5 m.

   a) Determine the surface area of the prism.

   b) Determine the volume of the prism.

6. A box of crackers has a volume of 5000 cm^3. If its length is 25 cm and its width is 8 cm, what is its height?

7. The Great Pyramid of Giza is the only surviving wonder of the Seven Wonders of the Ancient World. When the Great Pyramid of Giza was built its square base had side lengths of 229 m and its height was 146 m.

   a) Determine the volume of this famous pyramid, to the nearest cubic metre.

   b) Determine its surface area, to the nearest square metre.

8. A juice container is a right prism with a base area of 140 cm^2. The height of the container is 35 cm.

   a) Find the volume of the juice container.

   b) How many litres of juice will the container hold?

C

9. Phil has built a garden shed in the shape shown.

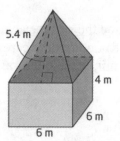

   a) Calculate the volume of the shed, to the nearest cubic metre.

   b) Phil plans to paint the outside of the shed, including the roof but not the floor. One can of paint covers 16 m^2. How many cans of paint will Phil need?

   c) If one can of paint costs $19.95, what is the total cost, including 6% GST and 8% PST?

10. The curator of a museum recently purchased the frustum of a pyramid shown. He plans to use the frustum to display ancient artifacts. The frustum is the part remaining from a pyramid after the top portion has been removed by making a cut parallel to the base of the pyramid.

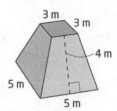

   a) Determine the surface area of the frustum.

   b) Calculate the total cost of painting the frustum with paint that costs $9.50/m^2 including GST and PST. It is not necessary to paint the bottom of the frustum.

8.4 Surface Area of a Cone

Principles of Mathematics 9, pages 444–450

A

1. Calculate the surface area of each cone. Round to the nearest square unit.

a)

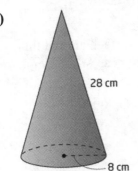

3 m

2 m

b)

28 cm

8 cm

c)

17 cm

15 cm

d)

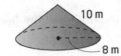

10 m

8 m

2. a) Find the slant height of the cone.

b) Calculate the surface area of the cone. Round to the nearest square metre.

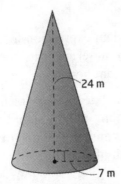

24 m

7 m

B

3. A funnel is shaped like a cone.

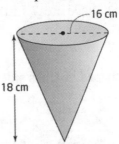

16 cm

18 cm

a) How much aluminum, to the nearest square centimetre, is needed to make the funnel?

b) What assumptions have you made?

4. One cone has base radius 5 cm and height 7 cm. Another cone has a base radius of 7 cm and height 5 cm.

a) Do the cones have the same slant height?

b) Do the cones have the same surface area? If not, predict which cone has the greater surface area. Explain your reasoning.

c) Determine the surface area of each cone to check your prediction. Round your answer to the nearest tenth of a centimetre. Were you correct?

5. The lateral area of a cone with radius 5 cm is 120 cm^2.

a) Determine the slant height of the cone, to the nearest centimetre.

b) Determine the height of the cone, to the nearest centimetre.

6. The height of a cone is tripled. Does this triple the surface area? Justify your answer.

7. The radius of a cone is tripled. Does this triple the surface area? Justify your answer.

8. A cube-shaped box has sides 16 cm in length.

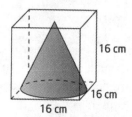

16 cm
16 cm
16 cm

a) What are the dimensions of the largest cone that fits inside this box?

b) What is the slant height of this cone? Round your answer to the nearest centimetre.

c) What is the surface area of this cone, to the nearest square centimetre?

9. A cone just fits inside a cylinder. The volume of the cylinder is 5600 cm³. The diameter of the cylinder is 18 cm.

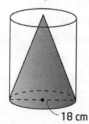

18 cm

a) What are the dimensions of this cone? Round your answers to the nearest centimetre.

b) What is the slant height of this cone? Round your answer to the nearest centimetre.

c) What is the surface area of this cone, to the nearest square centimetre?

C

10. The frustum of a cone is the part that remains after the top portion has been removed by making a cut parallel to the base. Calculate the surface area of this frustum, to the nearest square metre.

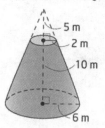

5 m
2 m
10 m
6 m

11. Calculate the surface area of this frustum, to the nearest square metre.

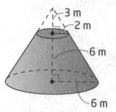

3 m
2 m
6 m
6 m

12. Create a problem involving the surface area of a cone. Solve the problem. Exchange with a classmate.

13. Suppose the cube in question 8 has side lengths of y.

a) Write expressions for the dimensions of the largest cone that fits inside this box.

b) What is a formula for the surface area of this cone?

14. a) Find an expression for the radius of a cone in terms of its lateral area and its slant height.

b) If the lateral area of a cone is 120 cm² and its slant height is 13 cm, determine its radius, to the nearest tenth of a centimetre.

8.5 Volume of a Cone
Principles of Mathematics 9, pages 451–456

A

1. Determine the volume of each cone. Round your answer to the nearest cubic unit, when necessary.

    a)

    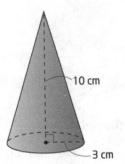
    10 cm
    3 cm

    b)

    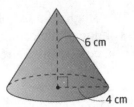
    6 cm
    4 cm

    c)

    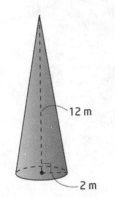
    12 m
    2 m

    d)

    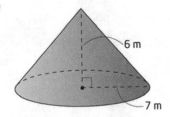
    6 m
    7 m

2. Determine the volume of each cone. Round your answer to the nearest cubic unit, when necessary.

    a)

    5 cm
    2 cm

    b)

    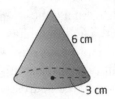
    6 cm
    3 cm

    c)

    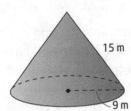
    15 m
    9 m

    d)

    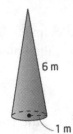
    6 m
    1 m

B

3. Giacomo has a water cup in the shape of a cone. The water cup has a radius of 6.4 cm and a slant height of 11.4 cm. How much water can the paper cup hold, to the nearest tenth of a cubic centimetre?

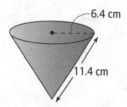

4. Sophia has constructed a cone-shaped funnel from paper. The funnel has a volume of 62 cm^3 and a radius of 4 cm. What is the height of the paper cup? Round your answer to the nearest centimetre.

5. Nadia has constructed a sand pile in the shape of a cone. The sand pile has a volume of 80 cm^3 and a height of 10 cm. What is the radius of the sand pile? Round your answer to the nearest centimetre.

6. A cone just fits inside a cylinder with volume 600 cm^3. What is the volume of the cone?

7. Create a problem involving the volume of a cone. Solve it. Exchange your problem with a classmate.

8. A cone has a volume of 80 cm^3. What is the volume of a cylinder that just holds the cone?

9. A cone-shaped storage unit holds 300 m^3 of salt. The unit has a base radius of 7 m. Round your answers to the nearest metre, if necessary.

a) Estimate the height of the storage unit.

b) Calculate the height.

c) How close was your estimate?

10. A candle is in the shape of a frustum. Calculate the volume of the candle to the nearest tenth of a cubic centimetre.

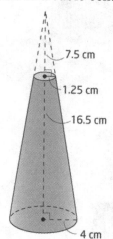

C

11. A cone has a height of 6 cm and a base radius of 5 cm. Another cone has a height of 5 cm and a base radius of 6 cm.

   a) Predict which cone has the greater volume. Explain your prediction.

   b) Calculate the volume of each cone to the nearest cubic centimetre. Was your prediction correct?

12. a) Express the height of a cone in terms of its volume and its radius.

   b) If a cone holds 1.5 L and its radius is 15 cm, what is its height? Round your answer to the nearest tenth of a centimetre.

13. a) Express the radius of a cone in terms of its volume and its height.

   b) If a cone holds 2 L and its height is 16 cm, what is its radius? Round your answer to the nearest tenth of a centimetre.

14. A cone-shaped glass holds 500 mL of water. If the height of the glass is 10 cm, determine the radius of the glass, rounded to the nearest tenth of a centimetre.

15. A cone-shaped sand pile has a volume of approximately 300 m^3. If the radius of the sand pile is 6 m, determine the height of the sand pile, rounded to the nearest tenth of a metre.

8.6 Surface Area of a Sphere

Principles of Mathematics 9, pages 457–461

A

1. Determine the surface area of each sphere. Round your answer to the nearest square unit.

    a)

    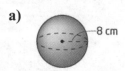
    8 cm

    b)

    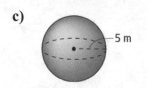
    50.3 mm

    c)

    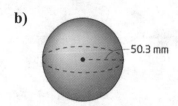
    5 m

    d)

    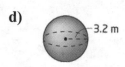
    3.2 m

2. A sphere has a surface area of 47.5 cm². Find its radius. Round your answer to one decimal place.

3. A sphere has a surface area of 65.8 cm². Find its diameter. Round your answer to one decimal place.

B

4. A soccer ball has a diameter of 25.4 cm.

    a) How much synthetic leather is required to cover this ball? Round your answer to the nearest tenth of a square centimetre.

    b) If the synthetic leather costs $25/m², what does it cost to cover the soccer ball?

5. A volleyball has a diameter of 26.4 cm.

    a) How much leather is required to cover this ball? Round your answer to the nearest tenth of a square centimetre.

    b) If the leather costs $32/m², what does it cost to cover the soccer ball?

6. Martie has a globe of the earth in her house. The diameter of the globe is 28 cm.

    a) Calculate the surface area of the globe. Round your answer to the nearest square centimetre.

    b) If the paper material to cover the surface area of the globe costs $2/m², what does it cost to cover the globe?

7. The world's largest rotating globe, excluding the Earth itself, is Eartha, located within the headquarters of the Delorme mapping corporation in Yarmouth, Maine. The globe has a diameter of 12.5 m. Calculate the surface area of Eartha. Round your answer to the nearest square metre.

8. Asteroids are rocky and metallic objects that orbit the sun but are too small to be considered planets. They are known as minor planets. The diameter of Ceres, the largest asteroid, is approximately 1000 km. Calculate its surface area, to the nearest square kilometre.

9. Joe is creating a Snow Globe. The ball has a diameter of 20 cm and will be covered with glass. Calculate the surface area of the Snow Globe, to the nearest square centimetre.

10. The radius of a sphere is 12 cm.

   a) Predict how much the surface area increases if the radius increases by 3 cm.

   b) Calculate the change in the surface area, to the nearest square centimetre.

   c) How accurate was your prediction?

C

11. Use Technology

   a) Write the formula to calculate the surface area of a sphere in terms of the diameter, d.

   b) Use a graphing calculator to graph the surface area of a sphere versus its diameter by entering the surface area formula.

   c) Describe the relationship.

   d) Use the TRACE feature to determine

   • the surface area of a sphere with diameter 8.5 cm, to the nearest square centimetre

   • the diameter of a sphere with surface area 60 cm^2, to the nearest tenth of a centimetre

12. Use Technology Refer to question 11.

   a) Determine an algebraic expression for the diameter of a sphere in terms of its surface area.

   b) Use your expression from part a) and a graphing calculator to graph the relationship between the diameter and the surface area.

   c) Describe the relationship.

   d) Use the graphing calculator to find the diameter of a sphere with surface area 600 cm^2. Round to the nearest tenth of a centimetre.

13. A spherical balloon is blown up from a diameter of 15 cm to a diameter of 60 cm. By what factor has its surface area increased? Explain your reasoning.

14. Which has the greater surface area: a sphere of radius 8 cm or a cube with edges of length 16 cm?

8.7 Volume of a Sphere
Principles of Mathematics 9, pages 462–469

A

1. Calculate the volume of each sphere. Round your answers to the nearest cubic unit.

   a)

   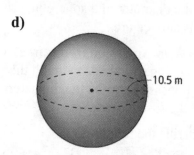
   15.3 cm

   b)

   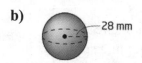
   28 mm

   c)

   4.3 m

   d)

   10.5 m

2. A beach ball has a diameter of 30 cm. Calculate its volume to the nearest cubic centimetre.

   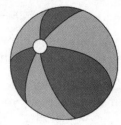

B

3. A baseball has a diameter of 7.5 cm. Calculate the volume of the baseball. Round your answer to the nearest cubic centimetre.

4. The diameter of the moon is 3476 km. Calculate the volume of the moon. Round your answer to the nearest cubic kilometre.

5. Mary found a sphere-shaped pebble on the shore of a lake. The pebble has a diameter of 6 cm. What is the volume of the pebble to the nearest cubic centimetre.

6. A ball just fits inside a plastic cube with edges 9 cm.

   a) Calculate the volume of the ball, to the nearest cubic centimetre.

   b) Calculate the volume of the cube.

   c) Determine the amount of empty space.

7. A gemologist is designing a ring for a customer. The gemstone to be used in the ring is spherical in shape and has a diameter of 50 mm. Calculate the volume of the gemstone to the nearest cubic millimetre.

8. A spherical glass fixture has a diameter of 25 cm.

  a) Calculate the volume of the glass fixture to the nearest tenth of a cubic centimetre.

  b) Calculate the surface area of the glass fixture to the nearest tenth of a square centimetre.

9. Tennis balls are stacked four high in a rectangular prism package. The diameter of one ball is 6.5 cm.

  a) Calculate the volume of the rectangular prism package.

  b) What is the minimum amount of material needed to make the box?

  c) Determine the amount of empty space in the rectangular prism package.

  d) What assumptions have you made?

10. A cylindrical silo has a hemispherical top (half a sphere). The cylinder has a height of 30 m and a base diameter of 8 m.

  a) Estimate the total volume of the silo.

  b) Calculate the total volume, to the nearest cubic metre.

  c) The silo should be filled to no more than 80% capacity to allow for air circulation. How much grain can be put in the silo?

  d) A truck with a bin measuring 8 m by 4 m by 3.5 m delivers grain to the farm. How many truckloads would fill the silo to its recommended capacity?

C

11. A propane tank beside a cottage is in the shape of a cylinder with a hemisphere at both ends. The tank has a radius of 0.4 m and a length of 2 m. Calculate the volume of the tank, to the nearest tenth of a cubic metre.

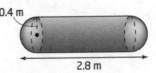

0.4 m

2.8 m

12. The diameter of the Earth is about 12 800 km. The diameter of Venus is about 12 100 km.

  a) Calculate the volume of the Earth, to the nearest square kilometre.

  b) Calculate the volume of Venus, to the nearest square kilometre.

  c) How much larger is the Earth than Venus?

  d) What assumptions have you made?

13. Estimate and then calculate the radius of a sphere with a volume of 500 cm³. Round your answer to the nearest hundredth of a centimetre, if necessary.

14. If the surface area of a sphere is tripled from 250 cm² to 750 cm², by what factor does its volume increase? Round your answer to one decimal place.

15. A sphere just fits inside a cube with sides of length 6 cm.

  a) Estimate the ratio of the volume of the sphere to the volume of the cube.

  b) Calculate the volumes of the sphere and the cube and their ratio.

  c) How does your answer compare to your estimate?

1. Determine the perimeter and area of each right triangle. Round answers to the nearest tenth of a unit or square unit.

   a)

   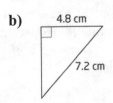

   10.3 cm
   5.7 cm

   b)

   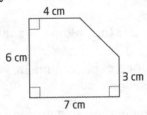

   4.8 cm
   7.2 cm

2. A 8-m ladder is leaning against a vertical wall. The top of the ladder is 7 m up the wall. How far from the wall is the base of the ladder? Round to the nearest tenth of a metre.

3. Calculate the perimeter and area of the figure. Round answers to the nearest tenth of a unit or square unit, if necessary.

   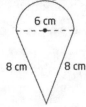

   4 cm
   6 cm
   3 cm
   7 cm

4. Calculate the perimeter and area of the figure. Round answers to the nearest tenth of a unit or square unit.

   6 cm
   8 cm   8 cm

5. The diagram shows the track for a bicycle race. The track consists of two parallel line segments with a semicircle at each end. The track is 10 m wide.

   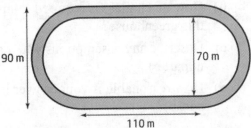

   90 m   70 m
   110 m

   a) Ismail bikes on the inner edge of the track. How far does he bike in one lap, to the nearest tenth of a metre?

   b) Carey bikes on the outer edge. How far does he bike in one lap, to the nearest tenth of a metre?

   c) Find the difference between the distances biked by Ismail and Carey.

6. Calculate the surface area of each object. Round answers to the nearest square unit.

   a)

   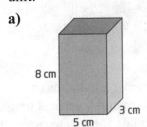

   8 cm
   3 cm
   5 cm

   b)

   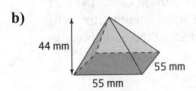

   44 mm
   55 mm
   55 mm

7. a) Calculate the volume of the greenhouse.

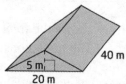

40 m
5 m
20 m

b) How much glass is required to make this greenhouse?

c) Describe any assumptions you made in part b).

d) How reasonable is your answer in part b)?

8. A cylindrical paint can holds 3.73 L and has a radius of 8.4 cm. Calculate the height of the can, to the nearest centimetre.

9. Calculate the surface area of a cone with a slant height of 15 cm and a height of 13 cm. Round to the nearest square centimetre.

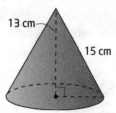

13 cm
15 cm

10. The cone portion of a pylon has a diameter of 26 cm and a vertical height of 38 cm. Calculate the surface area of the cone portion of the pylon, to the nearest square centimetre. Assume that the bottom of the cone is complete.

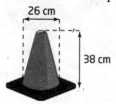

26 cm
38 cm

11. A conical flower vase holds 120 mL. If the height of the vase is 15 cm, determine its radius, to the nearest tenth of a centimetre.

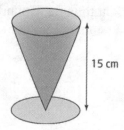

15 cm

12. Calculate the volume of a cone that just fits inside a cylinder with a base radius of 6 cm and a height of 11 cm. Round to the nearest cubic centimetre. How does the volume of the cone compare to the volume of the cylinder?

13. A ball has a diameter of 23.4 cm. Calculate the amount of material required to cover the ball, to the nearest tenth of a square centimetre.

14. The diameter of Mars is about 6 794 km.

a) Calculate the area of the Northern Hemisphere of Mars, to the nearest square kilometre.

b) What assumptions have you made?

15. Calculate the volume of a tennis ball with a diameter of 8 cm, to the nearest tenth of a cubic centimetre.

16. The tennis ball in question 14 is packaged so that it just fits inside a cube-shaped box.

a) Estimate the amount of empty space inside the box.

b) Calculate the amount of empty space.

c) How close was your estimate?

9.1 Investigate Measurement Concepts

Principles of Mathematics 9, pages 478–483

A

1. Explore the different rectangles that you can form with a perimeter of 22 units.

   a) What are you to investigate?

   b) Choose a strategy that you can carry out on grid paper. Record the areas of five different rectangles.

Rectangle	Width (units)	Length (units)	Perimeter (units)	Area (square units)
1			22	
2			22	
3			22	
4			22	
5			22	

2. Explore the different rectangles that you can form with an area of 18 square units.

   a) What are you to investigate?

   b) Choose a strategy that you can carry out using elastics on a geoboard. Record the perimeter of each rectangle.

Rectangle	Width (units)	Length (units)	Perimeter (units)	Area (square units)
1				18
2				18
3				18

3. You are designing a rectangular garage that is to have an area of 36 m². Using a geoboard, let the distance between the pegs represent 1 m.

   a) With an elastic, construct different rectangles to represent the garage's perimeter. Record the dimensions of each rectangle you create in a table. Calculate the perimeter of each rectangle.

Rectangle	Width (m)	Length (m)	Perimeter (m)	Area (m²)
1				36
2				36
3				36

   b) Explain how the perimeter affects the cost of the garage.

   c) Which shape would be the most economical for the garage? Why?

   d) Is cost the only factor when choosing a shape for the garage.

B

4. You are designing a rectangular room in an office that is to have an area of 64 m². Using a geoboard, let the distance between the pegs represent 1 m.

   a) With an elastic, construct different rectangles to represent the room's area. Record the dimensions of each rectangle you create in a table. Calculate the perimeter of each rectangle.

Rectangle	Width (m)	Length (m)	Perimeter (m)	Area (m²)
1				64
2				64
3				64
4				64

   b) Explain how the perimeter affects the cost of the garage.

   c) Which shape would be the most economical for the garage? Why?

   d) Is cost the only factor when choosing a shape for the garage.

5. **Use Technology** Reg is making a garden in his back yard. He was to put a fence around his garden. He has 25 m of fencing. Use *The Geometer's Sketchpad®* to investigate the dimensions of the rectangular garden with the greatest area than Reg can enclose with this fencing.

6. **Use Technology** Arin wants to put a fence around the swimming pool in her yard. He has 49 m of fencing. Use *The Geometer's Sketchpad®* to investigate the dimensions of the rectangular swimming pool with the greatest area than Arin can enclose with this fencing.

7. Meredith is enclosing a rectangular area for dogs with 48 m of fencing at a local park. Use a table or a spreadsheet to investigate the greatest area that Meredith can enclose.

Rectangle	Width (m)	Length (m)	Perimeter (m)	Area (m²)
1	1	23	48	23
2	2	22	48	44
3			48	
4			48	

	A	B	C	D	E
1	Rec-tangle	Width (m)	Length (m)	Perim-eter (m)	Area (m)
2	1	1	=24-B2	48	=B2*C2
3	2	=B2+1	=24-B3	48	=B3*C3
4	3			48	
5	4			48	

C

8. Pyal is enclosing a rectangular area for his lawn with 72 m of fencing. Use a table or a spreadsheet to investigate the greatest area that Pyal can enclose.

9. What happens to the area when you change the shape of an enclosure. Suppose each toothpick represents a 1-m length of fence.

a) Use 48 toothpicks to build enclosures with the greatest area, using the following shapes:

- triangle
- rectangle
- hexagon
- octagon
- circle

b) Find the area of each enclosure in part a). Round your answers to one decimal place, when necessary.

c) Does the shape of the enclosure affect its area? Write a brief report of your findings.

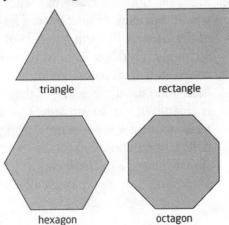

triangle

rectangle

hexagon

octagon

9.2 Perimeter and Area Relationships of a Rectangle
Principles of Mathematics 9, pages 484–490

A

1. What dimensions will provide the maximum area for a rectangle with each perimeter?

   a) 28 m

   b) 40 m

   c) 48 m

   d) 65 m

2. A rectangular table is being constructed using oak wood. The perimeter of the table is to be 10.0 m.

   a) Sketch three different tables that have a perimeter of 10.0 m.

   b) What table dimensions will give the maximum area for the table?

3. A rectangular swimming area is to be enclosed using 78 m of rope.

   a) What are the dimensions of the rectangle of maximum area?

   b) Suppose 39 barriers, each 2 m long, are used instead. Can the same area be enclosed? Explain.

   c) How much more area can be enclosed if the rope is used instead of the barriers?

B

4. A fence is to be built with prefabricated sections that are 2.6 m in length. What is the maximum rectangular area that you can enclose with

   a) 28 pieces?

   b) 52 pieces?

5. A fence is being built using the materials in question 4, but now there is an existing wall that will be used as one of the boundaries. Draw a diagram and label the dimensions of the maximum rectangular area that you can enclose with

   a) 28 pieces

   b) 52 pieces

   For the fence materials in each of parts a) and b), how much additional area does using an existing border provide?

6. Fred is adding a rectangular fenced in area to the back of his house. The back of the house will form one side of the rectangle. Fred has 20 m of fencing to use. Conduct an investigation to determine the dimensions of the enclosure of maximum area. Use any tools: toothpicks, geoboards, grid paper, tables, or technology such as spreadsheets, *The Geometer's Sketchpad*®, or a graphing calculator.

7. A farmer is adding a rectangular corral to the side of his barn. The barn will form one side of the rectangle. The area of the corral is to be 50 m². One possible rectangle is given.

a) Investigate other possible rectangles with an area of 60 m². Copy and complete the table or use a spreadsheet like the one shown.

Rectangle	Width (m)	Length (m)	Area (m²)	Length of Fence Used (m)
1	1	50	50	52
2	2		50	
3			50	
4			50	

	A	B	C	D	E
1	Rec-tangle	Width (m)	Length (m)	Area (m²)	Length of Fence Used (m)
2	1	1	=50/B2	50	=C2+2*B2
3	2	=B2+1	=50/B3	50	=C3+2*B3
4	3			50	
5	4			50	

b) What dimensions use the minimum length of fence to enclose the corral?

c) What is the minimum length of fence that can be used to enclose the corral?

8. Sanjay has prepared a proposal for a client. In the proposal, he reports how 40 m of fencing can be used to fence an enclosure on

• four sides
• three sides, using a wall at the back of the property as the fourth side
• two sides, using the wall at the back and an existing hedge on an adjacent side

Draw diagrams for each of the three scenarios in Sanjay's proposal and calculate the maximum area that can be enclosed in each case.

9. Pose a problem involving the relationship between the perimeter and the area of a rectangular swimming pool. Solve the problem and then have a classmate solve it.

C
10. Describe a situation in which it is important to know
a) the maximum area of a rectangle for a given perimeter
b) the minimum perimeter of a rectangle for a given area

11. Conduct an investigation to determine the dimensions of the rectangular rug with area 42 m² and minimum perimeter. Round the dimensions to two decimal places.

12. A rectangular balcony with an area of 32 m² is to be enclosed on three sides. Minimizing the perimeter will minimize the cost of the material to be used for the balcony enclosure. Conduct an investigation to determine the shape of the balcony enclosure with the minimum perimeter.

13. Conduct an investigation to find the dimensions of the triangle of maximum area that can be inscribed in a circle with
a) diameter 10 cm
b) diameter 16 cm
c) diameter 22 cm
Round you answers to two decimal places, when necessary.

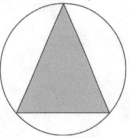

9.3 Minimize the Surface Area of a Square-Based Prism
Principles of Mathematics 9, pages 491–497

A

1. Determine the dimensions of the square-based prism box with each volume that requires the least material to make. Round the dimensions to the nearest tenth of a centimetre, when necessary.

   a) 729 cm^3

   b) 1331 cm^3

   c) 800 cm^3

   d) 1300 cm^3

   e) 750 cm^3

   f) 548 cm^3

2. Determine the surface area of each prism you found in question 2, to the nearest square centimetre.

3. These square-based prisms all have the same volume. Rank them in order from least to greatest surface area. Explain your reasoning.

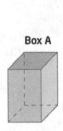
Box A

Box B

Box C

B

4. Jacinth has been asked to design a square-based prism container to transport hot food. To keep heat loss to a minimum, the total surface area must be minimized.

   a) Find the dimensions of the container with volume 150 000 cm^3 that has minimum heat loss. Round the dimensions to the nearest tenth of a centimetre.

   b) What other factors might Jacinth consider?

5. Determine the dimensions of a square-based prism container with volume 4300 cm^3 and minimum heat loss. Round the dimensions to the nearest tenth of a centimetre.

6. Cereal is packaged in a square-based prism box.

   a) The box contains 5564 cm^3 of cereal. What dimensions for the box require the least amount of cardboard? Round the dimensions to the nearest tenth of a centimetre.

   b) Does cereal usual come in a box shaped like the one you found in part a)? Suggest reasons for this.

7. Martie is mailing a cell phone charger in a small cardboard squared-based prism box. The box must have a capacity of 1500 cm³ and Martie wants to use the minimum amount of cardboard when she mails the box.

   a) What should the dimensions of the box be, to the nearest hundredth of a centimetre?

   b) What is the minimum amount of cardboard that Martie will need, to the nearest tenth of a square centimetre?

8. Create a problem that involves designing a square-based prism with a minimum surface area. Solve the problem. Exchange with a classmate.

9. A laundry soap manufacturer wants its large box of laundry detergent to be a square-based prism with a capacity of 5.5 L.

   a) What should the dimensions of the box be to require the minimum amount of cardboard to construct the box? Round the dimensions to one decimal place.
   Hint: 1 L = 1000 cm³.

   b) Determine the least amount of cardboard required to construct this box. Round to nearest square centimetre.

10. A storage container is a square-based prism with a capacity of 9.6 L. The storage container was designed to use the minimum amount of material when it was constructed.

    a) Determine the dimensions of the storage container, to the nearest hundredth of a centimetre.

    b) Determine the amount of material that was used in the construction of the storage container, to the nearest tenth of a centimetre.

11. Refer to question 10. The company has also designed a line of storage containers with a capacity of 9.6 L that do not have lids.

    a) Carry out an investigation to determine the dimensions of a lidless box with minimum surface area and a capacity of 9.6 L. Round your answer to the nearest tenth of a centimetre.

    b) Compare the results to those in question 10. Are the dimensions the same or different?

    c) Does the lidless box require more, less, or the same amount of material to construct, compared to the box with a lid?

C

12. a) Determine the dimensions of a square-based prism box of orange juice that holds 175 mL of juice and requires the least amount of material. Round the dimensions to the nearest tenth of a centimetre.

b) Suggest reasons why boxes of orange juice are not usually manufactured with the dimensions you found in part a).

c) Write a letter to the manufacturer recommending a new design for its boxes of orange juice, keeping your results from parts a) and b) in mind.

13. a) Determine the dimensions of a box of microwave popcorn that has a capacity of 32.5 cm^3 and requires the least amount of material. Round the dimensions to the nearest tenth of a centimetre.

b) Suggest reasons why boxes of microwave popcorn are not usually manufactured with the dimensions you found in part a).

c) Write a letter to the manufacturer recommending a new design for its boxes of microwave popcorn, keeping your results from parts a) and b) in mind.

14. How would you arrange 48 interlocking cubes in a square-based prism with the smallest surface area possible?

9.4 Maximize the Volume of A Square-Based Prism

Principles of Mathematics 9, pages 498–503

A

1. The three square-based prisms have the same surface area. Rank the prisms in order of volume from greatest to least.

Box A   Box B   Box C

2. Determine the dimensions of the square-based prism with maximum volume for each surface area. Round the dimensions to the nearest tenth of a unit when necessary.

   a) 294 cm^2

   b) 864 m^2

   c) 600 cm^2

   d) 1536 m^2

   e) 1500 cm^2

   f) 1800 m^2

3. Determine the volume of each prism in question 2, to the nearest cubic unit, when necessary.

4. Use a table or a spreadsheet to conduct an investigation to find the dimensions of the square-based prism box with maximum volume that can be made with 850 cm^2 of cardboard. Round dimensions to the nearest tenth of a centimetre.

B

5. a) Determine the surface area and volume of the square-based prism box shown.

   38 cm
   14 cm
   14 cm

   b) Determine the dimensions of a square-based prism box with the same surface area but with maximum volume. Round the dimensions to the nearest tenth of a centimetre.

   c) Calculate the volume of the box in part b) to verify that it is greater than the volume of the box in part a). Round your answer to the nearest cubic centimetre.

6. a) Determine the surface area and volume of the square-based prism box shown. Round your answers to the one decimal place when necessary.

   1.8 m
   2.4 m
   2.4 m

   b) Determine the dimensions of a square-based prism box with the same surface area but with maximum volume. Round the dimensions to the nearest tenth of a metre.

   c) Calculate the volume of the box in part b) to verify that it is greater than the volume of the box in part a). Round your answer to the nearest cubic metre.

7. **a)** Determine the surface area and volume of the square-based prism box shown. Round your answers to the one decimal place when necessary.

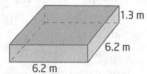

1.3 m

6.2 m

6.2 m

b) Determine the dimensions of a square-based prism box with the same surface area but with maximum volume. Round the dimensions to the nearest tenth of a metre.

c) Calculate the volume of the box in part b) to verify that it is greater than the volume of the box in part a). Round your answer to the nearest metre.

8. Helen is building a square-based prism cedar chest with a lid to hold blankets. She has 16 m² of cedar wood available.

a) Determine the dimensions of the cedar chest with maximum volume, the nearest tenth of a metre.

b) Determine the volume of Helen's cedar chest to the nearest cubic metre.

9. Ranjit is building a square-based prism storage box with a lid to hold tools. He has 20 m² of plywood available.

a) Determine the dimensions of the storage box with maximum volume, the nearest tenth of a metre.

b) Determine the volume of Ranjit's storage box to the nearest cubic metre.

C

10. Jane is packaging a stereo system to be shipped to her cousin. She has 16 000 cm² of cardboard and will put shredded paper around the speakers to protect them during shipping.

a) What are the dimensions of the square-based prism box with maximum volume? Round the dimensions to the nearest tenth of a centimetre.

b) What is the volume of this box? Round to the nearest cubic centimetre.

c) If the stereo system measures 35 cm by 35 cm by 44 cm, how much empty space is left in the box?

d) What assumptions have you made in solving this problem?

11. Philip has a piece of plywood that measures 150 cm by 300 cm. He wants to construct a square-based prism box to hold his gardening equipment. Philip wants to maximize the volume of the box and to keep the waste of plywood to a minimum.

a) Determine the dimensions of the box with maximum volume that he can construct including a lid. Round to the nearest tenth of a centimetre.

b) Draw a scale diagram on grid paper to show how Dylan should cut the plywood.

c) Describe any assumptions you have made in solving this problem.

9.5 Maximize the Volume of a Cylinder
Principles of Mathematics 9, pages 504-509

A

1. Determine the dimensions of the cylinder with the maximum volume for each surface area. Round the dimensions to the nearest hundredth of a unit.

   a) 1400 cm^2

   b) 20 m^2

   c) 3000 mm^2

   d) 400 cm^2

   e) 80 m^2

   f) 4500 mm^2

2. Determine the volume of each cylinder in question 1. Round to the nearest cubic unit.

3. A chemical company wants to make a cylindrical storage container of sheet metal. 80 m^2 of material is available.

   a) Determine the dimensions of the container with maximum volume. Round the dimensions to the nearest tenth of a metre.

   b) Determine how many litres of a chemical this container can hold. Hint: 1 m^3 = 1000 L.

   c) Describe any assumptions you have made in solving this problem.

B

4. A fuel company wants to make a cylindrical fuel tank of sheet metal.

   10 m^2 of material is available.

   a) Determine the dimensions of the fuel tank with maximum volume. Round the dimensions to the nearest tenth of a metre.

   b) Determine how many litres of a fuel this tank can hold.

   c) Describe any assumptions you have made in solving this problem.

5. A fertilizer company wants to make a cylindrical storage container out of metal to store fertilizer in. There are 30 m^2 of material available to make the container.

   a) Determine the dimensions of the storage container with maximum volume. Round the dimensions to the nearest tenth of a metre.

   b) Determine how many cubic metres of fertilizer this tank can hold.

6. Martin ships DVDs to his customers in cylindrical plastic containers. The DVDs are 12.2 cm in diameter and 2 mm thick. Martin wants the cylinder to hold as many DVDs as possible.

   a) What is the height of the optimal cylinder?

   b) How many DVDs will this cylinder hold?

   c) Describe any assumptions you have made.

7. A company is using plastic to create containers to store CDs in. They would like to use 1017 cm^2 of plastic to make each CD storage container.

   a) Determine the dimensions of the plastic storage container with maximum volume. Round the dimensions to the nearest hundredth of a centimetre.

   b) If CDs are each 2 mm in height, how many CDs will this container be able to hold?

C

8. You have a piece of sheet metal. Your task is to use this material to create a container with maximum volume to store water in.

   a) Which shape would have the greatest volume: a square-based prism or a cylinder?

   b) Justify your answer using a fixed surface area of 3500 cm^2.

9. An open-topped cylinder is to be made using 800 cm^2 of plastic.

   a) Describe how you would determine the dimensions of the cylinder of maximum volume.

   b) Determine the dimensions of the cylinder with the optimal volume. Round to the nearest tenth of a centimetre.

10. Suppose you have 3000 cm^2 of material to create a three-dimensional figure with the greatest volume. The material can be formed into a square-based prism, a cylinder, or a sphere.

   a) Predict which shape will produce the greatest volume.

   b) Determine the dimensions of each shape so that the volume is maximized. Round your answers to the nearest hundredth of a centimetre.

   c) Determine the volume of each shape. Round your answers to the nearest tenth of a cubic centimetre.

   d) Was your prediction correct? If not, which of the three shapes has the greatest volume for a given surface area? Will this always be true?

   e) Summarize your findings.

11. Use Technology You have a piece of sheet metal that measures 2 m by 3 m. Use a spreadsheet to investigate the dimensions of the cylinder with the greatest volume if

   a) the cylinder has a top and a bottom

   b) the cylinder has no top

   Round your answers to the nearest thousandth of a cubic metre.

9.6 Minimize the Surface Area of a Cylinder
Principles of Mathematics 9, pages 510–515

A

1. Determine the dimensions of the cylinder with minimum surface area for each volume. Round the dimensions, to the nearest tenth of a unit.

   a) 1400 cm^3

   b) 5 m^3

   c) 375 mm^3

   d) 10 cm^3

   e) 800 m^3

   f) 25 mm^3

2. Determine the surface area of each cylinder in question 1 to the nearest square unit.

3. A cylindrical container for potato chips is to have a volume 900 cm^3. What should its dimensions be to minimize the amount of material used to make it? Round the dimensions to the nearest tenth of a centimetre.

4. A cylindrical can of soup is to have a volume of 450 cm^3. What should its dimensions be to minimize the amount of material used to make it? Round the dimensions to the nearest tenth of a centimetre.

5. A cylindrical tank is designed to hold 6 L of a chemical.

   a) Determine the dimensions of the tank that requires the least material. Round the dimensions to the nearest tenth of a centimetre.
   Hint: $1 \text{ L} = 1000 \text{ cm}^3$

   b) Describe any assumptions you made in solving this problem.

B

6. A cylindrical can is designed to hold 355 mL of a soft drink.

   a) Determine the dimensions of the cylindrical soft drink can that requires the least material. Round the dimensions to the nearest tenth of a centimetre.
   Hint: $1 \text{ mL} = 1 \text{ cm}^3$

   b) Describe any assumptions you made in solving this problem.

7. A company is designing a cylindrical can to contain a fruit drink. The medium size can is designed to hold 500 mL of the fruit drink.

   a) Determine the dimensions of the medium size cylindrical fruit drink can that requires the least material. Round the dimensions to the nearest tenth of a centimetre.

   b) If aluminum costs $\$0.0015/\text{cm}^2$, find the cost of the aluminum to make 24 medium sized cans.

8. Refer to question 7. The company is also designing a large size cylindrical can which is designed to hold 700 mL of the fruit drink.

a) Determine the dimensions of the large size cylindrical fruit drink can that requires the least material. Round the dimensions to the nearest tenth of a centimetre.

b) If aluminum costs $0.0015/cm^2, find the cost of the aluminum to make 12 large sized cans.

9. Refer to question 7. The company is also designing a small size cylindrical can which is designed to hold 350 mL of the fruit drink.

a) Determine the dimensions of the small size cylindrical fruit drink can that requires the least material. Round the dimensions to the nearest tenth of a centimetre.

b) If aluminum costs $0.0015/cm^2, find the cost of the aluminum to make 36 small sized cans.

10. A recycling company is designing a cylindrical recycling bin with a lid. They are planning to create a container with a volume of 500 000 cm^3 that is as cost efficient as possible.

a) Determine the dimensions of the recycling bin that requires the least material. Round the dimensions to the nearest tenth of a centimetre.

b) If aluminum costs $0.001/cm^2, find the cost to make 10 recycling bins.

11. Gary is shipping computer cables to a customer. He needs a container with a volume of 300 cm^3 that is as cost efficient as possible. Should he use a square-based prism box or a cylinder for the cables? Justify your answer mathematically.

C

12. A movie theatre sells popcorn in an open cylindrical container. The medium size holds 1200 cm^3 of popcorn.

a) Determine the dimensions of the container that requires the least amount of cardboard, with or without technology. Round your answers to the nearest hundredth of a centimetre.

b) How much cardboard is required to make one container? Round your answer to the nearest square centimetre.

c) Describe any assumptions you have made in solving this problem.

13. a) For a given volume, predict which three-dimensional figure will have the minimum surface area: a cube, a cylinder with height equal to diameter, or a sphere.

b) Check your prediction using the formulas for volume and surface area and a fixed volume of 1300 cm^3. Round your answers to one decimal place.

Chapter 9 Review

Principles of Mathematics 9, pages 516–517

1. Glen is building a rectangular frame for a flower box with 30 m of lumber. Use toothpicks to investigate the greatest area that Glen can enclose.

   a) Let each toothpick represent 1 m of lumber. Construct different rectangles to represent the flower box's area. Record the dimension and the area in each case.

Rectangle	Width (units)	Length (units)	Perimeter (units)	Area (square units)
1			30	
2			30	

   b) How many different rectangles are possible?

   c) Which shape would you choose for the flower box? Give reasons for your choice.

2. A rectangular children's play area is to have an area of 36 m². The play area will be enclosed by edging bricks which will form the perimeter of the play area.

   a) On grid paper, sketch all the rectangles with whole-number dimensions and an area of 36 m².

   b) Record the dimensions and the perimeter in each case.

Rectangle	Width (units)	Length (units)	Perimeter (units)	Area (square units)
1				36
2				36

   c) Which shape would be the most economical for the garden? Why?

3. A mirror is to have an area of 4 m². What should the dimensions of the mirror be to minimize the amount of framing required to go around the outside?

4. What is the maximum area of a rectangular horse paddock that can be enclosed with 160 m of fencing in each case?

   a) The yard is enclosed on all four sides.

   b) The yard is enclosed on three sides.

5. A rectangular parking lot is to have an area of 800 m². The parking lot is surrounded by a chain-link fence.

   a) What are the dimensions of the parking lot that can be enclosed most economically? Round the dimensions to the nearest tenth of a metre.

   b) Give reasons why the parking lot might not be designed in the most economical shape that you determined in part a).

6. Cookies are to be packaged in a square-based prism box with a capacity of 950 cm³. Use a table like the one shown, or the spreadsheet you created in Section 9.3, to determine the dimensions of the box that requires the least amount of material. Round the dimensions to the nearest tenth of a metre.

Side Length of Square Base (cm)	Area of Square Base (cm²)	Height (cm)	Volume (cm³)	Surface Area (cm²)
6			950	
7			950	

7. Sea salt is packaged in a plastic-coated square-based prism box with a capacity of 802.125 mL.

    a) Determine the dimensions of the box that requires the minimum amount of material. Round the dimensions to the nearest tenth of a centimetre.

    b) Explain why these dimensions might not be the ones the manufacturer chooses.

8. A 2-L box of instant mashed potatoes is a square-based prism and is to be made from the minimum amount of cardboard. Determine the minimum amount of cardboard required, to the nearest square centimetre.

9. Use a table like the one shown, or the spreadsheet you created in Section 9.4, to investigate the dimensions of the square-based prism box with maximum volume that can be made from 3 m² of cardboard. Round the dimensions to the nearest hundredth of a metre.

Side Length of Base (m)	Area of Base (m²)	Surface Area (m²)	Height (m)	Volume (m³)
1		3		
2		3		

10. What are the dimensions of the square-based prism box with maximum volume that can be made from 3000 cm² of cardboard? Round the dimensions to the nearest tenth of a centimetre.

11. Suppose the cardboard in question 10 is a rectangular sheet that measures 30 cm by 100 cm. Explain why it may not be possible to make the shape you determined.

12. Use a table like the one shown, or the spreadsheet you created in Section 9.5 to investigate the dimensions of the cylinder with maximum volume that can be formed using 620 cm² of cardboard. Round your answer to the nearest hundredth.

Radius (cm)	Height (cm)	Volume (cm³)	Surface Area (cm²)
4			620
5			620

13. A manufacturer is trying to choose the best package for white rice. A square-based prism and a cylinder require the same amount of cardboard to make. Which shape should the manufacturer choose? Give reasons for your answer.

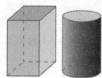

14. a) Use a table like the one shown, or the spreadsheet you created in Section 9.6, to determine the minimum amount of aluminum required to make a pop can with a capacity of 450 mL. Round your answers to the nearest hundredth.

Radius (cm)	Base Area (cm²)	Volume (cm³)	Height (cm)	Surface Area (cm²)
1				
2				

    b) What assumptions did you make in your solution?

1. **Perfect squares** If you take two of each of the numbers from 1 to 13, you now have 26 numbers. Write these numbers in pairs so that the sum of every pair of numbers is a perfect square.

2. **English** When you write the whole numbers in words, "one," "two," "three," and so on, what is the first word that has the letters in alphabetical order?

3. **River crossing** Two grade 6 students and two grade 9 students want to cross a river in a canoe. The canoe is big enough to hold the two grade 6 students or one grade 6 student and one grade 9 student. How many times must the canoe cross the river to get all the students to the other side?

4. **Measurement** The figure is made up of 11 identical squares. The area of the figure is 539 cm^2.

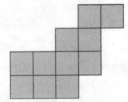

What is the perimeter of the figure?

5. **Whole numbers** Find 5 consecutive whole numbers whose sum is 405.

6. **Whole numbers** Jason chose a whole number less than 10. He multiplied the number by 6 and added 1. The result was a perfect square. What numbers could he have chosen?

7. **Asterisks** The rectangular shapes are made from asterisks.

Diagram 1   Diagram 2   Diagram 3

a) How many asterisks will there be in the 4th rectangle? the 5th rectangle?

b) How many asterisks will there be in the *n*th rectangle?

c) How many asterisks will there be in the 26th rectangle?

d) Which rectangle is made from 92 asterisks?

8. **Measurement** The squares are exactly the same size. The total area of the figure is 384 cm^2. What is the perimeter of the figure?

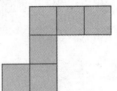

9. **Lifeguards** There are 12 h of lifeguard work available for the weekend. Three lifeguards have each agreed to work a whole number of hours. In how many different ways can the 12 h be divided so that each person works at least 2 h?

10. **Floor tiles** A rectangular floor is tiled with 36 square tiles. The tiles around the outside edge of the rectangle are red, and the tiles on the inside are white. How many red tiles are there? Is there more than one possible answer?

1. **Measurement** A square piece of paper is folded in half as shown. The perimeter of each new rectangle formed is 24 cm. What is the perimeter of the original square?

2. **Toothpicks** There are 20 toothpicks in a pile. In how many ways can they be organized into 3 groups, with an even number of toothpicks in each group?

3. **Triangle design** How many triangles are in the 1st row? The 2nd row? The 3rd row? The 4th row? If the pattern continues, how many triangles are in the 10th row? The 20th row? The 100th row? The *n*th row?

4. **Number pattern** Determine the pattern and write the next 3 rows.

   1 1 1
   1 2 3 2 1
   1 3 6 7 6 3 1
   1 4 10 16 19 16 10 4 1

5. **Picture border** A picture 20 cm by 20 cm is to be bordered by 1-cm squares. How many squares are needed for the border?

6. **Dividing grids** The diagram shows two ways to divide the grid into two congruent pieces using line segments that connect grid points.

   How many other ways are there, if rotations and reflections are not permitted?

7. **Geometry** This is a 4 by 4 square.

   One way to separate it into two congruent shapes, made up of smaller squares, is shown.

   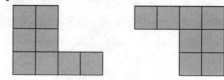

   Find at least five other ways.

8. **Latin Squares** The diagram shows a Latin Square. The numbers 1, 2, and 3 have been placed so that each number appears only once in each row and column.

1	2	3
2	3	1
3	1	2

   There are 11 other different Latin Squares that use the numbers 1, 2, and 3. Draw them.

1. **Measurement** This question was part of the Canada/U.S. qualifying test for the First World Puzzle Team Championship, held in 1992.

   How many triangles with side length 1 unit, with side length 2 units, with side length 3 units, with side length 4 units, and with side length 5 units are in this figure?

   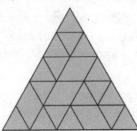

2. **Comparing models** The map shows the locations of 4 houses, the train station, and the airport.

   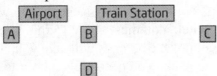

   Match each house with the correct number of the distance graph. Give reasons for your answer.

   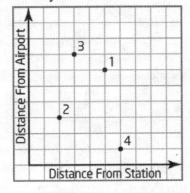

3. **Triangular numbers** the first 4 triangular numbers are shown.

   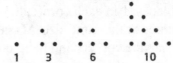

   What are the next 3 triangular numbers?

4. **Summer job** Jennifer works at a hardware store during her summer vacation. She earns $12.50/h for up to 40 h/week. She earns time-and-a-half for hours over 40 h/week. One week she worked 45 h. How much did she earn?

5. **Measurement** The perimeter of an isosceles triangle is 8 cm. The length of each side is a whole number. How long is the shortest side?

6. **Number puzzle** Place the digits 1, 2, 3, 4, 5, 6, and 7 in the circles so that the sum of each line of connected circles is the same.

7. **Grouping numbers** In how many different ways can you place the numbers 1, 2, 3, 4, 5, 6, 7, 8, and 9 into groups so that the sum of the numbers in each group is 15?

8. **TV watching** Sketch a graph to show the length of time you spend watching TV versus the day of the week.

1. **Bulletin board** To hang a picture on a bulletin board, Masao uses 4 thumbtacks, 1 in each corner. For two pictures of the same size, Masao can overlap the corners and hang both pictures with only 6 tacks.

   a) What is the minimum number of tacks Masao needs to hang 6 pictures of the same size in a row?

   b) Write an expression for finding the number of tacks needed to hang any number of pictures in a row.

2. **Driving distances** A delivery van and a bus left a highway garage at the same time and travelled in opposite directions. The van travelled at 80 km/h, and the bus travelled at 75 km/h. How far apart were the two vehicles after 3.5 h?

3. **Smallest sum** Use each of the digits 1, 3, 4, 6, 7, and 8 only once. Make the smallest possible sum by arranging the numbers as indicated in the diagram. What is the sum?

   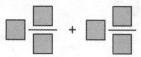

4. **Counterfeit coin** What is the minimum number of mass comparisons an inspector needs to make to find 1 counterfeit coin in a collection of 40 coins? Assume that the counterfeit coin is lighter than the others.

5. **Toothpicks** The trapezoids are made from toothpicks.

   a) How many toothpicks are in the fourth diagram? the fifth diagram?

   b) Describe the pattern in words.

   c) Write an expression that represents the number of toothpicks needed for the nth diagram in terms of n.

   d) Using the expression from part c) how many toothpicks are there in the 50th diagram? The 80th diagram?

6. **Leap year** If New Year's Day in a leap year is on a Tuesday, on what day of the week does July 1 fall?

7. **Cruise departure** The ship will leave the harbour at 08:30. You have to be on board 20 min before departure. It takes 25 min to drive to the ship from your hotel. You must allow 15 min to check out of the hotel. It will take you 20 min to pack. You need half an hour to eat breakfast and at least 45 min to shower and dress. For what time should you place your wake-up call?

8. **Coins** How many different combinations of coins have a value of $0.28? Copy and complete the table to find out.

Combinations	$0.25	$0.10	$0.05	$0.01
1	1	0	0	3
2	0	1	2	8
3				

9. **Estimating distances** About how many kilometres will you travel on school property this school year?

1. **Square design** The area of the large square is 64 cm^2.

   Each smaller square is formed by joining the midpoints of the sides of the next larger square. What is the area of the smallest square?

2. **Difference of squares** The whole number 5 can be written as the difference of the squares of two whole numbers.
   $$5 = 3^2 - 2^2$$
   What other whole numbers between 1 and 10 can be written as the difference of the squares of two whole numbers?

3. **Student council** In a student council election, there are 2 candidates for president: Ali and Beth. There are 3 candidates for vice-president: Connie, Devo, and Eleanor. There are 3 candidates for treasurer: Franco, Gino, and Helen. One possible set of winners is Beth, Dev, and Helen. How many others are there?

4. **Chores** Kim has two chores at home. Every 4 days, she must clean the gerbil cage. Every 6 days, she must clean the canary cage. Last Monday, she did both jobs. On what day of the week will she next do both jobs?

5. **Making change** List the different ways you can make change for a dollar using only quarters and nickels.

6. **Designs** The square has been divided into 8 triangles. One way to shade 4 of the 8 triangles is shown. How many other different ways to shade 4 triangles are there?

7. Copy the diagram. Fill in the boxes with the digits 2, 3, 4, and 5 to make the greatest possible sum.

8. **Shopping**. You spend $2.75 in a store and receive $7.25 change from $10.00. Notice that the arrangement of the digits in the amount you spent is a rearrangement of the digits in your change. Find 4 other pairs of amounts spent and change from $10.00 that share this property.

9. **Bus schedule** The Beach bus leaves every 20 min, and the Sand bus leaves every 45 min. If they leave together at noon, when is the next time that they will eave together?

10. **Guessing game** Is it possible to guess any number from 1 to 1024 in 10 guesses or fewer if you are told on each guess that it is correct, too large, or too small? Explain.

11. **Phone calls** About how many hours do all the high school students in Ontario spend on the telephone in a year?

1. **Order of operations** Use six 9s and the order of operations to write an expression that equals 100.

2. **Numbers** Find three consecutive whole numbers who sum is 144.

3. **Time** How many hours are in 1 000 000 s?

4. **Seating arrangements** Justine, Chris, and Meelang plan to travel together in a van. They will all sit in the front seat. In how many different arrangements can they sit in each of the following situations?
   a) all three can drive
   b) only Chris and Meelang can drive
   c) only Justine can drive

5. **Coin collection** In a collection of coins, the number of dimes and nickels add to 5. The numbers of dimes and quarters add to 7. The numbers of nickels and quarters add to 8. How many of each type of coin are there?

6. **Averages** The average of two numbers is 21. When a third number is included, the average of the three numbers is 23. What is the third number?

7. **Cutting cheese** A block of cheese, covered with wax, measures 12 cm by 12 cm by 10 cm. The block is cut into 2-cm cubes.
   a) How many cubes are there?
   b) How many cubes have wax on 3 faces?
   c) How many cubes have wax on 2 faces?
   d) How many cubes have no wax on them?

8. **Consecutive integers** Find 3 consecutive integers whose product is 1716.

9. **Squares** The numbers in the large squares are found by adding the numbers in the small squares. What are the numbers in the small squares?

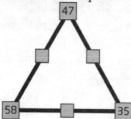

10. **Melting Ice** You fill a glass half full of water from the tap. Then, you add enough ice cubes to the water to fill the glass. Sketch a graph of temperature versus time from the moment you add the ice to the water until the moment when the ice has all melted.

11. **Train trip** Your train leaves at 08:15. The bus trip to the train station takes 25 min. The bus stop is a 5-min walk from your place. You should get to the train station to buy your ticket 15 min before the train leaves. It will take you 55 min to get dressed, eat breakfast, and pack. For what time should you set your alarm clock?

12. **Trees** Estimate the number of trees within a 2 km radius of your school.

13. **Making a cube** What is the edge length of a cube that can be made with 294 cm^2 of cardboard? What assumptions have you made?

14. **Islands** About how many islands are there in Ontario?

1. **Products** Determine the pattern and predict the next two lines.

   $101 \times 101 = \square$

   $202 \times 202 = \square$

   $303 \times 303 = \square$

2. **Team points** A team gets 2 points for a win, 1 point for a tie, and no points for a loss. The Bears have played 28 games. They have 27 points and 7 losses. How many wins do they have?

3. **Letters** Assume that the following pattern continues.

   A, BBB, CCCCC, DDDDDDD, …

   a) How many letter Ms will there be?

   b) How many letter Zs will there be?

4. **Buying chicken** Chicken pieces come in boxes of 6, 9, and 20. You can buy 21 pieces by buying two boxes of 6 pieces and one box of 9 pieces.

   $6 + 6 + 9 = 21$

   Can you buy

   a) 41 pieces?

   b) 42 pieces?

   c) 43 pieces?

   d) 44 pieces?

5. **Pattern** If the pattern continues, find the following product.

   $$\left(1 - \frac{1}{2}\right)\left(1 - \frac{1}{3}\right)\left(1 - \frac{1}{4}\right) \cdots \left(1 - \frac{1}{24}\right)$$

6. **Purchase price** The amount of a purchase is $12.43. How can the exact amount be paid without using a $10.00 bill, but using the smallest number of bills and coins?

7. **Pop machine** Students are allowed into the school at 08:00. Classes start at 09:00. There are 15-min breaks that begin at 10:30 and 14:30. Lunch is from 12:00 to 13:00. School is dismissed at 16:00. Students must leave the building by 17:00. Students are allowed to use the pop machine in the school cafeteria before and after school and during their breaks and lunch hour. The machine is filled twice a day, at 07:00 and 14:00. Sketch a graph of the number of cans in the machine versus time on a hot Monday in September.

8. **Measurement** The perimeter of the figure is 12 units.

   Sketch your answers to the following.

   a) Remove 1 square and keep the perimeter the same.

   b) Remove 2 squares and keep the perimeter the same.

   c) Remove 1 square and increase the perimeter by 2.

   d) Remove 2 squares and increase the perimeter by 2.

   e) Remove 2 squares and increase the perimeter by 4.

9. **Book pages** If you open a book and the product of the page numbers on the two facing pages is 45 156, what are the page numbers?

10. **GCF** The greatest common factor of two numbers, *m* and *n*, is 14.

    If $m = 2 \times 5 \times 7^2$, name three numbers that could be *n*.

1. **Consecutive numbers** The number 63 can be written as the sum of consecutive whole numbers as follows.

   $$63 = 20 + 21 + 22$$

   a) Find another way to write 63 as the sum of consecutive whole numbers.

   b) Find four consecutive whole numbers that add to 138.

2. **Number puzzle** Copy the diagram and fill in the squares with the numbers 1 to 8 so that consecutive numbers are not adjacent in any direction – horizontally, vertically, or diagonally.

3. **Calendar** In one year, December had exactly four Tuesdays and four Saturdays. On what day did December 1 fall that year?

4. **Railway crossing** A train travelling at 90 km/h passes a car sitting at a railway crossing. It took 45 s for the train to pass. How long was the train, in metres.

5. **Coffee shop** A coffee shop on the corner of a busy intersection is open 24 h a day. Sketch a graph of the number of customers in the shop versus the time of day.

6. **Line-up** You are standing in line at the cafeteria. You are the seventh from the front and eighth from the end. How many people are in the line?

7. **Perfect squares** The number 2601 is a 4-digit number that is a perfect square, because $51^2 = 2601$. What is the smallest 4-digit number that is a perfect square and that has all even digits?

8. **Library books** For all the books in your school library, estimate the total number of words.

9. **Car trip** The graph shows the speed of a car for 10 min. Write a story to explain the graph.

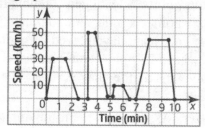

10. **Design** Each rectangular design is made with grey border squares and white interior squares. Each square has a side length of 1 unit.

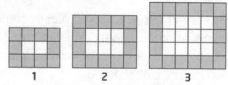

   a) How many grey squares are in the fourth diagram? the fifth diagram?

   b) Write an expression for the number of grey squares in terms of the length of the design, l.

   c) How many grey squares are there in the design with a length of 14? 40?

11. **Difference of squares** The number 16 can be written as the difference of two squares.

   $$16 = 25 - 9$$
   $$= 5^2 - 3^2$$

   What other whole numbers between 10 and 20 can be written as the difference of two squares?

1. **Birthday** Two days ago, Robert was 16 years old. Next year, Robert will be 19 years old. What is today's date and when in Robert's birthday?

2. **Animal speeds** This table shows the maximum speeds of some animals.

Animal	Maximum Speed (km/h)
Ostrich	80
Coyote	72
Elephant	40
Porcupine	18

   How many minutes less than a porcupine does a coyote take to run 1 km? What assumptions have you made?

3. **Apartments** An apartment building has six floors. The top floor has one apartment. Each of the other floors has twice the number of apartments as the floor above it. How many apartments are there?

4. **Walking** Sketch a graph that shows the distance you walk in a school day. Label the vertical axis "Distance Walked" and the horizontal axis "Time of Day." Represent a complete 24-h period, starting at midnight. Compare your graph with a classmate's and explain any differences.

5. **Calendar math** If two months in a row have a Friday the 13th, what months are they? Explain.

6. **Fence posts** Three sides of a triangular field are 40 m, 44 m, and 52 m. A fence is to be built around the field with a post in each corner and the posts 4 m apart. How many fence posts are needed?

7. **Piano tuners** About how many piano tuners are there in Canada?

8. **Compact discs** Tania has a collection of compact discs. When she puts them in piles of 2, she has 1 left over. She also has 1 left over when she puts them in piles of 3 and piles of 4. She has none left over when she puts them in piles of 7. What is the smallest number of compact discs she can have?

9. **Running** Lauryn and Yolanda had a 100-m race. Lauryn beat Yolanda by 10 m. For the second race, Yolanda suggested that Lauryn start 10 m behind the starting line. Yolanda thought this way of starting would give her a fair chance.
   a) Who won the race and by how much?
   b) What assumptions did you make?

10. **Bean toss** In a bean toss game, each person throws two bags.
    Scoring A and B gives 18 points.
    Scoring A and C gives 15 points.
    Scoring B and C gives 13 points.
    What will you score if you toss both bags in B?

11. **Sentence** Copy the sentence. Then, fill in the blank with a number, written in words, to make the sentence true.
    This sentence has _____ letters.

12. **Even numbers** Six consecutive even numbers are written on a piece of paper. If the sum of the first three numbers is 60, what is the sum of the last three?

13. **Books** How many books are in the library at your school?

1. **Perfect squares** When you add the digits of the number 45, you create a perfect square.
   $$4 + 5 = 9 \text{ or } 3^2$$
   How many other numbers between 1 and 100 have digits that add to give perfect squares?

2. **Measurement** Calculate the area of the figure, in square units, if each grid square represents 1 square unit.

   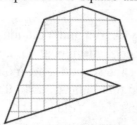

3. **Numbers** Use any of the arithmetic operations and brackets, if necessary, to combine each set of numbers so that they equal the number in brackets.
   a) 4, 5, 12   [8]
   b) 3, 7, 14   [10]
   c) 4, 6, 7, 8 [15]
   d) 3, 5, 6, 11 [19]

4. **Ages** The number 72 can be factored as follows.
   $$72 = 36 \times 2$$
   $$= 18 \times 2 \times 2$$
   $$= 9 \times 2 \times 2 \times 2$$
   $$= 3 \times 3 \times 2 \times 2 \times 2$$
   Use this technique to find the age of each person in a group of teenagers, if the product of their ages is 661 500.

5. **Squares** What is the total number of squares in this diagram?

6. **Perfect cubes** The number 8 is a perfect cube.
   $$2^3 = 2 \times 2 \times 2 = 8 \text{ or } 2^3 = 8$$
   The number 27 is also a perfect cube.
   $$3^3 = 3 \times 3 \times 3 = 27 \text{ or } 3^3 = 27$$
   You can write 8 as the sum of two consecutive odd numbers.
   $$3 + 5 = 8$$
   You can write 27 as the sum of three consecutive odd numbers.
   $$7 + 9 + 11 = 27$$
   a) The next perfect cube is 64 because $4^3 = 64$. Write 64 as the sum of 4 consecutive odd numbers.
   b) The next perfect cube is 125. Write 125 as the sum of five consecutive odd numbers.
   c) The next perfect cube is 216. Write 216 as the sum of six consecutive odd numbers.
   d) How does the square of the number that is cubed fit into the sum of the consecutive odd numbers?
   e) Use this pattern to write 7^3 as the sum of seven consecutive odd numbers.

7. **Placing counters** The diagram shows how 20 counters have been placed in 8 squares to that there are 6 counters in each row of 3 squares.

   Rearrange the counters so that there are 7 counters in each row of squares.

Answers
Principles of Mathematics 9 Exercise and Homework Book

Prerequisite Skills

Lowest Common Denominator, page 1

1. a) 12 **b)** 10 **c)** 72
2. a) 30 **b)** 56 **c)** 10
3. a) 15 **b)** 8 **c)** 24
4. a) 9 **b)** 60 **c)** 80
5. a) 6 **b)** 15
6. a) 18 **b)** 60
7. a) $\dfrac{9}{12}, \dfrac{10}{12}$ **b)** $\dfrac{25}{40}, \dfrac{16}{40}$
8. a) $\dfrac{8}{24}, \dfrac{18}{24}, \dfrac{15}{24}$ **b)** $\dfrac{12}{24}, \dfrac{16}{24}, \dfrac{9}{24}$

Add and Subtract Fractions, page 2

1. a) 1 **b)** $1\dfrac{1}{2}$ **c)** $\dfrac{3}{5}$ **d)** $\dfrac{1}{4}$
2. a) $\dfrac{7}{8}$ **b)** $1\dfrac{5}{12}$ **c)** $\dfrac{11}{14}$
3. a) $1\dfrac{7}{12}$ **b)** $1\dfrac{3}{20}$ **c)** $\dfrac{20}{21}$
4. a) $\dfrac{1}{6}$ **b)** $\dfrac{3}{14}$ **c)** $\dfrac{3}{10}$
5. a) $\dfrac{13}{30}$ **b)** $\dfrac{8}{21}$ **c)** $\dfrac{19}{36}$
6. a) $3\dfrac{14}{15}$ **b)** $2\dfrac{1}{12}$ **c)** $\dfrac{17}{35}$
7. a) $8\dfrac{7}{12}$ h **b)** $\dfrac{2}{3}$ h **c)** $\dfrac{7}{12}$ h

Multiply and Divide Fractions, page 3

1. a) $\dfrac{6}{35}$ **b)** $\dfrac{4}{9}$ **c)** $\dfrac{3}{10}$ **d)** $\dfrac{7}{15}$
2. a) $1\dfrac{1}{4}$ **b)** $\dfrac{13}{30}$ **c)** $11\dfrac{1}{7}$ **d)** $17\dfrac{1}{10}$
3. a) $\dfrac{3}{4}$ **b)** $1\dfrac{1}{14}$ **c)** $\dfrac{15}{49}$ **d)** $2\dfrac{7}{10}$
4. a) $2\dfrac{2}{9}$ **b)** $\dfrac{1}{4}$ **c)** $\dfrac{1}{3}$ **d)** $\dfrac{69}{91}$
5. $\dfrac{1}{2}$
6. 4

Add Integers, page 4

1. a)

$-3 + 5 = 2$

b)

$-4 + 2 = -2$

c)

$5 + (-4) = 1$

d)

$4 + (-6) = -2$

2. a)

$-1 + (-3) = -4$

b)

$-2 + 2 = 0$

c)

$3 + (-3) = 0$

d)

$0 + (-5) = -5$

3. a) -2 **b)** 3 **c)** -1 **d)** -7
4. a) 0 **b)** 0 **c)** -3 **d)** -8
5. a) -10 **b)** 2 **c)** -1 **d)** -2
6. a) -6 **b)** 6 **c)** -3 **d)** -4
7. a) 1 **b)** -12 **c)** 2 **d)** -5
8. a) -4 **b)** 2 **c)** -12 **d)** -8
9. a) 7 **b)** -6 **c)** -1 **d)** -2
10. 5°C
11. $39

Subtract Integers, page 5

1. a) 2 **b)** -2 **c)** 7 **d)** 7
2. a) 0 **b)** 0 **c)** -9 **d)** 6
3. a) -4 **b)** 8 **c)** -10 **d)** -8
4. a) 5 **b)** -2 **c)** 0 **d)** -7
5. a) 3 **b)** 9 **c)** 7
6. a) 2 **b)** -3 **c)** 8
7. a) -3 **b)** -6 **c)** -10 **d)** -3
8. a) -1 **b)** -3 **c)** -10 **d)** -2
9. a) and d) both equal 5; b) and e) both equal -3;
c) and f) both equal -5
10. -18°C
11. -7°C

Multiply and Divide Integers, page 6

1. a) 35 **b)** -12 **c)** -18 **d)** 16
2. a) 0 **b)** -28 **c)** -42 **d)** 48
3. a) 3 **b)** -4 **c)** -8 **d)** 3
4. a) 0 **b)** -5 **c)** -4 **d)** 7
5. a) -48 **b)** 0 **c)** 18
6. a) -60 **b)** 48 **c)** 24
7. a) $-1, 1, -2, 2, -3, 3, -6, 6, -9, 9, -18, 18$

b) –1, 1, –3, 3, –5, 5, –15, 15

8. a) –1, 1, –2, 2, –3, 3, –4, 4, –6, 6, –8, 8, –12, 12, –24, 24

b) –1, 1, –2, 2, –3, 3, –5, 5, –6, 6, –15, 15, –30, 30

9. Answers will vary. For example:

a) $(-4) \times 2$ and $(-16) \div 2$ **b)** $(-5) \times 3$ and $(-30) \div 2$

10. a) $\times 4$; 64, 256 **b)** $\div 2$; –50, –25

c) $\times (-5)$; –500, 2500

Distributive Property, page 7

1. a) 355 **b)** 177 **c)** 92 **d)** 156
2. a) 4.08 **b)** 2.88 **c)** 10.35 **d)** 5.82
3. a) 828 **b)** 645 **c)** 762 **d)** 834
4. a) 21.6 **b)** 6.86 **c)** 26.12 **d)** 39.76
5. a) 205 **b)** 291 **c)** 344 **d)** 774
6. a) 312 **b)** 1212 **c)** 2050 **d)** 3240
7. a) 1386 **b)** 908 **c)** 1542 **d)** 2397
8. a) 9.6 **b)** 39 **c)** 24.6
9. a) 56.63 **b)** 24.12 **c)** 72.32
10. a) 6.34 **b)** 20.96 **c)** 77.67
11. a) 630 **b)** 1160 **c)** 2350
12. a) 18 600 **b)** 21 000 **c)** 26 800

Order of Operations, page 8

1. a) 41 **b)** –4 **c)** 17 **d)** –5
2. a) 29 **b)** 33 **c)** 43 **d)** –12
3. a) 9 **b)** 77 **c)** 20 **d)** 6
4. a) –36 **b)** 2 **c)** 43 **d)** –8
5. a) 1 **b)** 1 **c)** –3 **d)** –36
6. a) 3 **b)** 9.9 **c)** 0.96 **d)** 6.22
7. a) 0.7 **b)** 5.9 **c)** 1.85 **d)** 26.2

8. a) $(16 \div 4 - 5) \times 2^2 = -4$

b) $(16 \div 4) - (5 \times 2^2) = -16$

c) $16 \div (4 - 5) \times 2^2 = -64$

9. a) $4 - 2 \times 3 = -2$ **b)** $20 \div (5 - 9) = -5$

c) $(10 - 3) \times (-2) = -14$

Bar Graphs, page 9

1. a) The graph shows that the shopping mall had the fewest number of visitors on Monday and the most visitors on Saturday.
b) The number of visitors increases from Monday to Saturday then drops on Sunday.
2. a) Graphs will vary.
b) Attendance is fairly constant from Monday through Friday, then increases over the weekend.
3. a) The graph shows that the museum had the fewest visitors in January and the most visitors in August.
b) The number of visitors increases from January to August then decreases through December.
4. a) Graphs will vary.
b) Answers will vary. For example: The taxes are lower in the Prairie Provinces.

Measures of Central Tendency, page 10

1. a) mean: 14.8; median: 15; mode: 15
b) mean: 31.6; median: 31; mode: 30
c) mean: 54.4; median: 55; mode: 55
d) mean: 42.8; median: 43; mode: 43
e) mean: 85.6; median: 85; mode: 88
f) mean: 23.4; median: 24; mode: 21
2. a) mean: 33.5; median: 33; mode: 32
b) mean: 54.5; median: 54.5; mode: 54
c) mean: 84; median: 84.5; mode: 85
d) mean: 65; median: 66; mode: 68
e) mean: 45; median: 45.5; mode: 47
f) mean: 93; median: 93.5; mode: 90
3. a) mean: 21.9; median: 23; mode: 23
b) mean: 36.6; median: 36; mode: 34
c) mean: 68.6; median: 66; mode: 64
d) mean: 48.6; median: 48; mode: 48
4. a) mean: 2.16; median: 2.1; mode: 1.9
b) mean: 4.06; median: 4.3; mode: 4.3
c) mean: 6.78; median: 6.45; mode: 6.4
d) mean: 8.77; median: 8.8; mode: 8.8
5. mean: 13.74; median: 13.75; mode: 12.7
6. The mean, since the numbers are centralized.
7. mean: 68.425; median: 68.9; mode: 69.4
8. The median, since there is an outlier.

Scatter Plots, page 11

1.– 4. Graphs will vary.

Linear Relationships, page 12

1. a)

Oranges (kg)	Cost ($)
1	0.75
2	1.50
3	2.25

b) (0, 0) This point shows the cost $0, for 0 kg of oranges.

2. a)

Time (h)	Cost ($)
1	1.50
2	3.00
3	4.50
4	6.00

b) (0,0) This point shows the cost $0, for 0 h of parking.
3. a) Graphs will vary. **b)** week 6
c) (0, 6) This point shows the height of the plant, 6 cm, at week 0.
4. a) Graphs will vary. **b)** 3.5 h **c)** 6 km
d) (0, 0) This point shows the distance, 0 km, for 0 h.

Rational Numbers, page 13

1. a) $\dfrac{3}{-5}$ **b)** $\dfrac{-5}{-8}$ **c)** $\dfrac{-1}{-4}$ **d)** $\dfrac{-12}{5}$
2. a) 0.8 **b)** –0.7 **c)** –0.375 **d)** 2.75

3. a) $\frac{7}{5}$ **b)** $\frac{9}{10}$ **c)** $-\frac{29}{9}$ **d)** $-\frac{43}{10}$

4. Answers will vary. For example:

a) $\frac{5}{-8}$, $-\frac{5}{8}$, -0.625 **b)** $\frac{4}{3}$, $1\frac{1}{3}$, $\frac{8}{6}$

c) $-\frac{3}{4}$, $\frac{-3}{4}$, $\frac{3}{-4}$

5. Answers will vary. For example:

a) $\frac{6}{-4}$, $-\frac{6}{4}$, $-\frac{3}{2}$ **b)** $\frac{4}{-12}$, $\frac{-4}{12}$, $-\frac{1}{3}$

c) $\frac{12}{10}$, 1.2, $\frac{6}{5}$

6. a)

b) -3.2, -3, $-\frac{2}{5}$, $1\frac{3}{10}$, 2.5, 4

7. a) $\frac{2}{-5} < \frac{-3}{8}$ **b)** $\frac{5}{-3} > \frac{-7}{2}$ **c)** $\frac{5}{-4} = \frac{-15}{12}$

Rates, page 14

1. a) 93.75 km/h **b)** 5 km/h **c)** 1.25 m/s
2. a) 2 km/h **b)** 90 km/h **c)** 95 km/h
3. a) \$0.26/lime **b)** \$35.00/pair of jeans
c) \$1.25/cornmeal muffin
4. a) \$1.20/bottle of water **b)** \$0.60/apple
c) \$4.50/mug
5. a) \$0.004/g **b)** \$0.003/g **c)** \$0.0045/g
6. a) 5 mL/cookie **b)** 200 pages/min
c) 30 rotations/min
7. Brand A
8. Brand B
9. Brand A
10. Brand B
11. a) Terri **b)** \$0.50/hour
12. a) Colette **b)** \$0.25/hour

Ratio and Proportion, page 15

1. a) 2:7 **b)** 1:3 **c)** 5:8 **d)** 5:2
2. a) 2:3 **b)** 20:7 **c)** 4:11 **d)** 10:9
3. a) 7:20 **b)** 13:20 **c)** 7:13
4. 525 mL frozen concentrate, 975 mL water
5. a) 3:10 **b)** 9:5 **c)** 6:1
6. a) 9:44 **b)** 15:22 **c)** 5:44
7. a) 300 mL **b)** 1200 mL
8. 120 people
9. 250 people
10. 140 dogs

Percents, page 16

1. a) 5% **b)** 12.5% **c)** 60% **d)** 35% **e)** 124%
2. a) 75% **b)** 62.5% **c)** 60% **d)** 160%
3. a) 45.5% **b)** 33.3% **c)** 44.4% **d)** 28.6%
e) 166.7%
4. a) 0.29 **b)** 0.385 **c)** 0.08 **d)** 1.15
5. a) 5.7% **b)** 146 cm

6. a) 30% **b)** \$112.49
7. a) oxygen 6 kg, carbon 1.2 kg, hydrogen 0.64 kg, nitrogen 0.16 kg
b) oxygen 15 kg, carbon 3 kg, hydrogen 1.6 kg, nitrogen 0.4 kg
8. a) 140% **b)** \$44.00

Powers, page 17

1. a) 4^6 **b)** 7^8 **c)** 3^4 **d)** 11^3
2. a) 2.8^5 **b)** 6.1^3 **c)** 3.4^5 **d)** 1.7^6
3. a) $(-1)^3$ **b)** $(-6)^5$ **c)** $(-3)^4$ **d)** $(-7)^6$
4. a) x^4 **b)** y^2 **c)** m^3 **d)** d^5
5. a) 49 **b)** 1024 **c)** 10 000 **d)** 1 **e)** 125 **f)** 256
6. a) 27.9841 **b)** 5.37824 **c)** 0.027 **d)** 0.0625
7. a) 146.41 **b)** 1157.625 **c)** 3652.264 **d)** 428.49
8. a) 4^2 **b)** 2^4
9. a) 27^2 **b)** 9^3 **c)** 3^6
10. a) 8^3 **b)** 7^4 **c)** 10^9
11. a) 243 **b)** 8 **c)** 9

Classify Triangles, page 18

1. a) equilateral **b)** scalene **c)** isosceles
2. a) obtuse **b)** right **c)** acute
3. a) right, isosceles **b)** scalene, acute
c) scalene, obtuse **d)** equilateral, acute
4. a) $\triangle ABC$, $\triangle ACD$, $\triangle BCD$
b) $\triangle ABC$ is obtuse, $\triangle ACD$ is obtuse, $\triangle BCD$ is obtuse
5. a) $\triangle MNO$, $\triangle MNP$, $\triangle NOP$
b) $\triangle MNO$ is right and isosceles, $\triangle MNP$ is obtuse and scalene, $\triangle NOP$ is acute and scalene

Classify Polygons, page 19

1. a) pentagon, irregular **b)** pentagon, regular
c) triangle, irregular **d)** octagon, regular
e) quadrilateral, irregular **f)** triangle, irregular
g) pentagon, irregular
2. a) rectangle; Two pairs of opposite sides have equal lengths, and all four angles are 90°.
b) square; It has four equal sides and all four angles are 90°.
c) parallelogram; Two pairs of opposite sides have equal lengths and are parallel. The quadrilateral contains no right angles.
d) rhombus; All sides are marked as equal. The quadrilateral has no right angles.
e) trapezoid; No sides are marked as equal. One pair of opposite sides is parallel.
3. a) ABCF is a rectangle. CDEF is a trapezoid.
b) MNOR is a square. OPQR is a parallelogram.

Angle Properties, page 20

1. 78°
2. 39°
3. 58°
4. a) $x = 110°$, $y = 70°$ **b)** $d = 25°$ **c)** $m = 32°$

5. a) $a = 97°$, $b = 83°$, $c = 97°$
b) $x = 48°$, $y = 132°$, $z = 48°$
6. a) $x = 62°$ **b)** $y = 78°$ **c)** $z = 78°$
7. a) $x = 82°$, opposite angles; $y = 98°$, co-interior angles; $z = 98°$, opposite angles
b) $x = 117°$, supplementary angles; $y = 63°$, opposite angles; $z = 63°$, corresponding angles

Calculate Perimeter and Circumference, page 21
1. a) 18.8 cm **b)** 19.4 cm **c)** 20 m **d)** 88 mm
e) 21 m **f)** 16 cm
2. a) 15.1 m **b)** 57.2 mm **c)** 21.4 cm **d)** 38.6 m
3. 13.2 m
4. 14.4 m

Apply Area Formulas, page 22
1. a) 53.29 cm^2 **b)** 26.52 m^2 **c)** 11 m^2 **d)** 56.8 cm^2
e) 9.2 m^2
2. a) 15.1 cm^2 **b)** 24.6 m^2
3. a) 58.1 cm^2 **b)** 9.8 cm^2
4. a) 13.6 m^2 **b)** 86 m^2 **c)** 5529 mm^2 **d)** 92 cm^2

Calculate Surface Area and Volume, page 23
1. a) 150 cm^2 **b)** 122 m^2 **c)** 478 cm^2 **d)** 283 m^2
2. a) 125 cm^3 **b)** 84 m^3 **c)** 754 cm^3 **d)** 1257 m^3
3. a) surface area: 294 m^2; volume: 343 m^3
b) surface area: 215.9 m^2; volume: 207.2 m^3
c) surface area: 837.5 cm^2; volume: 1847.7 cm^3
d) surface area: 1759.3 m^2; volume: 3694.5 m^3
4. surface area: 368.9 m^2; volume 374.4 m^3

Use *The Geometer's Sketchpad®*, page 24
1.–5. Answers will vary.

Compare Figures, page 25
1. a) Container A: surface area 1020 cm^2, volume 2700 cm^3; Container B: surface area 2100 cm^2; volume 5000 cm^3
b) Container B **c)** Container B
2. a) Container A: surface area 228 cm^2, volume 288 cm^3; Container B: surface area 264 cm^2; volume 216 cm^3
b) Container B **c)** Container A
3. a) Container A: surface area 1825 cm^2, volume 5850 cm^3; Container B: surface area 2513 cm^2; volume 12 566 cm^3
b) Container B had the greater surface area and volume.
4. a) Container A: surface area 224.7 cm^2, volume 243 cm^3; Container B: surface area 157.5 cm^2; volume 67.5 cm^3
b) Container A **c)** Container A

5. a) Container A: surface area 84 cm^2, volume 24 cm^3; Container B: surface area 217 cm^2; volume 283 cm^3
b) Container B **c)** Container B
6. a) Container A: volume 339 cm^3; Container B: volume 240 cm^3; Container A has the largest capacity.
b) Container A: surface area 254 ^{2}; Container B: surface area 256 cm^2; Container A requires the least amount of material to construct it.

Chapter 1
1.1 Focus on Problem Solving, page 27
1. a) 18, 23, 28; add 5 to the previous term
b) 54, 162, 486; multiply the previous term by 3
c) 32, 256, 8192; multiply the two previous terms
d) 13, 17, 19; the terms are the prime numbers in order
2. 15
3. a) $0.\overline{027}$, $0.\overline{054}$, $0.\overline{081}$, ...
b) If the numerator is less than 37, then a group of three digits repeats that is the product of the numerator and 27.
c) $0.\overline{675}$ $(675 = 25 \times 27)$
4. a) $0.\overline{09}$, $0.\overline{18}$, $0.\overline{27}$, ...; If the numerator is less than 11, then a group of two digits repeats that is the product of the numerator and 9.
b) If the number is less than 111, then a group of three digits repeats that is the product of the numerator and 9.
c) If the number is less than 11 111, then a group of five digits repeats that is the product of the numerator and 9.
5. 7

6. a) 2 **b)** 5 **c)** 9 **d)** 54 **e)** $\dfrac{n^2 - 3n}{2}$

7. a) Answers will vary.
b) Answers will vary. For example, ask my parents, use the Internet to find perpetual calendars, count back.
8. 300
9. T = 6, H = 9, A = 2, W = 3, S = 5, E = 7, Y = 1
10.

5	3	2	1	6	8	4	7	9
7	1	8	4	5	9	3	6	2
6	4	9	3	7	2	1	5	8
9	5	4	7	8	3	2	1	6
2	7	3	5	1	6	8	9	4
8	6	1	2	9	4	5	3	7
3	9	6	8	4	5	7	2	1
4	2	7	6	3	1	9	8	5
1	8	5	9	2	7	6	4	3

1.2 Focus on Communicating, page 28

1. a) Subtract 3 from the previous term; 9, 6.

b) Subtract 2 from the previous term; −14, −16.

c) Add $\dfrac{1}{6}$ to the previous term; $\dfrac{2}{3}$, $\dfrac{5}{6}$.

d) Multiply the previous term by −3; 324, −972.

e) Add the two previous terms; 32, 52.

f) ⌣⌣ ⌣⌣ ∿∿∿∿∿∿∿ ∿∿∿∿∿∿∿∿∿∿∿∿∿

2. Yes; the area of the triangle on the hypotenuse equals the sum of the areas of the triangles on the other two sides.

3. a) The rectangle is divided into thirds horizontally and three of these rows are shaded to show $\dfrac{2}{3}$. Then, the rectangle is divided into fifths vertically and three of these columns are shaded to show $\dfrac{3}{5}$. The overlap of the shading shows the product. Since six parts are double shaded, $\dfrac{2}{3} \times \dfrac{3}{5} = \dfrac{6}{15}$, or $\dfrac{2}{5}$.

b) $5 \times \dfrac{1}{2} = 2\dfrac{1}{2}$

4. Anna: tennis; Bryce: baseball; Coral: hockey; Deepak: swimming

5. The best location would be 3.5 m from the end of the recycling line and a perpendicular distance of 4 m from the line.

1.3 Focus on Connecting, page 29

1.

50¢	2¢	1¢	Values ($)
5	0	0	2.50
4	1	0	2.02
4	0	1	2.01
3	2	0	1.54
3	1	1	1.53
3	0	2	1.52
2	3	0	1.06
2	2	1	1.05
2	1	2	1.04
2	0	3	1.03
1	4	0	0.58
1	3	1	0.57
1	2	2	0.56
1	1	3	0.55
1	0	4	0.54
0	5	0	0.10
0	4	1	0.09
0	3	2	0.08
0	2	3	0.07
0	1	4	0.06
0	0	5	0.05

2. Answers will vary depending on the dimensions of the classroom. A possible estimate can be made using the formula Number of CD players = Volume of classroom ÷ Volume of one CD player (332 cm^3).

3. Add the number of parallelograms with different numbers of triangles: 166.

4. Guess and Test. Start by guessing that Rae ate one piece, then Kees ate four pieces and Jason ate three pieces, then Ming ate three pieces, then Anil ate two pieces and Edgar ate two pieces. This works since $1 + 4 + 3 + 3 + 3 + 2 + 2 = 15$. Then, rewrite each person's share as a fraction of the birthday cake.

Rae = $\dfrac{1}{15}$, Kees = $\dfrac{4}{15}$, Jason = $\dfrac{3}{15}$ or $\dfrac{1}{5}$,

Ming = $\dfrac{3}{15}$ or $\dfrac{1}{5}$, Anil = $\dfrac{2}{15}$, Edgar = $\dfrac{2}{15}$. This can also be solved algebraically by expressing all amounts in terms of Jason, summing to 15, and solving the resulting equation.

5. Answers will vary.

6. 14

7. Answers will vary.

8.

7	9	3	6	8	5	2	1	4
1	2	5	3	7	4	6	8	9
6	4	8	1	2	9	5	7	3
9	7	4	2	6	1	3	5	8
8	5	1	7	9	3	4	6	2
3	6	2	5	4	8	7	9	1
4	1	7	8	5	2	9	3	6
5	8	9	4	3	6	1	2	7
2	3	6	9	1	7	8	4	5

1.4 Focus on Representing, page 30

1. 2 km west of the starting point

2. Three floors with 12, 6, and 3 offices on the floors. The minimum is three offices because the next highest floor would have 1.5 offices, which is not possible.

3. 435

4. a) 5 **b)** $2\dfrac{2}{5}$

5. a) Add 2 to the x-coordinate and subtract 1 from the y-coordinate. D(6, −3), E(8, −4), F(10, −6)

b) Multiply the coordinates by −1. S(−1, −2), T(1, 2), U(−1, −2)

c) Add 1 to the x-coordinate and 2 to the y-coordinate. G(4, 8), H(5, 10), I(6, 12)

6. (−1, 7), (−1, −3)

7. If AB is not one of the equal sides, then vertex C can lie anywhere on the perpendicular bisector of AB except the point on AB. If AB is one of the equal sides, then the only possibilities for C are (5, −2), (−3, 6), (−7, 2), and (1, −6).

1.5 Focus on Selecting Tools and Computational Strategies, page 31

1. a) 8 squares divided into 2 columns gives 4 squares in each column.

b) 15 squares divided into 5 columns gives 3 squares in each column.
2. a) 35, 38 **b)** 3072, 12 288
c) −8, −10 **d)** 324, −2916

3. a) $-\dfrac{4}{5}$ **b)** $\dfrac{7}{20}$ **c)** $-\dfrac{4}{9}$ **d)** $\dfrac{5}{21}$

4. a) $\dfrac{1}{2}$ **b)** $-\dfrac{3}{20}$ **c)** $\dfrac{3}{16}$ **d)** $\dfrac{1}{10}$

5. a) $-\dfrac{3}{20}$ **b)** $-\dfrac{9}{10}$ **c)** $-\dfrac{1}{20}$ **d)** −2

6. 3971
7. about 111.6 cm
8. $2^{n-1} + 1$

1.6 Focus on Reasoning and Proving, page 32
1. Let the consecutive numbers be $n-2$, $n-1$, n, $n+1$, $n+2$. Then, the sum is $n-2+n-1+n+n+1+n+2 = 5n$, which is divisible by 5.
2. Answers may vary. Since a textbook is made by folding sheets of paper in half, there will always be an even number of pages because the number of pages equals two times the number of sheets.

3. a) 6 is an even number not divisible by 4. $\dfrac{6}{4} = 1.5$

b) 3 and 5 are odd numbers. $3 + 5 = 8$, which is an even number.

c) $\dfrac{1}{2} \times \left(-\dfrac{3}{4}\right) = -\dfrac{3}{8}$ is a negative product, not positive.

4. 9 (7, 19, 26, 37, 56, 61, 63, 91, 98)
5. a) 1, 4, 9, 16
b) The sums are consecutive perfect squares.
c) n^2
6. Answers will vary.
7. a) 2 **b)** 2 **c)** 6 **d)** 6 **e)** 14 **f)** 14
g) The sum of consecutive powers of two is two less than the next power of two.
h) $2^1 + 2^2 + 2^3 + 2^4 = 30$; $2^5 - 2 = 30$
$2^1 + 2^2 + 2^3 + 2^4 + 2^5 = 62$; $2^6 - 2 = 62$
i) Answers may vary.
8. a) 9 **b)** 14 **c)** 13 **d)** 46

1.7 Focus on Reflecting, page 33
1. 4

2. $3\dfrac{1}{4}$

3. a) 33 **b)** 25 **c)** 8 **d)** 50
e) 33 numbers are divisible by 3, and 25 numbers are divisible by 4. However, 8 of these numbers are divisible by both 3 and 4. Subtract 8 from 33 + 25 to get 50. You could check by using a hundred chart and circling numbers that are divisible by 3 or 4.
4. a) 271 **b)** 181 **c)** 35 **d)** 417

e) 271 numbers contain the digit 5, and 181 numbers contain the digit 0. But 35 numbers contain both 5 and 0, so subtract 35 from 271 + 181 to get 417.
5. a) 5 moves
b) $-40 + 70 = 30$; $30 + (-55) = -25$; $-25 + 40 = 15$; $15 + (-25) = -10$; $-10 + 10 = 0$. Also, you could use a number line.
6. 6
7. Answers will very. Consider how many people are in Ontario and how many people drink bottled water.
8.

2	3	1	8	7	6	4	9	5
8	7	9	4	2	5	1	6	3
5	6	4	1	3	9	2	7	8
4	9	2	6	5	8	3	1	7
7	1	5	3	4	2	9	8	6
6	8	3	9	1	7	5	2	4
9	2	6	5	8	3	7	4	1
1	5	7	2	6	4	8	3	9
3	4	8	7	9	1	6	5	2

Chapter 1 Review, page 34
1. a) 15, 18, 21; add 3 to the previous term
b) 64, 128, 256; multiply the previous term by 2
c) 25, 34, 45; add consecutive odd integers to the previous term
d) −7, −17, −29; subtract consecutive even integers from the previous term
2. a) The x-coordinate increases by 3 and the y-coordinate increases by 2. D(10, 8), E(13, 10), F(16, 12)
b) The x-coordinate decreases by 4 and the y-coordinate decreases by 2. J(−8, −1), K(−12, −3), L(−16, −5)
c) The x-coordinate decreases by 3 and the y-coordinate decreases by 2. S(−15, −7), T(−18, −9), U(−21, −11)

3. a) $\dfrac{3}{4}$, $\dfrac{7}{8}$, 1 **b)** $-\dfrac{3}{4}$, −1, $-1\dfrac{1}{4}$

4. Answers will vary. Consider the dimensions of the milk jug to find the volume. Then, consider the dimensions of and volume of a quarter. The number of quarters will be the quotient of the two volumes.
5. 204; solve a simpler problem, make a diagram
6. a) The new volume is eight times the old volume.
b) The same is true for any cube.
7. a) $(12 + 3) \div 5 - 2 = 1$

b) $\left(\dfrac{1}{3} - \dfrac{1}{4}\right) + \dfrac{5}{6} \times \dfrac{1}{2} - \dfrac{5}{12} = \dfrac{1}{12}$

8. a) $\dfrac{7}{20}$ **b)** $1\dfrac{4}{15}$ **c)** $\dfrac{8}{21}$ **d)** $\dfrac{22}{35}$

9. a) 302 **b)** 113th term
10. 28; Answers will vary. Use a calculator.

Chapter 2

2.1 Hypotheses and Sources of Data, pages 35–36

1. a) Most people's favourite colour is not blue.
b) Teenagers do not spend more time listening to rock music than to classical music.
c) Bob's favourite type of ice cream is not chocolate.
d) Most students do not study mathematics.
2. Answers will vary. Examples:
a) Hypothesis: Children tend to grow to have the same shoe size as their fathers. Opposite: Children do not tend to grow to have the same shoe size as their fathers.
b) Hypothesis: As the cost of a movie ticket increases, the number of people renting DVDs increases. Opposite: As the cost of a movie ticket increases, the number of people renting DVDs does not increase.
c) Hypothesis: As the altitude of a city increases, the length of time to boil water increases. Opposite: As the altitude of a city increases, the length of time to boil water does not increase.
d) Hypothesis: As the age of a university student increases, the average of the student's marks increases. Opposite: As the age of a university student increases, the average of the student's marks does not increase.
3. a) Primary: The Student Council president gathers the data.
b) Secondary: The student uses data from the Internet.
c) Primary: The researcher gathers the data.
d) Secondary: the teacher uses data gathered by Statistics Canada.
4. Answers about advantages will vary.
a) primary; data are up-to-date
b) secondary; Internet search is fast and easy
c) primary; opinions of customers are found
d) secondary; data are accessible
5. Answers will vary. Examples:
a) Most students in the school prefer to spend time rollerblading rather than ice skating in their leisure time.
b) Survey the school. Primary data are best since the population is small and secondary data may not be available.
6. a) Primary: Anoja gathered the data herself.
b) Answers will vary. Examples: Brown-eyed students' favourite subject is History. Most students have blue eyes.
c) Survey a larger sample.
7. a) Secondary: Elliot did not gather the data himself.
b) Answers will vary. Examples:
Most employees who state that their favourite colour is green also state that their favourite animal is a cat. Most employees' favourite animal is a dog.

c) Survey a larger sample.
8. Answers will vary. Examples:
a) The higher the resolution of the camera, the more it will cost.
c) primary if you collect prices from Web sites for individual suppliers; secondary if you find price surveys with data gathered by someone else
d) Visit a camera store to research resolutions and prices.
9. Answers will vary. Example:
a) The higher the altitude of a mountain, the lower the temperature.
10. Answers will vary. Example:
a) The difference between the Olympic records for men and women in the 100-m freestyle swimming race has decreased over the years.

2.2 Sampling Principles, pages 37–38

1. a) all children **b)** all cars
c) all sporting goods stores **d)** all teenagers
2. a) people's heights and weights, sample
b) colours of cars in car dealership, census
c) sizes of painting in Art Gallery, census
d) marks on exam, census
3. Answers will vary. Examples:
a) Survey every fifth student at the school.
b) Randomly select 2% of the teenagers in every high school across Ontario.
c) Select households to survey by any random method, and then ask the people surveyed where they were born.
d) Use a random number generator to select telephone numbers within Ontario and then ask the people in those homes what their favourite TV program is.
4. a) non-random sample; could be biased since Chartered Accountants at this one company may not be representative of all newly qualified Chartered Accountants
b) simple random sample; could be biased since the sample excludes anyone who does not have a telephone listing
c) systemic random sampling
d) non-random sample; biased because it includes only people who have chosen to spend some of their free time going to a museum
5. Answers may vary. Example: by gender, by age, by number of years worked
6. a) all Canadian musicians
b) Answers will vary. Example: Randomly select 15% of the musicians in each province and territory.
7. a) all health club members
b) Answers will vary. Example: Randomly select a starting point on the list of members, and then select every 5th person until you have a total of 100.

8. a) members of the school clubs

b) Answers will vary. Example: Write each club member's name on a slip of paper, put the slips in a box, and then randomly draw 20% of the slips out of the box.

9. Year 1, 149; Year 2, 133; Year 3, 115; Year 4, 103

10. Sampling techniques will vary. Examples:

a) all students in the school

b) all people in the community

c) all drivers in Canada

d) all teenagers in Ontario

e) all digital imaging companies in Canada

f) propane prices at all vendors in the community

11. Answers will vary.

12. Answers will vary.

13. The sample is representative only of people who are willing to respond to the questions being asked in the survey and then mail back the survey. The sample excludes anyone who does not have the time or does not want to complete the survey.

14. a) Employees at small companies have a greater chance of being selected than employees at large companies.

b) The sample is likely to have a greater proportion of employees from small companies than the population does.

2.3 Use Scatter Plots to Analyse Data, pages 39–40

1. a) independent: physical activity; dependent: heart rate

b) independent: mass of a letter; dependent: cost of postage

c) independent: age of the tree; dependent: height of the tree

d) independent: age of a car; dependent: value of a car

2. a)

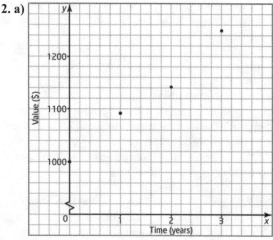

b) As the time increases, so does the value of the mutual fund investment.

3. a) independent: Instructional Hours; dependent: Student's Score

b)

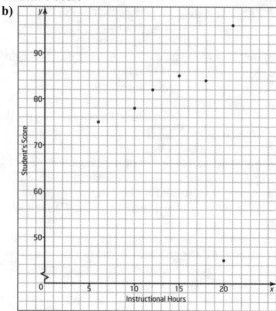

c) As the number of instructional hours increases, so does the student's score.

d) The outlier is (20, 45). The scatter plot indicates a linear correlation, except for this point.

4. a) independent: Price of T-shirt; dependent: Monthly Sales

b)

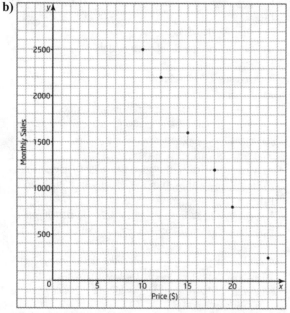

c) As the price of a T-shirt increases, the monthly sales of T-shirts decrease.

5. a) independent: Speed; dependent: Stopping Distance

b)

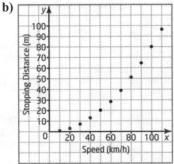

c) As the speed increases, so does the stopping distance.

6. a) independent: Speed; dependent: Fuel Economy

b)

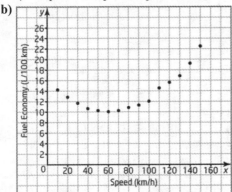

c) 60 km/h

7. a)

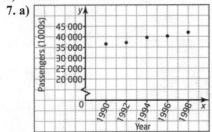

b) The number of passengers of Canadian air-carriers is increasing.

8. Answers will vary. Examples:

a) As a person's arm length increases, so does the leg length.

b) Answers will vary. **c)** Answers will vary.

d) Improve accuracy of measurements; use a larger sample.

9. a)

Item	Fat (mg/g)	Energy (kJ/g)
Chocolate Chunk Cookies	265	21.6
Butterfly Wing Cookies	289	22.1
Digestive Biscuits	213	20.8
Pure Butter Shortbreads	303	22.7
Vanilla Wafers	233	19.1

b)

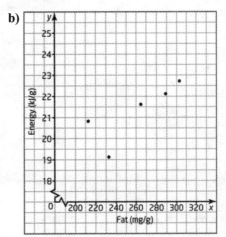

c) The point for Digestive Biscuits is an outlier due to the low fat content. However, this point represents valid data that should not be discarded.

d) Answers will vary. Example: Cookies can have a high energy content without a high fat content.

2.4 Trends, Interpolation, and Extrapolation, pages 41–43

1. a)

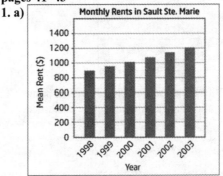

b) Rents increased every year. **c)** about $1500

2. a)

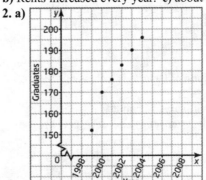

b) The number of graduates increased every year.

c) about 223

3. a)

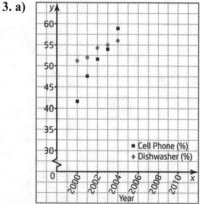

b) about 83%; about 64%

4. a) independent: Year; dependent: Taxes

b)

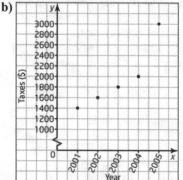

c) Taxes increased every year.

d) (2005, 3000) is an outlier. However, this point represents valid data that should not be discarded.

5. a)

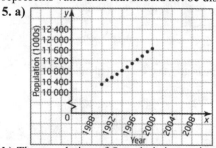

b) The population of Ontario is increasing.

c) 13 000 000

6. a) Graphs will vary. **b)** about 8.1

7. a) independent: income; dependent: pet expenses

b)

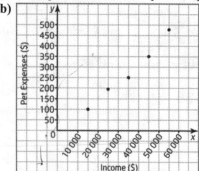

c) As income increases, pet expenses also increase. Reasons for trend may vary. For example, as people earn more, they might buy more expensive pet food or spend more on toys and grooming.

d) $300 **e)** $500 **f)** $50 000

8. a)

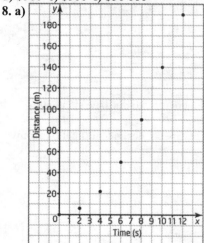

b) about 110 m

9. a) **b)** about 2 s

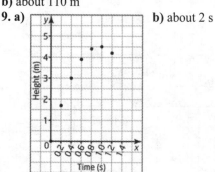

10. a)

Summaries may vary. For example, the average weekly earnings are increasing yearly. The average weekly earnings in Ontario and Alberta are greater than in Canada as a whole. Alberta's weekly earnings are increasing faster than in Ontario and all of Canada.

b) Canada, $750; Ontario, $800; Alberta, $800

2.5 Linear and Non-Linear Relations, pages 44–46

1. a) Yes; the points lie close to a straight line.

b) No; the points lie close to a curve.

2. a) Linear; the points lie along a straight line.
b) Non-linear; the points lie along a curve.
3. a) No; the points follow a curve.
b) Yes; the points lie close to a straight line.
4. a) No; there is no apparent pattern.
b) No; there are not enough points to find a good line of best fit.
5. a)

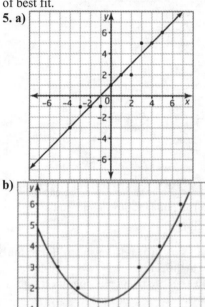

b)

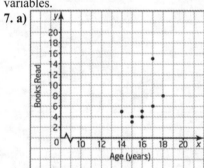

6. a), b) Graphs will vary.
c) A non-linear relationship exists between the variables.
7. a)

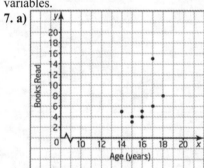

b) A linear relationship exists between the variables if the outlier is ignored.
c) The outlier is the point (17, 15). The scatter plot indicates a linear correlation, except for this point.

8. a), b)

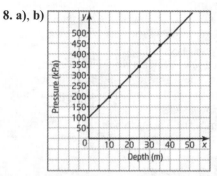

c) As the depth increases, the water pressure increases.
d) 474 kPa **e)** 690 kPa
9. Answers will vary.
10. a) Linear; each time x increases by 1, y increases by 2.
b) Non-linear; h does not change by a constant amount each time t increases by 1.
c) Non-linear; d does not change by a constant amount each time t increases by 1.

2.6 Distance-Time Graphs, pages 47–48
1. a) moving away at a constant speed
b) no movement
c) moving closer at decreasing speed, then slowing down and stopping
d) moving away at decreasing speed, then slowing down and stopping
2. Answers will vary. Examples:
a) Vaughn walks from school to the library, picks up a library book, and then walks back toward school but stops at a friend's house.
b) Brandon leaves home and runs at a constant speed for 2 min, stops for 1 min, and then walks in the same direction at a constant speed for 5 min.
3. a)   **b)**

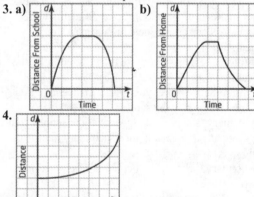

4.

5. a) 2 h **b)** 1 km
c) stopping at the dock directly across the lake
d) on the way to the dock

6. a) Move away from the wall at a constant speed for 2 s, stop for 3 s, and then walk back toward the wall at the same speed for 2 s.
b) The sloped line segments would be steeper.
c) The sloped line segments would be less steep.
7. After starting out, the car increases in speed, and then slows down and stops.
8. a) 1.25 km/h, 0 km/h, 1 km/h
b)

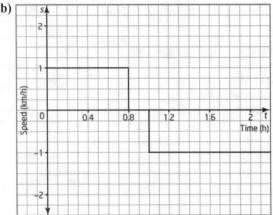

c) The steeper the slope of the distance-time graph, the faster is the speed of the swimmer.
d) the rate at which the swimmer swims back toward the starting dock
9. Answers will vary.

Chapter 2 Review, pages 49–50
1. Answers will vary. Examples:
a) Hypothesis: As the temperature in a city during the winter decreases, the amount of electricity used by the residents increases. Opposite: As the temperature in a city during the winter decreases, the amount of electricity used by the residents does not increase.
b) Hypothesis: Students with larger shoe sizes have higher marks in English. Opposite: Students with larger shoe sizes do not have higher marks in English.
2. a) Internet use has not more than tripled in the last 20 years.
b) If you practise more, your performance in a game will improve or stay the same.
3. a) Primary; a survey of students at the school could give more accurate results than secondary data would.
b) Secondary; primary data could take a lot of time to collect.
4. a) employees working for the chain store
b) Randomly select 15% of the employees in each store.
c) Survey all employees at the nearest store.
d) Employees at the nearest store have the same work conditions. These employees may not have the same concerns and opinions as employees at other stores.
5. a) employees in the office

b) Answers will vary. Example: Randomly select 25% of the employees in each department.
6. a) clients of the travel company
b) Answers will vary. Example: Randomly select one name on a list of the travel agent's clients, and then select every 50th person before and after that name.
7. a)

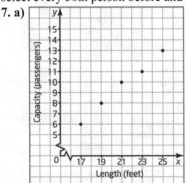

b) As the length of the boat increases, the capacity also increases. The points follow a line, so the relationship is linear.
c) 9 **d)** 16
8. a) Graphs will vary. The relationship is linear; the points lie close to the line.
b) Graphs will vary. The relation is non-linear; the points follow a curve.
9. Answers will vary.
10. a)

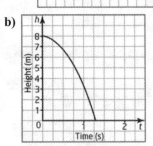

b)

11. a) moving closer at constant speed
b) moving away with increasing speed
c) moving closer at decreasing speed, stopping for moment, and then moving away with increasing speed

12. part a); the points lie on a line.

Chapter 3
3.1 Build Algebraic Models Using Concrete Materials, pages 51–52
1. Tile models may vary.
2. Tile models may vary.
3. a) $x^2 + 2x + 4$ **b)** $2x^2 + 3x$ **c)** $x^2 + 5$ **d)** $2x + 4$
4. a) 5 m **b)** 3 m **c)** 2 m **c)** $3x$ metres **d)** $2x$ metres
5. a) 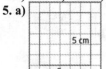 **b)** 25 cm^2, 5^2 cm^2

6. a) **b)** 27 cm^3, 3^3 cm^3

7. a) 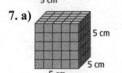 **b)** 125 cm^3, 5^3 cm^3
c) 5^2 cm^2, 25 cm^2

8. a) 8 cm **b)** 512 cm^3, 8^3 cm^3 or 2^9 cm^3
9. a) 150 cm^2 **b)** 294 cm^2
10. a) 16 cm^2 **b)** 4 cm **c)** 64 cm^3, 4^3 cm^3 or 2^6 cm^3
11. a) 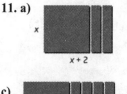 **b)**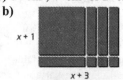

c)  **d)**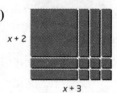

12. a) 2 cm, 4 cm **b)** 120 cm^2
13. 9

3.2 Work With Exponents, pages 53–54

1. a) 5^6 **b)** $(-3)^4$ **c)** 2.03^5 **d)** $\left(-\dfrac{2}{3}\right)^3$

2. a) $2 \times 2 \times 2 \times 2$
b) $(-4) \times (-4) \times (-4) \times (-4) \times (-4)$
c) $0.7 \times 0.7 \times 0.7$ **d)** $\left(-\dfrac{3}{4}\right) \times \left(-\dfrac{3}{4}\right)$

3. a) 8 **b)** 16 **c)** −16 **d)** −216 **e)** $\dfrac{81}{256}$

4. a) $-\dfrac{8}{27}$ **b)** 12.167 **c)** 1 **d)** −1 **e)** −1

5. a) 24 **b)** 960 **c)** 256 **d)** 1

6. a) 12 **b)** 20 **c)** 32 **d)** $-\dfrac{1}{6}$ **e)** 240 **f)** −45

7. a) 45 **b)** 19.6 **c)** 144 **d)** 150.8 **e)** 18.1 **f)** 0
8. a) 3, 9, 27, 81, 243, 729
b) The final digits are in the sequence 3, 9, 7, 1, 3, 9, ….
c) 7
9. a)

Time (min)	Population of Staphylococcus aureus
0	200
60	400
120	800
180	1600
240	3200

b)
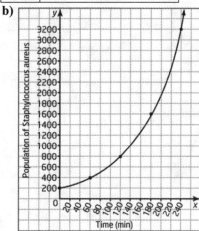

c) 819 200, 3 355 443 200
10. a)

Time (min)	Population of Streptococcus pneumoniae
0	100
20	200
40	400
60	800
80	1600
100	3200

b)
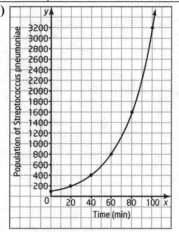

11. a) 5 000 000 **b)** 5 000 000

12. a)

Number of Half-Life Periods	Time (days)	Amount of Iodine-131 Remaining (mg)
0	0	200
1	8	$200\left(\dfrac{1}{2}\right)^1 = 100$
2	16	$200\left(\dfrac{1}{2}\right)^2 = 50$
3	24	$200\left(\dfrac{1}{2}\right)^3 = 25$
4	32	$200\left(\dfrac{1}{2}\right)^4 = 12.5$

b)

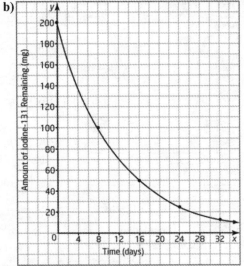

The graph decreases very quickly and then slows down as it gets closer to 0.
c) 3.125 mg **d)** 61 days
13. a) 3.45×10^{10} **b)** 5.12×10^{-9}

3.3 Discover the Exponent Laws, pages 55–56
1. a) $4^5 = 1024$ **b)** $(-2)^6 = 64$ **c)** $2.5^6 = 244.140\,625$

d) $(-1)^{40} = 1$ **e)** $\left(\dfrac{2}{3}\right)^7 = \dfrac{128}{2187}$ **f)** $\left(-\dfrac{3}{5}\right)^5 = -\dfrac{243}{3125}$

2. a) $8^2 = 64$ **b)** $(-5)^3 = -125$ **c)** $3.2^3 = 32.768$

d) $(-1)^{15} = -1$ **e)** $\left(\dfrac{3}{4}\right)^3 = \dfrac{27}{64}$ **f)** $\left(-\dfrac{2}{5}\right)^2 = \dfrac{4}{25}$

3. a) $5^6 = 15\,625$ **b)** $(-4)^6 = 4096$

c) $(0.2)^6 = 0.000\,064$ **d)** $(-1)^{18} = 1$ **e)** $\left(\dfrac{1}{5}\right)^4 = \dfrac{1}{625}$

f) $\left(-\dfrac{5}{6}\right)^6 = \dfrac{15\,625}{46\,656}$

4. a) $3^7 = 2187$ **b)** $4^2 = 16$ **c)** $2^{12} = 4096$ **d)** $2^2 = 4$
5. a) $3^3 = 27$ **b)** $4^5 = 1024$ **c)** $0.2^3 = 0.008$
d) $(-3)^1 = -3$ **e)** $6^{10} = 60\,466\,176$ **f)** $(-5)^4 = 625$

6. a) x^8 **b)** y^2 **c)** m^{12} **d)** d^8 **e)** a^4b^4 **f)** c^4d^3
7. a) $15x^7y^5$ **b)** $2a^4b$ **c)** $m^{10}n^6$ **d)** $-8c^9$
8. a) $2dm^4$ **b)** g^3h^4 **c)** xy^4
9. a) 8 **b)** $2x^2y^2$; 8 **c)** Answers will vary.

10. a) $\dfrac{1}{512}, \dfrac{1}{4096}$

b) $\left(\left(\dfrac{1}{2}\right)^3\right)^3$; Answers may vary for 12 tails in a row:

possibilities are $\left(\left(\dfrac{1}{2}\right)^2\right)^6, \left(\left(\dfrac{1}{2}\right)^3\right)^4, \left(\left(\dfrac{1}{2}\right)^4\right)^3$, and

$\left(\left(\dfrac{1}{2}\right)^6\right)^2$.

11. a) $\dfrac{1}{6}$ **b)** $\dfrac{1}{7776}$ **c)** $\dfrac{1}{2}$ **d)** $\dfrac{5}{6}$

12. a) $\dfrac{1}{4}$ **b)** $\left(\dfrac{1}{4}\right)^4 = \dfrac{1}{256}$ **c)** $\left(\dfrac{1}{4}\right)^7 = \dfrac{1}{16\,384}$

13. a) $8 \times 10^7 = 80\,000\,000$ **b)** $7 \times 10^5 = 700\,000$
c) $2 \times 10^4 = 20\,000$ **d)** $2.3 \times 10^2 = 230$

14. $x^2, x, \dfrac{1}{x}, \dfrac{1}{x^2}$

15. a) Answers will vary. **b)** Answers will vary.

3.4 Communicate With Algebra, pages 57–59
1. a) coefficient: 3, variable x
b) coefficient: -5, variable: y
c) coefficient: 1, variable: dm
d) coefficient: -4, variable: ab
2. a) coefficient: -1, variable: w^3y^2
b) coefficient: -0.2, variable: e^5f
c) coefficient: $\dfrac{2}{3}$, variable: x^5

d) coefficient: $-\dfrac{3}{8}$, variable: y^4

3. a) monomial **b)** binomial **c)** trinomial
d) monomial **e)** trinomial **f)** binomial
4. a) 1 **b)** 3 **c)** 1 **d)** 8 **e)** 4 **f)** 8 **g)** 0 **h)** 0
5. a) 1 **b)** 2 **c)** 3 **d)** 9 **e)** 5 **f)** 8
6. $2w + t$
7. a) Variable chosen may vary; c **b)** $0.45c$
c) \$9 **d)** \$6300
8. a) $2b + f$, where b represents the number of baskets and f represents the number of free throws.
b) 17
9. a) $c - 2i$, where c represents the number of correct answers and i represents the number of incorrect answers.
b) 16
10. a) $10g + 5s$

b)

Term	Variable	Coefficient	Meaning
$10g$	g	10	g: number of gold memberships she sells 10: bonus she gets per membership
$5s$	s	5	s: number of silver memberships she sells 5: bonus she gets per membership

c) $350

11. a) $80o + 50d + 25b$

b)

Term	Variable	Coefficient	Meaning
$80o$	o	80	o: the number of orchestra seats sold 80: the earnings per orchestra seat
$50d$	d	50	d: the number of dress circle seats sold 50: the earnings per dress circle seat
$25b$	b	25	b: the number of balcony seats sold 25: the earnings per balcony seat

c) $21 750 **d)** $23 900

12. a) $400 + 0.15v + 200p$, where v represents the value of the boat and p represents the number of passengers.

b) $30 400

13. a) Answers will vary. For example: s: swim, c: cycle, r: run

b)

Part of the Race	Speed (km/h)	Distance (km)	Time (h)
swim	1.5	s	$\dfrac{s}{1.5}$
cycle	30	c	$\dfrac{c}{30}$
run	12	r	$\dfrac{r}{12}$

c) $\dfrac{s}{1.5} + \dfrac{c}{30} + \dfrac{r}{12}$ **d)** 12 h 3 min 24 s

3.5 Collect Like Terms, pages 60–61

1. a) like **b)** unlike **c)** unlike **d)** like **e)** like
f) unlike
2. Answers will vary
3. $5x$ and $-3x$, $-3mn$ and $5mn$, 8 and -5, $4a^5$ and $7a^5$, $-2x^3$ and $2x^3$, and $6a^2b^2$ and $-3a^2b^2$
4. a) $8x + 6$ **b)** $2y + 2$ **c)** $3m + 1$ **d)** $n - 6$ **e)** $5x^2 + 9$
f) $3a - 2b$
5. a) $7x^2 + 7x$ **b)** $2a - 2$ **c)** $2m^2 - 2m - 1$
d) $4w^3 + 6w^2 - w$

6. a) $a^2 - 3ab - b^2$ **b)** $m^3n^2 + m^2n^3$ **c)** $-7x^2y - 3x + 2$
d) $7r^4 + r^2 - 3$
7. a) $2(w + 5w)$ or $2(6w)$ or $12w$, where w is the width of the garden
b) 240 m **c)** width: 15 m; length: 75 m **d)** $5w^2$
e) 4500 m^2 **f)** width: 10 m; length: 50 m
8. Diagrams may vary.
a) $6x + 4$ **b)** $2y + 1$ **c)** $6c^2 - c$
9. a) $4x$ **b)** x^2 **c)** 20 m
10. a)

Store	Profit ($)	Profit (or Loss) After 2 Months ($)
North End	$1500x - 3200$	-200
South End	$1300x - 900$	1700
West End	$2150x - 1100$	3200
East End	$1700x - 5000$	-1600
Central	$1850x - 800$	2900

$6000
b) $8500x - 11\,000$ **c)** $6000; the same **d)** $91 000
11. $5x$
12. a) John multiplied the like terms instead of adding them.
b) Answers will vary. Example: Substitute any value for x into the original expression and into the simplified expression.
c) $2x^2 + 5x$. Verify by substituting a value for x into the expressions.
13. 1806

3.6 Add and Subtract Polynomials, pages 62–64

1. a) $8x + 5$ **b)** $10m - 1$ **c)** $-2n + 1$ **d)** $10k + 9$
e) $13r + 2$
2. a) $x + 2$ **b)** $4m + 1$ **c)** $2s - 7$ **d)** $2d - 2$ **e)** $r + 12$
f) $3t - 12$
3. a) $7x + 2$ **b)** $12y - 7$ **c)** $6p^2 + 5p - 2$
d) $5m^2 - 6mn - n^2$ **e)** $3a + 3b$ **f)** $5p^2 + p + 3q$
4. a) $180\,000 + 170b$ **b)** $231 000
5. a)

b) $6w + 6$
c) $w(2w + 3)$
d) 18 m; 14 m^2
6. a) $120\,000 + 0.6n$
b) silver status: $150 000, gold status: $165 000, platinum status: $180 000
c)

Status	Employee
silver	Susan and Kelvin
gold	Kelvin
platinum	Kelvin

7. missing expressions: step 2: $-4x - 5y$;
step 3: $-6x - 4y$
8. missing expressions: step 2: $-x - 3y$;
step 3: $3x + 7y$
9. a) Cruz: $80\,000 + 35g + 25a$;
Gortan: $60\,000 + 20g + 18a$;
McKinnon: $100\,000 + 42g + 30a$

b) $240\ 000 + 97g + 73a$ **c)** \$266 700
10. a) Jack: \$1200; Yaling: \$1 050; Stacia: \$1125;
Meisrain: \$1325; Janet: \$1250
b) $4050 + 38\ 000c$

3.7 The Distributive Property, pages 65–66
1. a) $3x + 6$ **b)** $4x - 20$ **c)** $-2x - 8$ **d)** $-5x + 20$
2. a) $8a + 12$ **b)** $18b - 24$ **c)** $-6m - 5$ **d)** $-4r + 3$
3. a) $x^2 + 4x$ **b)** $a^2 - 5a$ **c)** $-z^2 + 3z$ **d)** $-2b^2 + b$
4. a) $-3w^2 - 5w$ **b)** $-3m^2 + 2m$ **c)** $12q^2 + 28q$
d) $14d^2 + 35d$
5. a) $3m + 6$ **b)** $5d - 15$ **c)** $-6h - 10$ **d)** $-12r + 3$
6. a) $5q - 20$ **b)** $7b - 42$ **c)** $-20t - 28$ **d)** $-35c + 15$
7. a) $3x^2 + 15x + 12$ **b)** $5x^2 - 15x + 10$
c) $4m^3 + 12m^2 + 20m$ **d)** $5a^3 + 5a^2 - 20a$
e) $3x^2 + 21x + 9$
8. a) $-4x^2 - 4x + 4$ **b)** $5a^2 - 5a + 20$ **c)** $-r^2 - r + 5$
d) $20x + 30$ **e)** $-16b + 60$
9. a) $8x + 2$ **b)** $a - 23$ **c)** $1.3c - 1.9$ **d)** $-22d + 4$
e) $7k^2 + 3k$
10. a) $75 + 25t$, where t is the time, in hours.
b) \$162.50 **c)** $150 + 50t$
d) \$325. Yes, the answer makes sense because it is
doubled.
11. a) $-1.8h^2 - 0.1h$ **b)** $6a - 17$ **c)** $3r - 28$
d) $10a^2 + 17a - 16$ **e)** $4g^2 - 3g - 9$
12. a) $14x + 6$ **b)** $12x^2 + 9x$
c) Perimeter: $28x + 12$, Area: $48x^2 + 36x$
d) Yes. Double the old perimeter is $2(14x + 6)$ or
$28x + 12$.
e) No. Double the old area is $2(12x^2 + 9x)$ or
$24x^2 + 18x$, which is not equal to the new area.
13. $SA = 2lw + 2hw + 2lh$

14. a) $4x + \dfrac{17}{12}$ **b)** $-4a + \dfrac{23}{20}b$ **c)** $4m + \dfrac{26}{15}$

d) $a - \dfrac{23}{6}c$

15. a) $15x^2 + 24x$ **b)** $4m^2 + 40m$ **c)** $2a^3 + 30a^2$
d) $-14b + 10$ **e)** $-y - 13$ **f)** $-5c - 5$
16. a) $x^2 + 7x + 12$ **b)** $a^2 + 11a + 30$ **c)** $b^2 + 10b + 21$
d) $w^2 + 10w + 16$ **e)** $d^2 + 3d - 10$
17. a) $z^2 - 3z - 18$ **b)** $m^2 + m - 20$ **c)** $y^2 - 2y - 15$
d) $h^2 - 12h + 32$ **e)** $p^2 - 6p + 9$
18. a) $x^3 + 5x^2 + 10x + 8$ **b)** $y^3 - y^2 - 17y - 15$

Chapter 3 Review, pages 67–68
1. Models will vary. **a)** 5 **b)** $3x$ **c)** $x + 5$ **d)** 2
2. a) 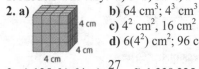 **b)** 64 cm^3; 4^3 cm^3
  c) 4^2 cm^2, 16 cm^2
  d) $6(4^2)$ cm^2; 96 cm^2

3. a) 125 **b)** 64 **c)** $\dfrac{27}{64}$ **d)** 1.338 225 557 8

4. a) $3^6 = 729$ **b)** $5^3 = 125$ **c)** $4^3 = 64$ **d)** $2^4 = 16$
e) $(-3)^6 = 729$ **f)** $5^3 = 125$

5. a)

Time (min)	Population of E. coli
0	400
20	800
40	1 600
60	3 200
80	6 400
100	12 800
120	25 600

b)

(graph: Population of E. coli vs Time (min))

c) 13 107 200; 6 710 886 400
6. a) a^8b^6 **b)** d^4 **c)** m^2 **d)** y^8
7. a) coefficient: 6, variable: x
b) coefficient: -5, variable: y
c) coefficient: 7, variable: none
d) coefficient: 4, variable: a^5b^3
e) coefficient: 1, variable: dm

f) coefficient: $\dfrac{2}{3}$, variable: x^2y^3

8. a) $4w + 2o$, where w represents a win and o
represents an overtime win. **b)** 24
9. a) 4 **b)** 5 **c)** 6 **d)** 0
10. a) 1 **b)** 4 **c)** 2 **d)** 3
11. a) like **b)** unlike **c)** like **d)** unlike **e)** like
f) like
12. a) $6x^2$, $-5x^2$ **b)** $6y^2$, $5y^2$, $-4y^2$; $-4y^3$, $-2y^3$
13. a) $7x + 11y$ **b)** $d - 2m$ **c)** $a^2 - 3a - 3$
d) $w^2 + 3y^2$ **e)** $7d - 3e - 16f$ **f)** $11a^3 - 7ab + 5b^2 - 3$
14. a) $11x - 1$ **b)** $9y - 5$ **c)** $10p^2 + p + 1$
d) $3m^2 - 4mn + 3n^2$ **e)** $4a + 7b$
15. $14x + 4$
16. a) $5x + 10$ **b)** $-4y + 12$ **c)** $6m^2 + 8m$
d) $-8g^2 + 12g$
17. a) $23x + 42y$ **b)** $6y - 6w - 3$ **c)** $17a - 3b$
d) $24c + 28$

Chapter 4
4.1 Solve Simple Equations, pages 69–70
1. a) $x = 3$ **b)** $y = 8$ **c)** $m = 3$ **d)** $c = 6$
2. a) $x = 4$ **b)** $y = 6$ **c)** $a = 5$ **d)** $b = 20$
3. a) $x = 3$ **b)** $g = 2$ **c)** $h = 7$ **d)** $c = -2$
4. a) $d = -7$ **b)** $k = 3$ **c)** $u = -4$ **d)** $w = -10$
5. a) $x = 2$ **b)** $w = 2$ **c)** $p = 4$ **d)** $h = -1$
6. a) $q = 2$ **b)** $a = 13$ **c)** $m = 2$ **d)** $b = 1$
7. a) $a = -10$ **b)** $c = 7$ **c)** $d = 5$ **d)** $h = -15$

8. a) $r = 7$ **b)** $v = -1$ **c)** $g = 1$ **d)** $j = -4$

9. The variable used may vary.
a) $15d = 120$ **b)** $d = 8$

10. a) $h = \dfrac{2}{3}$ **b)** $k = \dfrac{1}{5}$ **c)** $w = \dfrac{5}{7}$

11. a) $d = -\dfrac{1}{2}$ **b)** $r = -\dfrac{22}{15}$ **c)** $t = \dfrac{14}{15}$

12.

Step	Explanation
$5x - 4 = 6$	
$5x - 4 + 4 = 6 + 4$	Add 4 to both sides.
$5x = 10$	Simplify by adding integers.
$\dfrac{5x}{5} = \dfrac{10}{5}$	Divide both sides by 5.
$x = 2$	Divide integers to give the solution for x.

13. a) $a = 30°$, $b = 60°$, $c = 90°$
b) $a = 20°$, $b = 60°$, $c = 100°$
14. The variable used may vary.
a) $15n + 250 = 2000$
b) $n = 116.\overline{6}$; The committee can afford 116 T-shirts.
15. a) $2000 + 840n = 10\ 400$, where n is the number of litres.
b) 10 L

4.2 Solve Multi-Step Equations, pages 71–72

1. a) $x = 2$ **b)** $y = 3$ **c)** $a = -3$ **d)** $m = 4$
2. a) $w = 5$ **b)** $k = -2$ **c)** $b = 1$ **d)** $d = -3$
3. a) $t = -5$ **b)** $c = -5$ **c)** $x = 2$ **d)** $n = 1$
4. a) $x = -3$ **b)** $q = 4$ **c)** $t = 7$ **d)** $u = 4$

5. a) $r = 2$ **b)** $y = \dfrac{15}{2}$ **c)** $v = -4$ **d)** $y = 2$

6. $x + 4x = 180°$, where x is the measure of the smaller angle, in degrees; $36°$, $144°$
7. $10°$, $30°$, $50°$

8. a) $x = \dfrac{5}{3}$ **b)** $h = -\dfrac{3}{2}$ **c)** $m = -4$ **d)** $p = -13$

9. equilateral triangle: 8, 8, 8; rectangle: 7 by 5
10. $108°$, $36°$, $36°$
11.

Step	Explanation
L.S. $= 3(x + 4) + 6$	
$= 3[(-3) + 4] + 6$	Substitute the root into the left side.
$= 3(1) + 6$	Simplify the expression inside the brackets.
$= 3 + 6$	Multiply.
$= 9$	Add.
R.S. $= 9 - (x + 3)$	
$= 9 - [(-3) + 3]$	Substitute the root into the right side.
$= 9 - (0)$	Simplify the expression inside the brackets.
$= 9$	Subtract.

12. a) 20 cm, 20 cm, 30 cm
b) The perimeter is the sum of the sides and this must be 70 cm. So, write and solve the equation $2x + 2x + 3x = 70$.
13. 1350 cm^2

14. a) $x = -12$ **b)** $k = -\dfrac{10}{3}$ **c)** $m = -\dfrac{1}{4}$ **d)** $d = \dfrac{3}{5}$

4.3 Solve Equations Involving Fractions, pages 73–74

1. a) $x = -5$ **b)** $a = -3$ **c)** $m = 8$
2. a) $k = 2$ **b)** $k = 5$ **c)** $p = 4$

3. a) $y = -7$ **b)** $p = -17$ **c)** $h = \dfrac{7}{4}$

4. a) $n = -\dfrac{1}{2}$ **b)** $c = -5$ **c)** $w = -11$

5. a) $h = 9$ **b)** $d = -10$ **c)** $x = -7$
6. a) $p = 15$ **b)** $k = -37$ **c)** $s = 12$

7. a) $m = \dfrac{59}{9}$ **b)** $k = \dfrac{5}{2}$ **c)** $c = -\dfrac{13}{14}$ **d)** $n = \dfrac{7}{5}$

e) $w = 17$
8. 12 m
9. a) The error is in the second line,
$4(x + 5) = 3(x - 2)$. The numerators on each side of the first line were multiplied by their own denominators. The correct step should be to multiply both sides by 12 (the lowest common denominator).
b) The third line is incorrect. In the previous line, the denominators and the 10 were eliminated instead of being simplified. The third line should be $2(2y + 4) = 5(y - 3)$.
10. 18 cm
11. a) $86°F$ **b)** $25°C$

12. a) $a = \dfrac{3}{2}$ **b)** $u = -\dfrac{18}{11}$ **c)** $w = \dfrac{57}{29}$

13. a) height 4.0 m; base 2.0 m **b)** 4 m^2

4.4 Modelling With Formulas, pages 75–76

1. a) $d = \dfrac{C}{\pi}$ **b)** $t = \dfrac{d}{v}$ **c)** $I = A - P$

2. a) $m = \dfrac{y - b}{x}$ **b)** $y = \dfrac{-Ax - C}{B}$ **c)** $a = \dfrac{F}{m}$

d) $R = \dfrac{V}{I}$

3. a) $s = \sqrt[3]{V}$ **b)** $R = \dfrac{P}{I^2}$ **c)** $h = \dfrac{V}{\pi r^2}$

4. a) $l = \dfrac{P - 2w}{2}$ **b)** $s = \sqrt{A}$ **c)** $h = \dfrac{2A}{b}$

d) $a = \sqrt{c^2 - b^2}$

5. a) 6.6 pounds; 1.1 pounds **b)** $w = \dfrac{m}{2.2}$

c) 3.6 kg

6. a)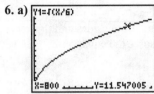

b) Linear. When the equation is graphed, a straight line results.

c) 1.4 kg; 11 pounds

7. a) $s = \sqrt{\dfrac{A}{6}}$ **b)** 11.5 cm

8. a) <<tech art 2-Chapter 4 Answers>>; 11.5 cm
b) Non-linear. Since the graph is curved, the relation is non-linear.

9. $r = \dfrac{I}{Pt}$, $t = \dfrac{I}{Pr}$

10. a) $s = \sqrt[3]{V}$

b)

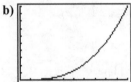 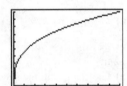

c) Answers will vary. Both graphs show a non-linear relationship.
d) Answers will vary. In the first graph, $V = s^3$, the graph opens upward. In the second graph, $s = \sqrt[3]{V}$, the graph opens sideways.

11.

Step	Explanation
$F = \dfrac{Gm_1m_2}{d^2}$	Start with the original formula.
$Fd^2 = Gm_1m_x$	Multiply both sides of the equation by d^2.
$\dfrac{Fd^2}{F} = \dfrac{Gm_1m_2}{F}$	Divide both sides of the equation by F.
$d^2 = \dfrac{Gm_1m_2}{F}$	Simplify.
$\sqrt{d^2} = \sqrt{\dfrac{Gm_1m_2}{F}}$	Take the square root of both sides.
$d = \sqrt{\dfrac{Gm_1m_2}{F}}$	Simplify to isolate d.

4.5 Modelling With Algebra, pages 77–78

1. a) $4n$ **b)** $n + 3$ **c)** $\dfrac{1}{3}n$ **d)** $3n - 4$

2. a) $5n$ **b)** $2n + 6$ **c)** $n - 2$ **d)** $\dfrac{3}{5}n$

3. a) $5n = 85$; the variable n represents any number
b) $a + 8 = 177$; the variable a represents the area
c) $2n + 3 = 33$; the variable n represents any number
d) $x - 1 + x + x + 1 = 168$; the variable x represents any number
4. a) 17; this represents the number that equals 85 when multiplied by 5
b) 169; this represents the area that when increased by 8 equals 177
c) 15; this represents the number that, when multiplied by 2, is three less than 33
d) 56; the sum of this number and the two numbers on either side, 55 and 57, is 168
5. Natasha: 565; Krysten: 315
6. Justin: $57.50; Kieran: $37.50
7. Jacinth: 17; Naomi: 13
8. $8000
9. 39, 40, 41
10. a) length = 20 m; width = 10 m **b)** 60 m
c) 22.4 m
11. Jessica: 20; Letitia: 40; Sally: 48
12. a) $8.5t + 2m$, where t represents the time, in hours, and m represents the number of memberships.
b) $145 **c)** 195 **d)** 20 h
13. Azra, $85; Anoja, $170; Amani, $195
14. Alicia: 534 coins; Wayne 178 coins
15. front width: 9 m; back width: 3 m
16. triple the height
17. a) $E = 7.5t + 0.75g$, where E represents the earnings, in dollars; t represents the time, in hours; and g represents the number of pairs of sunglasses.
b) $63.75 **c)** 40

Chapter 4 Review, pages 79–80
1. a) $x = 4$ **b)** $f = 10$ **c)** $h = 5$ **d)** $k = 12$
2. a) $x = 3$ **b)** $y = -1$ **c)** $f = -11$ **d)** $m = -3$
3. a) $x = 2$ **b)** $p = -1$ **c)** $w = -\dfrac{1}{3}$ **d)** $u = \dfrac{3}{4}$
4. a) $5.95 + 2.95m = 23.65$, where m represents the number of magazines John can afford.
b) $m = 6$
5. a) $x = 3$ **b)** $c = 4$ **c)** $r = -5$ **d)** $g = -2$
6. a) $a = -1$ **b)** $b = 6$ **c)** $n = 6$ **d)** $d = -2$
7. 10°, 50°, 120°
8. a) $x = 7$ **b)** $b = 26$ **c)** $m = \dfrac{21}{2}$ **d)** $d = -\dfrac{19}{3}$
9. a) $r = 1$ **b)** $p = \dfrac{14}{5}$ **c)** $q = -7$ **d)** $b = \dfrac{7}{2}$
10. a) $x = 32$ **b)** $y = 26$ **c)** $b = -17$ **d)** $v = -27$
11. a) $m = \dfrac{F}{a}$ **b)** $I = \dfrac{V}{R}$ **c)** $r = \sqrt{\dfrac{A}{\pi}}$ **d)** $w = \dfrac{P - 2l}{2}$
e) $x = \dfrac{y - b}{m}$
12. a) 200 W **b)** 4 Ω **c)** 30 V

13. Suresh: 13 years; Hakima: 26 years; Saad: 9 years
14. a) $49.50 **b)** 64
15. a) $52.20 **b)** 100 **c)** 80

Chapter 5
5.1 Direct Variation, pages 81-82
1. a) 90 **b)** 15 **c)** 8
2. a) $C = 75w$
b) the cost per 1 m of width for the patio **c)** $525
3. a)

Mass of Potatoes, m (kg)	Cost, C ($)
0	0.00
1	2.18
2	4.36
3	6.54
4	8.72
5	10.90

b) 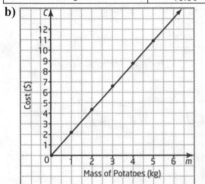 **c)** $C = 2.18m$

4. a) To get the cost of a boat rental, multiply the time the boat is rented, in hours, by $9.50. The cost, C, in dollars, of renting the boat varies directly with the time, t, in hours, for which the boat is rented.
b) 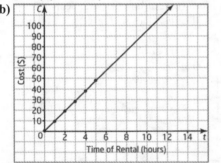 $C = 9.5t$

c) Answers will vary. Example: about $110. **d)** $114
5. a) To get the cost of a rental, multiply the time, in hours, rented by $8. The cost, C, in dollars, of renting, varies directly with the time, t, in hours, for which the canoe is rented.

b) 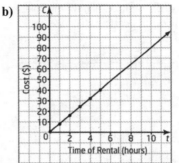 $C = 8t$

c) Answers will vary. For example: $60. **d)** $64
6. a) To get the cost of parking, multiply the time, in days, parked by $14.50. The cost, C, in dollars, of parking, varies directly with the time, t, in days, for which the vehicle is parked.
b) 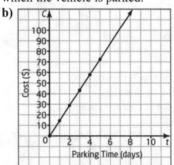 $C = 14.5t$

c) Answers will vary. For example: $90. **d)** $87
7. a)

Cookies Bought, n (packages)	Cost, C ($)
0	0.00
1	3.50
2	7.00
3	10.50
4	14.00

b) 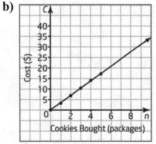 **c)** $C = 3.50n$

8. a) This relationship is a direct variation because the pay that Alison receives varies directly with the time she works.
b) $P = 9.75t$ **c)**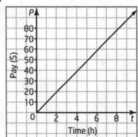

9. Answers will vary. Example: Consider the cost, in dollars, of taking a taxi for a certain distance, in kilometres.

10. a)

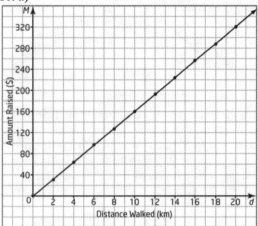

b) $M = 16d$ **c)** $400

11. a) $V = 100t$, where V is the volume of water, in litres, and t is the time, in minutes. The constant of variation represents the constant average rate of change of volume: 100 L/min.

b)

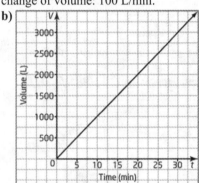

c) 3000 L **d)** 1000 min

12. $l = 0.220g$, where l is the number of litres and g is the number of Canadian gallons.

5.2 Partial Variation, pages 83–84

1. a) Direct variation: the equation is of the form $y = kx$.

b) Partial variation: the equation is of the form $y = mx + b$.

c) Partial variation: the equation is of the form $y = mx + b$

d) Direct variation: the equation is of the form $y = kx$.

2. a)

x	y
0	4
1	7
2	10
3	13
4	16
7	25

b) 4, 3 **c)** $y = 3x + 4$

d)

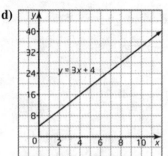

e) The graph is a straight line that intersects the *y*-axis at (0, 4). The *y*-values increase by 3 as the *x*-values increase by 1.

3. a)

x	y
0	-3
1	1
2	5
3	9
4	13
8	29

b) −3, 4 **c)** $y = 4x - 3$

d)

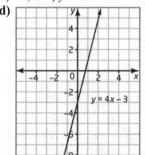

e) The graph is a straight line that intersects the *y*-axis at (0, −3). The *y*-values increase by 4 as the *x*-values increase by 1.

4. a) $200, $3 × number of people

b) $C = 3n + 200$ **c)** $500

5. a)

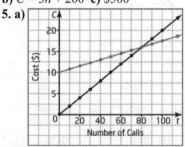

b) A: direct variation; B: partial variation

c) In both cases, C represents the cost of the cellular phone plan and n represents the number of calls.
A: $C = 1.50n$; B: $C = 0.25n + 25$

d) Plan A is cheaper when fewer than 20 phone calls are made. Plan B is cheaper when more than 20 phone calls are made.

6. a) The fixed cost is $50 and could represent, for example, the cost of paper, ink, and overhead.

b) From the table, it costs \$400 to print 200 newsletters, so the variable cost to print one newsletter is \$400 ÷ 200 = \$2.
c) $C = 2n + 50$ **d)** \$2450 **e)** 125
7. Answers will vary. Example: Consider the cost of renting a truck for a day. It costs a \$50 flat fee and \$0.50 per km.
8. a) fixed cost: \$825; variable cost: $15n
b) $C = 15n + 825$ **c)** \$3075 **d)** 175
9. a)

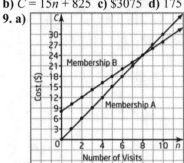

b) A: direct variation; B: partial variation
c) In both cases, C represents the cost of a membership and n represents the number of visits.
A: $C = 3n$; B: $C = 2n + 8$
d) Membership A is cheaper when fewer than eight visits are made. Membership B is cheaper when more than eight visits are made.

5.3 Slope, pages 85–86
1. 1.25
2. 0.73
3. a) $\dfrac{2}{3}$ **b)** $-\dfrac{3}{4}$ **c)** 0 **d)** not possible
4. Answers will vary. Examples:
a) B(5, 7) **b)** B(2, −1) **c)** B(3, −1) **d)** B(−5, −4)
5. Yes it does; otherwise the slopes would be different.
6. 0.2
7. 0.143
8. 1.3
9. a) 8 **b)** Yes.
10. a) steep **b)** medium **c)** shallow

5.4 Slope as a Rate of Change, pages 87–89
1. 40 km/h
2. 4 flaps/s
3. 72 beats/min
4. a) −5 **b)** The height decreases by 5 m/min.
5. a) −0.083
b) The atmospheric pressure decreases by 0.083 mbar/m.
6. 5¢/year
7. 2 m/year
8. a) Cyclist B, by 10 km/h

b) It is the time at which they have travelled the same distance. If they are travelling in the same direction, it is the time at which cyclist A passes cyclist B.
9. No.
10. a) The graph is a line starting at (0, 0) and passing through (20, 200).
b) 30 s

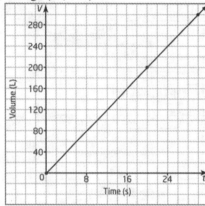

11. a) 0.2 km/min
b)

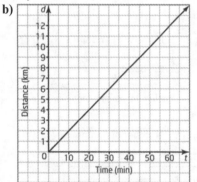

c) The rate of change is Selam's average running speed. It is also the slope of the graph.
12. a)

Time (h)	Price of Piano ($)
0	1350.00
4	1215.00
8	1093.50
12	984.15

b) Graphs may vary depending on scales chosen.
c) The graph is decreasing and it is curved because the rate of change changes at each interval.
13. a)

Time (h)	Cost of Membership ($)
0	570
2	540
4	510
6	480
8	450

b) Graphs may vary depending on scales chosen.
c) The graph is decreasing and it is linear because the rate of change is constant.
14. a) 40π cm **b)** $C = 2\pi r$ **c)** 2π cm/cm

5.5 First Differences, pages 90–92
1. a) linear **b)** linear **c)** non-linear **d)** non-linear

e) linear **f)** non-linear
2. a) linear

x	y	First Differences
0	2	
1	6	4
2	10	4
3	14	4

b) non-linear

x	y	First Differences
−3	−4	
−1	−1	3
1	1	2
3	4	3

3. a) linear **b)** non-linear

4. a)

Height (cm)	Painted Area (cm²)
0	0.00
1	0.25
2	1.00
3	2.25
4	4.00

b) non-linear

5. a) linear; $S = 4n + 1$; 29 segments

b) non-linear: 49 tiles

6. a)

Base Side Length	Number of Triangles
1	1
2	4
3	9
4	16

non-linear; 49

b)

Base Side Length	Number of Segments
1	3
2	9
3	18
4	30

non-linear; 84

c)

Base Side Length	Number of Horizontal Lines in Shape
1	1
2	2
3	3
4	4

linear; 7; $y = x$

7. a)

Height (cm)	Wet Area (cm²)
0	0
1	19
2	36
3	51
4	64
5	75

b) non-linear

c) 96 cm²

8. a)

Figure Number	Number of Hexagons in Pattern
1	1
2	7
3	19
4	37

b) non-linear

5.6 Connecting Variation, Slope, and First Differences, pages 93–94

1. a) 2 **b)** 2 **c)** $y = 2x + 2$

2. a) $-\dfrac{1}{2}$ **b)** −1 **c)** $y = -\dfrac{1}{2}x - 1$

3. Tables and graphs may vary. Sample tables are shown.

a)

x	y
0	−2
1	1
2	4
3	7
4	10

slope = 3

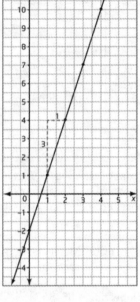

b)

x	y
0	1
1	−1
2	−3
3	−5
4	−7

slope = −2

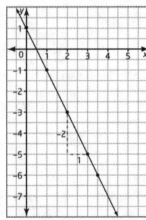

c)

x	y
0	0
1	0.5
2	1
3	1.5
4	2

slope = $\dfrac{1}{2}$

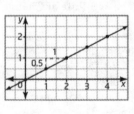

d)

x	y
0	−1
1	−1.5
2	−2
3	−2.5
4	−3

slope = −0.5

4. a)

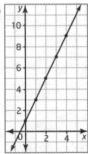

b) Each time the value of *x* increases by 1, the value of *y* increases by 2. The graph is a straight line that does not pass through (0, 0). This is a partial variation.

c) *y* = 2*x* + 1

5. a)

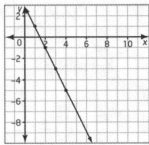

b) Each time the value of *x* increases by 1, the value of *y* decreases by 2. The graph is a straight line that does not pass through (0, 0). This is a partial variation.

c) *y* = −2*x* + 3

6.

Number of Rooms, *n*	Cost of Cleaning, *C* ($)
0	50
1	60
2	70
3	80
4	90

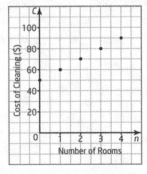

C = 10*n* + 50

7. a) The graph is a line starting at (0, 20) and passing through (1, 22) and (2, 24).

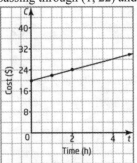

b) slope 2, cost of renting the bicycle for 1 h; vertical intercept 20, cost of renting the bicycle at the start of the rental

c) partial variation; graph is a straight line that does not pass through (0, 0)

d) *C* = 2*t* + 20

8. a) 2.2, 0 **b)** *d* = 2.2*t*

c)

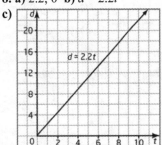

9.

x	y
−2	−3
−1	−1
0	1
1	3

y varies partially with *x*. As the value of *x* increases by 1, the value of *y* increases by 2.

y = 2*x* + 1

10.

x	y
−1	5
0	2
1	−1
2	−4

y varies partially with *x*. As the value of *x* increases by 1, the value of *y* decreases by 3. *y* = −3*x* + 2

11. Tables and graphs may vary. A sample table is shown.

x	y
0	2
1	5
2	8
3	11
4	14

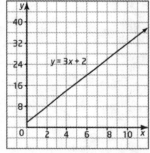

y varies partially with x. As the value of x increases by 1, the value of y increases by 3.

12. a) The relation is linear. As the value of t increases by 20 min, the volume of water increases by 30 kL.

b)

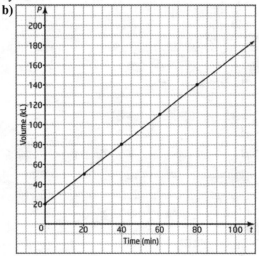

c) $\frac{3}{2}$, 1.5; constant; it represents that 1.5 kL of water fills the water tank every minute.

d) $V = 1.5t + 20$ **e)** 65 kL

Chapter 5 Review, pages 95–96

1. a)

Time Worked, t (h)	Pay, P ($)
0	0.00
1	10.50
2	21.00
3	31.50
4	42.00

b)

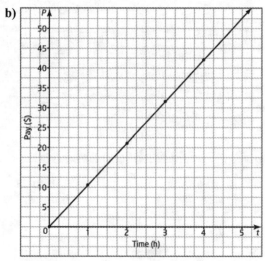

c) $P = 10.5t$

2. a) $d = 16t$; speed of 16 km/h **b)** 3.125 h

3. a) The volume of juice varies directly with the volume of water used to prepare it.

b) The graph is a line starting at (0, 0) and passing through (2, 2.5).

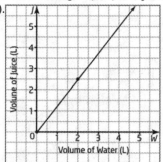

4. a) Partial variation: it is a straight line that does not pass through (0, 0).

b) Direct variation: it is a straight line that passes through (0, 0).

c) Neither: it is not a straight line.

5. a) Partial variation: it is a straight line that does not pass through (0, 0).

b) Direct variation: it is a straight line that passes through (0, 0).

c) Neither: it is not a straight line.

6. a)

x	y
0	5
1	9
2	13
3	17
4	21
8	37

b) 5, 4 **c)** $y = 4x + 5$

d) The graph is a straight line that starts at (0, 5) and rises upward to the right with a slope of 4.

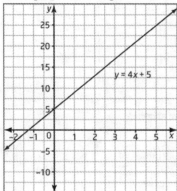

7. a) $25; 0.02b, where b is the number of business cards.
b) $C = 0.02b + 25$ **c)** $35
8. a) 0.375 **b)** 0.2
9. a) $\dfrac{4}{3}$ **b)** $-\dfrac{2}{7}$ **c)** 0 **d)** not possible

10. 3.5; the plant grows at a rate of 3.5 cm/month
11. a) yes **b)** no
12. a) linear **b)** non-linear
13. a) linear **b)** 5 **c)** $y = 5x - 4$
d)

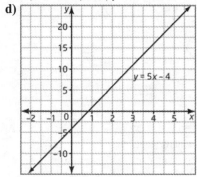

Chapter 6
6.1 The Equation of a Line in Slope
y-Intercept Form: $y = mx + b$, pages 97–99
1. a) slope = 3, y-intercept = -2
b) slope = -2, y-intercept = 4

c) slope = $\dfrac{3}{4}$, y-intercept = -5

d) slope = $-\dfrac{2}{5}$, y-intercept = 0

e) slope = 2, y-intercept = $-\dfrac{1}{3}$

f) slope = 0, y-intercept = 5
2. a) slope = 2, y-intercept = 1
b) slope = -3, y-intercept = -2
3. a) $y = 2x + 1$ **b)** $y = -3x - 2$

4. a) slope = $\dfrac{2}{3}$, y-intercept = -2

b) slope = $-\dfrac{3}{4}$, y-intercept = 3

5. a) $y = \dfrac{2}{3}x - 2$ **b)** $y = -\dfrac{3}{4}x + 3$

6. a) slope = 0, y-intercept = 2
b) slope = undefined, y-intercept = none, x-intercept = 3
c) slope = 0, y-intercept = -4
d) slope = undefined y-intercept = none, x-intercept -1
7. a) slope = 0, y-intercept = 1
b) slope = undefined, y-intercept = none, x-intercept = -2
c) slope = 0, y-intercept = 0, x-intercept = all real numbers
d) slope = undefined, y-intercept = all real numbers, x-intercept = 0
8. a) $y = 1$ **b)** $x = -2$ **c)** $y = 0$ **d)** $x = 0$
9. a) x-axis **b)** y-axis

10. a) $y = \dfrac{2}{5}x - 1$ 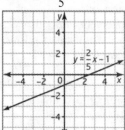 **b)** $y = -\dfrac{2}{3}x + 2$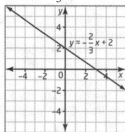

c) $y = -2$ 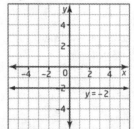 **d)** $x = 3$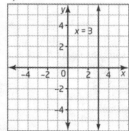

11. a) The person was an initial distance of 2 m from the sensor.
b) The person was walking at a speed of 0.4 m/s.
c) The person was walking away from the sensor. This is because on the graph, the person's distance from the sensor increases as time goes by.
d) 4 m

12. a)

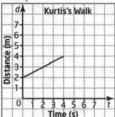

b)

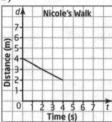

c)

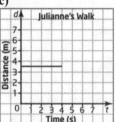

d)

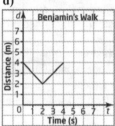

13. a) slope 0.5, d-intercept 2; The slope represents Christine's walking speed of 0.5 m/s away from the sensor. The d-intercept represents Christine's initial distance of 2 m away from the sensor; $d = \frac{1}{2}t + 2$.

b) slope = 100, d-intercept 0; The slope shows that the speed is 100 km/h. The d-intercept shows that when the trip began, the distance was 0 km; $d = 100t$.

14. a) x-intercept = 3; y-intercept = −6

b) x-intercept = −10; y-intercept = 4

6.2 The Equation of a Line in Standard Form:
Ax + By + C = 0, pages 100–101

1. a) $y = -x + 4$ **b)** $y = x + 2$ **c)** $y = -\frac{1}{4}x - \frac{3}{4}$

d) $y = \frac{1}{3}x - \frac{8}{3}$ **e)** $y = -\frac{2}{5}x - 2$ **f)** $y = \frac{3}{2}x + 3$

2. a) slope −1; y-intercept 4; the graph is a line crossing the y-axis at 4 and the x-axis at 4.

b) slope 1; y-intercept 2; the graph is a line crossing the y-axis at 2 and the x-axis at −2.

c) slope $-\frac{1}{4}$; y-intercept $-\frac{3}{4}$; the graph is a line crossing the y-axis at $-\frac{3}{4}$ and the x-axis at −3.

d) slope $\frac{1}{3}$; y-intercept $-\frac{8}{3}$; the graph is a line crossing the y-axis at $-\frac{8}{3}$ and the x-axis at 8.

e) slope $-\frac{2}{5}$; y-intercept −2; the graph is a line crossing the y-axis at −2 and the x-axis at −5.

f) slope $\frac{3}{2}$; y-intercept 3; the graph is a line crossing the y-axis at 3 and the x-axis at −2.

3. a) $C = 30n + 200$

b) fixed cost $200; variable cost $30 per person

c)

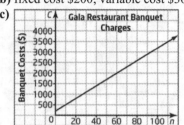

d) $3200

4. a) $C = 25n + 100$

b) fixed cost $100; variable cost $25 per table

c)

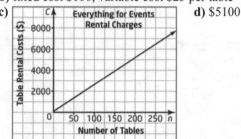

d) $5100

5. a) $C = 60m + 75$

b) fixed cost $75; variable cost $60 per bed

c)

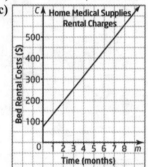

d) $375

6. a) $C = 10d + 50$

b) fixed cost $50; variable cost $10 per day

c)

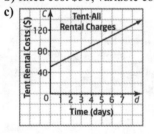

d) $120

7.

Step	Explanation
$2x + 3y - 6 = 0$	Start with the equation in standard form.
$3y = -2x + 6$	Subtract $2x$ from both sides and add 6 to both sides.
$\dfrac{3y}{3} = \dfrac{-2x+6}{3}$	Divide both sides by 3.
$y = -\dfrac{2}{3}x + 2$	Divide each term on the right by 3.

8.

Step	Explanation
$3x + 2y + 5 = 0$	Start with the equation in standard form.
$2y = -3x - 5$	Subtract $3x$ from both sides and subtract 5 from both sides.
$\dfrac{2y}{2} = \dfrac{-3x-5}{2}$	Divide both sides by 2.
$y = -\dfrac{3}{2}x - \dfrac{5}{2}$	Divide each term on the right by 2.

9.

Step	Explanation
$y = -\dfrac{3}{4}x + 2$	Start with the equation in slope y-intercept form.
$4 \times y = 4 \times \left(-\dfrac{3}{4}x + 2\right)$	Multiply both sides by 4.
$4y = -3x + 8$	Simplify.
$3x + 4y - 8 = 0$	Add $3x$ to both sides and subtract 8 from both sides.

10. a) $x - y - 5 = 0$ **b)** $x + y - 3 = 0$
c) $2x - y + 5 = 0$ **d)** $3x + y - 4 = 0$
e) $2x - 5y + 20 = 0$ **f)** $8x + 12y + 9 = 0$

6.3 Graph a Line Using Intercepts, pages 102–104
1. a) x-intercept 3; y-intercept 1
b) x-intercept -2; y-intercept -4
c) x-intercept -2.5; y-intercept 2.5
2. a) no x-intercept; y-intercept -3
b) x-intercept 2; no y-intercept
c) x-intercept 3; y-intercept -1.5
3. a)   **b)**

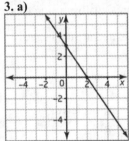
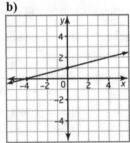

c)

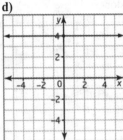

d)

e)

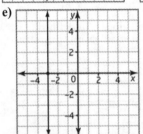

4. a) x-intercept 4; y-intercept 3
b) x-intercept 4; y-intercept 8
c) x-intercept 6; y-intercept -2
d) x-intercept -3; y-intercept 2
e) x-intercept 3; no y-intercept
f) no x-intercept; y-intercept 2
5. a) slope = 1   **b)** slope = -2

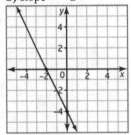

c) slope = -5 **d)** slope = 0

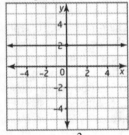

e) slope = undefined   **f)** slope = $-\dfrac{3}{4}$

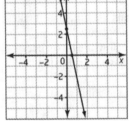
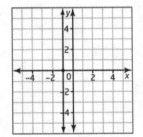
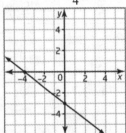
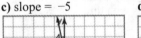

g) slope = 1

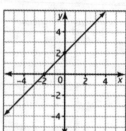

h) slope = $-\dfrac{1}{2}$

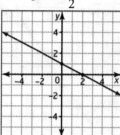

i) slope = 0

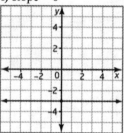

j) slope = undefined

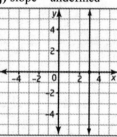

6. a) $-\dfrac{4}{5}$ **b)** $\dfrac{5}{2}$ **c)** 2 **e)** 0 **f)** undefined

7. a) c)

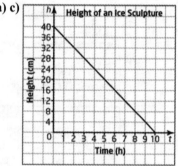

b) The slope should be negative because the ice sculpture's height decreases with time.
d) 24 cm; 18 cm
e) The t-intercept, 10, represents the time that it takes for the ice sculpture to melt completely.
f) The graph has no meaning below the t-axis because a melted ice sculpture cannot have negative length.
8. a) $10 000 **b)** 20 years
c) The slope -500, shows that the value of the car decreases by $500 each year.
9. a)

Time (years)	Car's Value
0	$10000.00
1	$7500.00
2	$5625.00
3	$4218.75
4	$3164.06
5	$2373.05

b) The relation is non-linear, because the points form a curve.

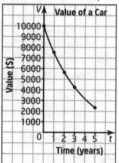

c) Answers will vary. Example: The car will be worth less than 30% of its value sometime after 4 years. It will never be worth $0 because 75% of a positive number is always another positive number.
d) No. Answers will vary. Example: It does not exist because the car's value will never reach 0.
e) Answers will vary. Example: The car's value depreciates faster in the system where its value each year is 75% of its value the preceding year. This is because 75% of $10000 is more than $500, which is the amount subtracted each year in the other model.
10. a) The relation is non-linear, because the points follow a curve.
b) one x-intercept; 3 **c)** one y-intercept; -3
d)-e) Answers will vary.

6.4 Parallel and Perpendicular Lines, pages 105–106

1. a) 2, 2, parallel **b)** 4, $-\dfrac{1}{4}$, perpendicular

c) 3, $\dfrac{1}{3}$, neither **d)** $\dfrac{1}{2}$, $\dfrac{1}{2}$, parallel

e) 1, -1, perpendicular **f)** 3, 2, neither
2. a) 0, 0, parallel **b)** 0, undefined, perpendicular
c) 0, 1, neither **d)** undefined, undefined, parallel
e) 1, -1, perpendicular **f)** undefined, -1, neither

3. a) -1, -1, parallel **b)** $-\dfrac{3}{2}$, $\dfrac{2}{3}$, perpendicular

c) -2, $-\dfrac{1}{2}$, neither **d)** -1, 1, perpendicular

4. a) parallel; $\dfrac{3}{4}$ and $\dfrac{6}{8}$ are equivalent

b) perpendicular; 3 and $-\dfrac{1}{3}$ are negative reciprocals

c) neither; 5 and -5 are unequal and are not negative reciprocals

d) parallel; 0.4 and $\dfrac{2}{5}$ are equivalent

e) perpendicular; $2\dfrac{1}{2}$ and $-\dfrac{2}{5}$ are negative reciprocals

f) neither; $-\dfrac{1}{2}$ and $\dfrac{1}{2}$ are unequal and are not negative reciprocals

g) perpendicular; since one line is vertical and the other line is horizontal, the lines must be perpendicular.

5. a) 3 **b)** –2 **c)** $\dfrac{2}{3}$ **d)** $-\dfrac{2}{5}$ **e)** $-\dfrac{2}{3}$ **f)** $\dfrac{5}{3}$

g) undefined **h)** 0

6. a) $-\dfrac{1}{3}$ **b)** $\dfrac{1}{2}$ **c)** $-\dfrac{3}{2}$ **d)** $\dfrac{5}{2}$ **e)** $\dfrac{3}{2}$ **f)** $-\dfrac{3}{5}$

g) 0 **h)** undefined

7.

Slope of a Line	Slope of a Parallel Line	Slope of a Perpendicular Line
4	4	$-\dfrac{1}{4}$
–3	–3	$\dfrac{1}{3}$
$\dfrac{2}{3}$	$\dfrac{2}{3}$	$-\dfrac{3}{2}$
0	0	undefined
undefined	undefined	0

8. a) $y = -\dfrac{3}{2}x + \dfrac{7}{2}$ **b)** $-\dfrac{3}{2}$ **c)** $-\dfrac{3}{2}$

d) Answers will vary. Example: Any two lines with slope $-\dfrac{3}{2}$.

9. a) $y = \dfrac{5}{2}x + 2$ **b)** $\dfrac{5}{2}$ **c)** $-\dfrac{2}{5}$

d) Answers will vary. Example: Any two lines with slope $-\dfrac{2}{5}$.

10. a) *x*-intercept: 9; *y*-intercept: 6

b)

Line Equation	x-intercept	y-intercept
$2x + 3y = 12$	6	4
$2x + 3y = 6$	3	2
$2x + 3y = -6$	–3	–2
$2x + 3y = -12$	–6	–4
$2x + 3y = -18$	–9	–6

c) Answers will vary.

11. a) The slope of AB is $-\dfrac{1}{2}$. The slope of AC is 0.

The slope of BC is 2. The slopes of lines AB and BC are negative reciprocals so ABC is a right triangle.

b) The slope of DE is $-\dfrac{1}{2}$. The slope of DF is $-\dfrac{7}{5}$.

The slope of EF is –5. No two pairs of slopes are negative reciprocals so no two of lines DE, DF, and EF are perpendicular. $\triangle$ DEF is not a right triangle.

c) The slope of MN is $\dfrac{2}{3}$. The slope of MO is $-\dfrac{1}{5}$.

The slope of NO is $-\dfrac{3}{2}$. The slopes of lines MN and NO are negative reciprocals so MNO is a right triangle.

12. a) Possible answers: (–4, 2); (–1, –1); (2, –1); (–1, –4); (–4, 5); (–7, 2)

b) There are many solutions. A few are listed in part a).

6.5 Find an Equation for a Line Given the Slope and a Point, pages 107–108

1. a) $y = 2x - 3$ **b)** $y = -4x - 14$ **c)** $y = \dfrac{3}{5}x - 4$

d) $y = -\dfrac{1}{4}x + \dfrac{13}{2}$

2. a) $y = -4$ **b)** $y = 3x - \dfrac{7}{4}$ **c)** $y = \dfrac{2}{3}x$

d) $y = \dfrac{1}{2}x - \dfrac{5}{2}$

3. a) $y = 5x - 7$ **b)** $y = -4x - 7$ **c)** $y = 2x - 4$

d) $y = -\dfrac{1}{3}x - \dfrac{4}{3}$ **e)** $y = 3$ **f)** $x = -3$

4. a) $y = \dfrac{1}{2}x$ **b)** $y = \dfrac{2}{5}x - \dfrac{11}{5}$ **c)** $y = -2x$

d) $y = -\dfrac{1}{3}x$

5. $y = -\dfrac{3}{5}x + \dfrac{9}{5}$

6. $y = \dfrac{5}{2}x - 2$

7. a) $C = 2d + 15$ **b)** \$45

c)

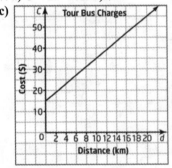

d) \$45

8. a)

Distance (km)	Cost ($)	First Differences
2	19	
3	21	2
4	23	2
5	25	2
6	27	2

b) 45 km **c)** \$36 **d)** Answers will vary.
9. a) 6 **b)** $C = 3d + 6$ **c)** Answers will vary.
10. a) Answers will vary. Example: It means that after 2 h of running towards the finish line, Ahmed has 15 km left to run.
b) This value shows that for each hour that Ahmed runs, his distance from the finish line decreases by 15 km. It is negative because it represents a decreasing distance per hour.
c) 45 **d)** $d = -15t + 45$
e) The d-intercept represents Ahmed's distance from the finish line just as he started his race.

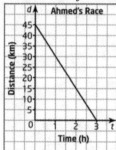

f) 3 h
g) Yes. Ahmed has run for 2 h at 15 km/h. So he has run 30 km. He still has 15 km to run. At 15 km/h this will take him another hour.
11. a) Answers will vary. Example: It means that after 2 h of driving towards Hamilton, Emeline has 300 km left to drive.
b) This value shows that for each hour that Emeline drives, her distance from the Hamilton decreases by 100 km. It is negative because it represents a decreasing distance per hour.
c) 500 **d)** $d = -100t + 500$
e) The d-intercept represents Emeline's distance from Hamilton just as she started her drive.

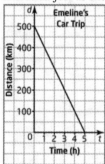

f) 5 h
g) No. Emeline has driven for 2 h at 100 km/h. So she has travelled 200 km. She still has 300 km to drive. At 100 km/h this will take her another 3 h.

6.6 Find an Equation for a Line Given Two Points, pages 109–111

1. a) $y = x + 1$ **b)** $y = -\frac{1}{2}x + 1$ **c)** $y = 3$ **d)** $x = 1$
2. a) $y = 2x - 2$ **b)** $y = -4x + 9$
c) $y = -\frac{5}{2}x - \frac{3}{2}$ **d)** $y = -\frac{5}{3}x + \frac{1}{3}$
3. a) $y = \frac{5}{3}x + 5$ **b)** $y = \frac{1}{2}x - 2$
4. a) $y = -2x + 4$ **b)** $y = -x - 2$
5. a) Dajanth is moving away from the sensor because he is farther away from it after 2 s than he was at the start.
b) 2.5 m/s **c)** $d = 2.5t + 2.5$
d) The d-intercept, 2.5, means that Dajanth's initial position was 2.5 m away from the motion sensor.
6. a) Helen is moving towards the sensor because she is closer to it after 8 s than she was at the start.
b) 1 m/s **c)** $d = -t + 8$
d) The d-intercept, 8, means that Helen's initial position was 8 m away from the motion sensor.
7. a) The point (2, 16.75) represents Patti's wage of \$16.75/h with 2 years of experience, and the point (5, 22.75) represents Susan's wage of \$22.75/h with 5 years experience.
b) slope 2; x-intercept 12.75; The slope represents the yearly wage increase, and the s-intercept represents the starting wage.
c) $s = 2n + 12.75$ **d)** \$32.75
e) \$52.75. Answers will vary.
8. a) Susu: $d = 2t + 6$; Meisrain: $d = -t + 12$
b) 2 s **c)** 10 m
d) Answers will vary. Example: Susu's distance has to equal Meisrain's distance, so set the right sides of the equations equal. Then, solve for t.
9. a) 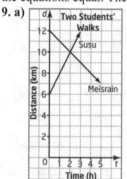 **b)** (2, 10)

c) Answers will vary. Example: The point of intersection shows that Susu and Meisrain were both 10 m away from the sensor after 2 s. This means that they must have crossed paths at this time and distance from the sensor.

10. a) $y = -\frac{33}{28}x + \frac{106}{28}$ **b)** $y = -\frac{25}{66}x - \frac{37}{66}$

6.7 Linear Systems, pages 112–114
1. a) $(-2, -3)$ **b)** $(3, -1)$ **c)** $(-2, 0)$ **d)** $(0, -2)$
2. a) $(2, 4)$ **b)** $(1, 1)$ **c)** $(-2, 1)$ **d)** $(-3, -7)$
3. a) $(-2, -1)$ **b)** $(1, 2)$ **c)** $(-2, -2)$
d) $(1, -2)$ **e)** $(1, -1)$ **f)** $(0, 4)$
g) $\left(\dfrac{32}{31}, \dfrac{7}{31}\right)$ **h)** $\left(-\dfrac{16}{13}, \dfrac{15}{13}\right)$

4. a) C represents the cost of operating each car, in dollars, and d represents the distance travelled, in kilometres.
b) $d = 4000$, $C = 3600$
c) The point of intersection represents the distance travelled when the cost of operating each car is the same.
d) gas-powered car
5. a) Printer A: $C = 225 + 6p$;
    Printer B: $C = 375 + 5.5p$
b) $(300, 2025)$ **c)** 300
d) Printer A is more economical for less than 300 pages. Printer B is more economical for more than 300 pages.
6. a) First Choice: $C = 2.50 + 0.40d$
    G.T.A. Taxi: $C = 3.25 + 0.25d$
b) $(5, 4.50)$
c) First Choice is more economical for less than 5 km. G.T.A. is more economical for more than 5 km.
7. The two equations represent the same line and are coincidental. The lines have the same slopes and the same y-intercepts.
8. $y = -\dfrac{5}{3}x - \dfrac{25}{3}$
9. a) $(5, 2)$ **b)** $(-1, 3)$ **c)** $(2, -3)$
10. $(1, 4, -2)$
11. The two lines never cross so no point of intersection exists. The lines have the same slopes, but different y-intercepts.
12. The two equations represent the same line and are coincidental. They have the same slopes and the same y-intercepts.

Chapter 6 Review, pages 115–116
1. a) slope 3; y-intercept -2
b) slope -2, y-intercept -2
c) slope 0; y-intercept 2
d) slope undefined; y-intercept none; x-intercept -3
2. a) slope 4; y-intercept 2
b) slope $-\dfrac{5}{6}$; y-intercept 4
c) slope 0; y-intercept 5
d) slope undefined; y-intercept none; x-intercept -2

3. a) $y = 2x - 3$

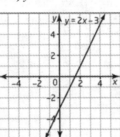

b) $y = -\dfrac{2}{3}x + 1$

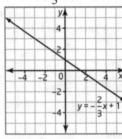

c) $y = 3$

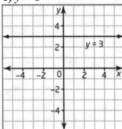

d) $x = 2$

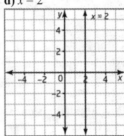

4. a) The slope is $\dfrac{1}{3}$ and the d-intercept is 2. The slope shows that the person is moving away from the motion sensor at a speed of $\dfrac{1}{3}$ m/s. The d-intercept shows that the person started 2 m away from the sensor.
b) $y = \dfrac{1}{3}x + 2$

5. a) $y = -3x + 4$ **b)** $y = \dfrac{2}{3}x + \dfrac{4}{3}$

6. a) $C = 35n + 50$
b) The slope is 35 and the C-intercept is 50. The slope shows that the electrician charges a variable cost of \$35/h and the C-intercept shows that the electrician also charges a base cost of \$50.
c) Graphs will vary depending on the scale chosen.
d) \$190
7. a) x-intercept 5; y-intercept 4
b) x-intercept 3; y-intercept -2
8. a) 6 **b)** 12
c) 1 bag of popcorn and 10 pops; 2 bags of popcorn and 8 pops; 3 bags of popcorn and 6 pops; 4 bags of popcorn and 4 pops; 5 bags of popcorn and 2 pops; also, any combination of bags of popcorn and pops that totals less than \$24.
9. a) x-intercept: 2; y-intercept: 5
b)

Line Equation	x-intercept	y-intercept
$2x - 5y = 20$	10	-4
$2x - 5y = 10$	5	-2
$2x - 5y = -10$	-5	2
$2x - 5y = -20$	-10	4
$2x - 5y = -30$	-15	6

c) Answers will vary. Example: To find the intercepts of a line perpendicular to a given line, interchange the values of x- and y-intercepts for the given line and multiply one of the intercepts by -1.

10. $y = \dfrac{3}{5}x - \dfrac{26}{5}$

11. $y = -\dfrac{4}{5}x + \dfrac{12}{5}$

12. $y = -\dfrac{1}{3}x - 2$

13. $y = -2x - 2$

14. $y = -6x + 10$

15. $(2, 1)$

16. $(1, 30)$. This means that both piano teachers charge \$30 for one hour of piano lessons.

Chapter 7

7.1 Angle Relationships in Triangles, pages 117–118

1. a) $111°$ b) $149°$ c) $127°$ d) $134°$
2. a) $65°$ b) $143°$ c) $152°$ d) $115°$
3. a) $170°$ b) $195°$ c) $155°$ d) $150°$
4. a) $110°$ b) $149°$ c) $120°$ d) $117°$
5. a) $x = 85°$
b) $x = 136°, y = 102°, z = 58°$
c) $w = 55°,\ x = 125°, y = 125°, z = 55°$
d) $w = 64°, x = 122°, y = 58°, z = 122°$
e) $a = 80°, b = 50°, c = 25°, d = 130°, e = 25°$
6. a) equilateral b) isosceles c) scalene
7. a) $157°$
b) interior angle, $67°$; exterior angle, $113°$
8. $w = 47°, x = 90°, y = 42°, z = 43°$
9. a) $30°, 60°,$ and $90°$ b) $60°, 60°,$ and $60°$
10. Answers will vary.

7.2 Angle Relationships in Quadrilaterals, pages 119–121

1. a) $a = 51°$ b) $b = 72°$ c) $c = 70°$ d) $d = 79°$
e) $e = 69°$ f) $f = 54°$
2. a) $112°$ b) $115°$ c) $87°$ d) $121°$
3. a) $88°$ b) $104°$ c) $76°$ d) $93°$
4. a) $\angle D = 133°$ b) $\angle C = 131°$ c) $\angle B = 105°$
d) $\angle A = 81°$
5. a) $\angle D = 117°$ b) $\angle C = 100°$ c) $\angle B = 88°$
d) $\angle A = 91°$
6. a) $x = 78°, y = 102°$
b) $w = 60°, z = 120°$
c) $a = 134°, b = 46°, c = 134°$
7. a) $x = 72°, y = 108°$
b) $a = 68°, b = 67°, c = 113°, d = 95°$
8. a) fourth angle measures $78°$
b) fourth angle measures $75°$
c) impossible since $\angle A + \angle B + \angle C = 364°$
9. a) impossible; sum of four acute angles is less than $360°$

b) Example: two $70°$ angles and two $110°$ angles
c) Example: two $100°$ angles, one $90°$ angle and one $70°$ angle
10. $90°$
11. $x = 49.5°, y = 93°, z = 110.5°, u = 107°, w = 73°$
12. a) Yes. b) Yes. c) Yes. d) No. e) Yes. f) No.
13 a) $72°, 72°, 108°, 108°$
b) $67.5°, 67.5°, 112.5°, 112.5°$

7.3 Angle Relationships in Polygons, pages 122–124

1. a) $1800°$ b) $2700°$ c) $3600°$ d) $3960°$
2. a) $135°$ b) $144°$ c) $154.3°$ d) $165°$
3. a) 10 b) 6 c) 13 d) 15
4. a) 6 b) 10 c) 8
5. a) equilateral triangle b) square
6.

Polygon	Number of Sides	Number of Diagonals From One Vertex	Number of Triangles in the Polygon	Sum of Interior Angles
pentagon	5	2	3	540°
hexagon	6	3	4	720°
octagon	8	5	6	1080°
dodecagon	12	9	10	1800°

7. a) Sum of the interior angles is $180°(3 - 2) = 180°$.

Since the angles are equal, each one measures $\dfrac{180°}{3}$
or $60°$.
b) Sum of the interior angles is $180°(4 - 2) = 360°$.

Since the angles are equal, each one measures $\dfrac{360°}{4}$
or $90°$.
8. a) $135°$ b) Answers will vary.
c) The angles do not change.
9. b) 7 c) $1440°$

10. a) $140°$ b) $156°$ c) $165°$ d) $\dfrac{180(n - 2)}{n}$

11. a) $156°$ b) $24°$ c) Answers will vary.
d) $144°$ e) $36°$
12. a) $150°$ b) Answers will vary.
c) The angles do not change.
13. $30°$

7.4 Midpoints and Medians in Triangles, pages 125–126

1. a) 5 cm b) 8 cm c) 10 cm d) 26 cm
2. a) 10 cm^2 b) 10 cm^2
3. a) 13 cm^2 b) 13 cm^2
4. a) 7.5 cm^2 b) 7.5 cm^2
5. 3.5 m
6. a) Answers will vary.
b) Fold along each of the medians and see if the equal sides line up.

c) Construct an equilateral triangle and the three medians and then measure the angles on either side of each of the medians.
d) The medians bisect each of the angles.
7. $\angle AXZ$ is acute when A is close to Z.
8. a) An isosceles triangle with interior angles 80°, 50°, and 50° is a counter-example.
b) An isosceles triangle with interior angles 20°, 80°, and 80° is a counter-example.
9. Since $\triangle DEF$ is an equilateral triangle, the median AF bisects $\angle DEF$. So in $\triangle DAF$, $\angle ADF = 60°$, $\angle AFD = 30°$, and $\angle ADF + \angle AFD + \angle DAF = 180°$. Therefore, $\angle DAF = 90°$. Similarly for $\triangle EAF$. Therefore, the perpendicular at A must pass through F.
10. Right bisectors intersect at one point in all triangles.
11. a) Medians intersect at one point in all triangles.
b) Yes; the circle's radius is the minimum distance from the intersection of the medians to any side of the triangle. The circle is inscribed in the triangle.

7.5 Midpoints and Diagonals in Quadrilaterals, pages 127–128
1. a) XY is parallel to WZ, YZ is parallel to XW
b) UV is parallel to TW, TU is parallel to WV
2. KD = 8 cm, LD = 10 cm, KM = 16 cm, LJ = 20 cm
3. AE = 11 cm, BE = 10 cm
4. 120 cm
5. 60 cm
6. when EFGH is a rectangle
7. a) False; any trapezoid that has unequal bases is a counter-example.
b) True; a line segment joining opposite midpoints creates two rectangles with equal heights and bases.
8. a) rhombus
b) The area of WXYZ is half the area of ABCD. The diagonals of WXYZ form four triangles that are congruent to the triangles outside WXYZ.
c) square
d) No; all the triangles are still congruent.
9. b) 90°
c) rectangle
d), e) Answers will vary. Example: The area of WXYZ if half the area of STUV.
10. Answers will vary. Example:
b) By the Pythagorean theorem,
$DG^2 + DE^2 = EG^2 = FG^2 + EF^2$.
So DG = FG.
c) $\triangle DEF$ and $\triangle FGE$ are congruent right triangles (DE = FD, DG = FG, and EG = GE). Therefore, $\angle DEG = \angle FEG$.
11. Answers will vary. Examples:
a) The area of QRST is half the area of MNOP.
b) Use geometry software to compare the areas.

12. In any rhombus ABCD, $\triangle ABC$ and $\triangle CDA$ are congruent (SSS), as are $\triangle ABD$ and $\triangle CDB$. Thus, $\angle CAB = \angle ACD$, $\angle CDB = \angle ABD$, $\angle ACB = \angle CAD$, and $\angle ADB = \angle CBD$. $\triangle ABE$ and $\triangle CDE$ are congruent (ASA), so DE = BE and AE = CE.
13. $\triangle EFG$ and $\triangle GHE$ are congruent (SSS). So, $\angle EFG = \angle GHE$. Since $\angle FGE$, $\angle GEF$, and $\angle EFG$ sum to 180°, $\angle HEG + \angle GEF + \angle EFG = 180°$. Therefore, EH is parallel to FG. Similarly, EF is parallel to GH.
14. $\triangle ABC$ and $\triangle AED$ are congruent (SAS). Therefore, AC = AD.

Chapter 7 Review, pages 129–130
1. a) $u = 113°$ **b)** $v = 138°$
c) $w = 113°$, $x = 78°$, $y = 35°$, $z = 102°$
d) $x = 29°$, $y = 84°$, $z = 67°$
2. The exterior angle would be greater than 180°.
3. a) any triangle
b) impossible; sum of exterior angles would be less than 360°
4. a) $x = 85°$
b) $a = 88°$, $b = 100°$, $c = 80°$, $d = 80°$, $e = 92°$
c) $x = 70°$, $y = 110°$, $z = 70°$
d) $a = 112°$, $b = 68°$, $c = 112°$, $d = 68°$, $e = 68°$
5. a) Example: three 85° angles
b) impossible: sum of interior angles would be less than 360°
6. a) 540° **b)** 900° **c)** 2340° **d)** 1620° **e)** 1080°
7. a) 120° **b)** 128.6° **c)** 150° **d)** 156°
8. a) 8 **b)** 9
9. Answers will vary.
10. GH connects the midpoints of DE and DF. Therefore, the base and altitude of $\triangle DGH$ are half those of $\triangle DEF$.
11. a) The median to the vertex opposite the unequal side of an isosceles triangle is an altitude. This divides the isosceles triangle into two congruent right triangles. Therefore, the median bisects the angle at the vertex.
b) False; any isosceles triangle is a counter-example.
12. Explanations will vary.
a) True **b)** False **c)** True **d)** False
13. Answers will vary.

Chapter 8
8.1 Apply the Pythagorean Theorem, pages 131–133
1. a) 5 cm **b)** 25 m **c)** 6.4 cm **d)** 9.4 m
2. a) 8 cm **b)** 17.0 m **c)** 6.8 cm **d)** 12.6 m
3. a) 28 cm^2 **b)** 41 m^2
4. a) 4.5 **b)** 3.2 **c)** 4.2 **d)** 5.4
5. 166 cm
6. 38 m
7. a) 86 m **b)** 300 m^2

c) Step 1: Use the Pythagorean theorem to find the length of the unknown side.
Step 2: Add the dimensions of the outer boundary to determine the perimeter.
Step 3: Use the formula for the area of a triangle.
8. 81 cm

9. a) $\sqrt{8}$; $\sqrt{12}$; $\sqrt{16}$; $\sqrt{20}$

b) $\sqrt{4} + \sqrt{8} + \sqrt{12} + \sqrt{16}$

c) As you add right triangles to the spiral pattern, the area will increase by $\sqrt{4 \times \text{number of triangles}}$.

10. a)

Length Side, a	Length Side, b	Hypotenuse
3	4	5
5	12	13
7	24	25
9	40	41
11	60	61
13	84	85
15	112	113

b) Answers will vary.

8.2 Perimeter and Area of Composite Figures, pages 134–136
1. a) 48 m **b)** 39.6 m **c)** 24.8 cm
2. a) 27.2 cm **b)** 29.2 cm **c)** 24.3 cm
3. a) 54 cm^2 **b)** 660 m^2 **c)** 38 cm^2 **d)** 46 m^2
4. a) 297 cm **b)** 5664 cm^2
c) Step 1: Use the Pythagorean theorem to find the length of the unknown sides.
Step 2: Add the dimensions of the outer boundary to determine the perimeter.
Step 3: To find the area, determine the area of the rectangular area and the area of the triangular area and then add the areas together.
5. a) 20.8 m **b)** 19.5 m^2
6. 300 mm^2
7. Answers will vary.
8. a) 2.8 m **b)** 11 m
9. 3600 cm^2
10. a) 32 m^2
b) The area of the swimming pool is four times the area of one of the triangular decks.
c) Yes. Answers will vary.
11. 75 cm^2

8.3 Surface Area and Volume of Prisms and Pyramids, pages 137–138
1. a) 337.6 cm^2 **b)** 85.8 cm^2
2. a) 4167 mm^3 **b)** 7 m^3
3. a) 908 mm^2 **b)** 192 cm^2
4. a) 1008 cm^3 b) 19 m^3
5. a) 94 m^2 **b)** 60 m^3
6. 25 cm
7. a) 2 552 129 m^3 **b)** 137 400 m^2
8. a) 4900 cm^3 **b)** 4.9 L

9. a) 198 m^3 **b)** 11 **c)** $250.17
10. a) 98 m^2 **b)** $693.50

8.4 Surface Area of a Cone, pages 139–140
1. a) 31 m^2 **b)** 905 cm^2 **c)** 1508 cm^2 **d)** 452 m^2
2. a) 25 m **b)** 704 m^2
3. a) 495 cm^2
b) Answers will vary. There is no aluminum being overlapped.
4. a) Yes.
b) No. The second cone. The slant height is the same for both, but in the expression πrs , the second cone has the greater radius.
c) 213.6 cm^2; 343.1 cm^2
5. a) 8 cm **b)** 6 cm
6. No. Answers will vary. Example: The formula for the surface area of a cone is $SA = \pi r^2 + \pi rs$. When the height is tripled only the term πrs is changed.
The term πr^2 remains unaltered. Hence, tripling the height of a cone does not triple the surface area.
7. No. Answers will vary. Example: The formula for the surface area of a cone is $SA = \pi r^2 + \pi rs$. When the radius is tripled the term πr^2 will be 9 times the size and the term πrs will triple. Hence, the surface area of the new cone will be more than three times the original cone.
8. a) radius 8 cm, height 16 cm **b)** slant height 18 cm
c) 653 cm^2
9. a) radius 9 cm, height 22 cm **b)** slant height 24 cm
c) 933 cm^2
10. 395 m^2
11. 307 m^2
12. Answers will vary.

13. a) height $= y$, radius $= \dfrac{y}{2}$, slant height $= \sqrt{\dfrac{5y^2}{4}}$

b) $SA = \dfrac{\pi y}{2}\sqrt{\dfrac{5y^2}{4}} + \dfrac{\pi y^2}{4}$

14. a) $r = \dfrac{\text{Lateral Area}}{\pi s}$ **b)** 2.9 cm

8.5 Volume of a Cone, pages 141–143
1. a) 94 cm^3 **b)** 101 cm^3 **c)** 50 m^3 **d)** 308 m^3
2. a) 19 cm^3 **b)** 49 cm^3 **c)** 1018 m^3 **d)** 6 m^3
3. 403.2 cm^3
4. 4 cm
5. 3 cm
6. 200 cm^3
7. Answers will vary.
8. 240 cm^3
9. a) Answers will vary. Example: 7 m
b) 6 m
c) Answers will vary.

10. 389.9 cm^3

11. a) Answers will vary. Example: The cone with base radius of 6 cm has the greater volume. The formula for the volume of a cone contains two factors of r and only factor of h. Hence, the volume is more dependent on r than on h.

b) Cone (height 6 cm, base radius 5 cm):
Volume = 157 cm^3
Cone (height 5 cm, base radius 6 cm):
Volume = 188 cm^3

12. a) $h = \dfrac{3V}{\pi r^2}$ **b)** 6.4 cm

13. a) $r = \sqrt{\dfrac{3V}{\pi h}}$ **b)** 10.9 cm

14. 6.9 cm

15. 8.0 m

8.6 Surface Area of a Sphere, pages 144–145

1. a) 804 cm^2 **b)** 31 794 mm^2 **c)** 314 m^2
d) 129 m^2
2. 1.9 cm
3. 4.6 cm
4. a) 2026.8 cm^2 **b)** $5.07
5. a) 2189.6 cm^2 **b)** $7.01
6. a) 2463 cm^2 **b)** $0.49
7. 491 m^2
8. 3 141 593 km^2
9. 1257 cm^2
10. a) Answers will vary. Example: 900 cm^2
b) 1018 cm^2
c) Answers will vary.

11. a) $SA = \pi d^2$ **b)**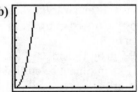

c) The diameter must be greater than 0. As the diameter increases, the surface area also increases in a non-linear pattern.
d) 227 cm^2, 4.4 cm

12. a) $d = \sqrt{\dfrac{SA}{\pi}}$ **b)**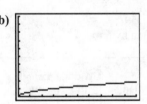

c) The diameter and the surface area must be greater than 0. The trend between the two variables is non-linear with the diameter increasing as the surface area increases but at a slow rate.
d) 13.8 cm

13. The surface area has increased by a factor of sixteen.
$$SA_{old} = 4\pi r^2$$
$$SA_{new} = 4\pi(4r)^2$$
$$= 4\pi(16r^2)$$
$$= 16(4\pi r^2)$$

14. The cube with edge length 16.

8.7 Volume of a Sphere, pages 146–148

1. a) 15 002 cm^3 **b)** 91 952 mm^3 **c)** 333 m^3
d) 4849 m^3
2. 14 137 cm^3
3. 221 cm^3
4. 21 990 642 870 km^3
5. 113 cm^3
6. a) 382 cm^3 **b)** 729 cm^3 **c)** 347 cm^3
7. 65 450 mm^3
8. a) 8181.2 cm^3 **b)** 1963.5 cm^2
9. a) 1098.5 cm^3 **b)** 760.5 cm^2 **c)** 523.3 cm^3
d) Answers will vary. Example: the tennis balls are packed closely together and the sides of the ball meet the rectangular prism package at the sides and at the top of the package.
10. a) Answers will vary.
b) 1642 m^3 **c)** 1313 cm^3 **d)** 12 truckloads
11. 1.3 m^3
12. a) 1 098 066 219 000 km^3
b) 927 587 170 500 km^3
c) 170 479 048 500 km^3
d) Answers will vary. Example: The Earth and Venus are perfect spheres.
13. Estimates will vary. Actual radius is 4.92 cm.
14. 5.2
15. a) Answers will vary. Example: 1:2
b) Volume of sphere = 113 cm^3
Volume of cube = 216 cm^3
Ratio: $\pi : 6$
c) Answers will vary.

Chapter 8 Review, pages 149–150

1. a) perimeter 27.8 cm; area 29.4 cm^2
b) perimeter 17.4 cm; area 13.0 cm^2
2. 3.9 m
3. perimeter 24.2 cm; area 37.5 cm^2
4. perimeter 25.4 cm; area 36.3 cm^2
5. a) 439.9 m **b)** 502.7 m **c)** 62.8 m
6. a) 158 cm^2 **b)** 8734 mm^2
7. a) 2000 m^3 **b)** 996 m^2
c) Answers will vary. Example: The side walls of the greenhouse are made of pieces of glass that are joined very closely.

d) Answers will vary. Example: The answer is fairly reasonable as when constructing a greenhouse, you want the pieces of glass to be as close together as possible.

8. 16.8 cm

9. 530.1 cm^2

10. 2173 cm^2

11. 2.8 cm

12. 415 cm^3; Volume$_{Cone}$ = $\frac{1}{3}$ × Volume$_{Cylinder}$

13. 1720.2 cm^2

14. a) 72 505 502 km^2 **b)** Mars is a sphere.

15. 268.1 cm^3

16. a) Answers will vary. Example: about 250 cm^3

b) 243.9 cm^3 **c)** Answers will vary.

Chapter 9

9.1 Investigate Measurement Concepts, pages 151–153

1. a) Investigate the dimensions of various rectangles with a perimeter of 22 units.

b) Answers will vary. Example:

Rectangle	Width (units)	Length (units)	Perimeter (units)	Area (square units)
1	1	10	22	10
2	2	9	22	18
3	3	8	22	24
4	4	7	22	28
5	5	6	22	30

2. a) Investigate the dimensions of various rectangles with an area of 18 square units using a geoboard.

b) Answers will vary. Example: Let the space between the two pins be 1 unit and use an elastic band to make different rectangles with an area of 18 square units. Start with a width of 1 unit and increase by intervals of one, and find the necessary length.

Rectangle	Width (units)	Length (units)	Perimeter (units)	Area (square units)
1	1	18	38	18
2	2	9	22	18
3	3	6	18	18

3. a)

Rectangle	Width (m)	Length (m)	Perimeter (m)	Area (m^2)
1	1	36	74	36
2	2	18	40	36
3	3	12	30	36
4	4	9	26	36
5	6	6	24	36

b) The greater the perimeter, the more expensive the garage; the smaller the perimeter, the lower the cost.

c) Rectangle 5 (a square) with dimensions 6 m by 6 m will be the most economical.

d) Answers will vary. Example: The quality of the material used to construct the garage and what will be stored in it.

4. a)

Rectangle	Width (m)	Length (m)	Perimeter (m)	Area (m^2)
1	1	64	130	64
2	2	32	68	64
3	4	16	40	64
4	8	8	32	64

b) The greater the perimeter, the more expensive the room; the smaller the perimeter, the lower the cost.

c) Rectangle 4 (a square) with dimensions 8 m by 8 m will be the most economical.

d) Answers will vary. Example: The quality of the material used to construct the room and what will be stored in it.

5. A rectangle with dimensions 5 m by 5 m encloses the greatest area for the same amount of fencing.

6. A rectangle with dimensions 7 m by 7 m encloses the greatest area for the same amount of fencing.

7. 144 m^2

8. 324 m^2

9. b) triangle: equilateral with each side 16 m, area: 110.9 m^2

rectangle: square with each side 12 m, area: 144 m^2

hexagon: regular with each side 8 m, area: 166.3 m^2

octagon: regular with each side 6 m, area: 173.8 m^2

circle: radius of 7.64 m, area: 183.4 m^2

c) Yes. Different shapes allow for different areas. The greatest area can be achieved by using a circle.

9.2 Perimeter and Area Relationships of a Rectangle, pages 154–155

1. a) 7 m by 7 m **b)** 10 m by 10 m **c)** 12 m by 12 m

d) 16.25 m by 16.25 m

2. a) Answers may vary. Example: 1 m by 4 m, 1.4 m by 3.6 m, 2.5 m by 2.5 m

b) 2.5 m by 2.5 m

3. a) 19.5 m by 19.5 m

b) No. 19.5 m cannot be created using 2-m barriers.

c) 19.25 m^2

4. a) 331.24 m^2 **b)** 1142.44 m^2

5. a) extra 331.24 m^2 **b)** extra 1142.44 m^2

18.2 m

36.4 m

33.8 m

67.6 m

6. 10 m by 5 m

7. a)

Rectangle	Width (m)	Length (m)	Area (m^2)	Length of Fence Used (m)
1	1	50	50	52
2	2	25	50	29
3	3	16.7	50	22.7
4	4	12.5	50	20.5
5	5	10	50	20

	A	B	C	D	E
1	Rec-tangle	Width (m)	Length (m)	Area (m^2)	Length of Fence Used (m)
2	1	1	=50/B2	50	=C2+2*B2
3	2	=B2+1	=50/B3	50	=C3+2*B3
4	3	=B3+1	=50/B4	50	=C4+2*B4
5	4	=B4+1	=50/B5	50	=C5+2*B5

b) 5 m by 10 m **c)** 20 m

8. 4 sides: a square with sides each 10 m; area 100 m^2

3 sides: a rectangle 20 m by 10; area 200 m^2

10 m

20 m

2 sides: a square with sides 20 m; area: 400 m^2

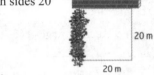

20 m

20 m

9. Answers will vary.
10. Answers will vary.
11. 6.48 m by 6.48 m
12. 4 m by 8 m
13. a) an equilateral triangle with side length 8.66 cm
b) an equilateral triangle with side length 13.86 cm
c) an equilateral triangle with side length 19.05 cm

9.3 Minimize the Surface Area of a Square-Based Prism, pages 156–158

1. a) 9 cm by 9 cm by 9 cm
b) 11 cm by 11 cm by 11 cm
c) 9.3 cm by 9.3 cm by 9.3 cm
d) 10.9 cm by 10.9 cm by 10.9 cm
e) 9.1 cm by 9.1 cm by 9.1 cm
f) 8.2 cm by 8.2 cm by 8.2 cm
2. a) 486 cm^2 **b)** 726 cm^2 **c)** 519 cm^2
d) 713 cm^2 **e)** 497 cm^2 **f)** 403 cm^2
3. C, A, B. Answers will vary.
4. a) cube with a side length of 53.1 cm
b) Answers will vary.
5. cube with a side length of 16.3 cm
6. a) 17.7 cm by 17.7 cm by 17.7 cm
b) Answers will vary.
7. a) 11.45 cm by 11.45 cm by 11.45 cm
b) 786.6 cm^2
8. Answers will vary.
9. a) 17.7 cm by 17.7 cm by 17.7 cm
b) 1880 cm^2
10. a) 21.25 cm by 21.25 cm by 21.25 cm
b) 2709.4 cm^2
11. a) 26.8 cm by 26.8 cm by 13.4 cm
b) different
c) The lidless box requires less material.
12. a) cube with a side length 5.6 cm
b) Answers will vary. Example: Cubical boxes are harder to hold.

c) Answers will vary.
13. a) 3.2 cm by 3.2 cm by 3.2 cm
b) Answers will vary. Example: The bags of microwave popcorn could not be folded to fit in the box.
c) Answers will vary.
14. Try to get the square-based prism to be as close to a cube in shape as possible. The dimensions are 4 by 4 by 3.

9.4 Maximize the Volume of A Square-Based Prism, pages 159–160

1. A, C, B
2. a) 7 cm by 7 cm by 7 cm
b) 12 m by 12 m by 12 m
c) 10 cm by 10 cm by 10 cm
d) 16 m by 16 m by 16 m
e) 15.8 cm by 15.8 cm by 15.8 cm
f) 17.3 m by 17.3 m by 17.3 m
3. a) 343 cm^3 **b)** 1728 m^3 **c)** 1000 cm^3
d) 4096 m^3 **e)** 3944 cm^3 **f)** 5178 m^3
4. 11.9 cm by 11.9 cm by 11.9 cm
5. a) 2520 cm^2; 7448 cm^3
b) 20.5 cm by 20.5 cm by 20.5 cm
c) 8615 cm^3
6. a) 28.8 m^2; 10.4 m^3 **b)** 2.2 m by 2.2 m by 2.2 m
c) 11 m^3
7. a) 109.1 m^2; 50.0 m^3 **b)** 4.3 m by 4.3 m by 4.3 m
c) 80 m^3
8. a) 1.6 m by 1.6 m by 1.6 m **b)** 4 m^3
9. a) 1.8 m by 1.8 m by 1.8 m **b)** 6 m^3
10. a) 51.6 cm by 51.6 cm by 51.6 cm
b) 137 388 cm^3 **c)** 83 488 cm^3
d) Answers will vary. Example: There is no empty space in the box. The stereo system would fit into the cube with enough room around the edges for the shredded paper. The shredded paper is tightly packed.
11. a) 86.6 cm by 86.6 cm by 86.6 cm
b)

c) Answers will vary. Example: Assume that Philip cuts the wood carefully to not waste any pieces, and glues pieces together.

9.5 Maximize the Volume of a Cylinder, pages 161–162

1. a) h = 17.24 cm, r = 8.62 cm
b) h = 2.06 m, r = 1.03 m
c) h = 25.24 mm, r = 12.62 mm
d) h = 9.22 cm, r = 4.61 cm
e) h = 4.12 m, r = 2.06 m
f) h = 30.90 mm, r = 15.45 mm
2. a) 4024 cm^3 **b)** 7 m^3 **c)** 12 629 mm^3

d) 616 cm^3 **e)** 55 m^3 **f)** 23 172 mm^3
3. a) r = 2.1 m, h = 4.2 m **b)** 58 189 L
c) Answers will vary. Example: No metal will be wasted in the building process, and no metal is being overlapped.
4. a) r = 0.7 m, h = 1.4 m **b)** 2155 L
c) Answers will vary. Example: No metal will be wasted in the building process, and no metal is being overlapped.
5. a) r = 1.3 m, h = 2.6 m **b)** 14 m^3
6. a) 12.2 cm **b)** 61 DVDs
c) Answers will vary. Example: Only the dimensions of the DVDs need to be considered; no extra space is left for the container's closing mechanism, the plastic container has no thickness.
7. a) r = 7.35 cm, h = 14.70 cm **b)** 73 CDs
8. a) Answers will vary.
b) cylinder: r = 13.6 cm, h = 27.2 cm, volume 15 805 cm^3;
square-based prism: s = 24.2 cm, volume 14 172 cm^3
9. a) Answers will vary. Example: Adjust the surface area formula for the new cylinder, isolate the height and run a few trials using a spreadsheet to find the maximum volume.
b) h = 9.2 cm, r = 9.2 cm, volume 2454 cm^3
10. a) Answers will vary.
b) square-based prism: s = 22.36 cm
cylinder: r = 12.62 cm, h = 25.24 cm
sphere: r = 15.45 cm
c) square-based prism: 11 179.3 cm^3
cylinder: 12 628.7 cm^3
sphere: 15 448.1 cm^3
d) The sphere has the greatest volume. Yes, this will always be the case.
e) For a given surface area:
volume of a sphere > volume of a cylinder
> volume of a square-based prism
11. a) r = 0.564 m, h = 1.128 m
b) r = 0.798 m, h = 0.798 m

9.6 Minimize the Surface Area of a Cylinder, pages 163–164
1. a) r = 6.1 cm, h = 12.2 cm **b)** r = 0.9 m, h = 1.8 m
c) r = 3.9 mm, h = 7.8 mm **d)** r = 1.2 cm, h = 2.4 cm
e) r = 5.0 m, h = 10.0 m **f)** r = 1.6 mm, h = 3.2 mm
2. a) 701 cm^2 **b)** 15 m^3 **c)** 287 mm^3
d) 27 cm^3 **e)** 471 m^3 **f)** 48 mm^3
3. r = 5.2 cm, h = 10.4 cm
4. r = 4.2 cm, h = 8.4 cm
5. a) r = 9.8 cm, h = 19.6 cm
b) Answers will vary. Example: No extra material will be needed to enclose the volume.
6. a) r = 3.8 cm, h = 7.6 cm
b) Answers will vary. Example: No extra material will be needed to enclose the volume.

7. a) r = 4.3 cm, h = 8.6 cm **b)** $12.55
8. a) r = 4.8 cm, h = 9.6 cm **b)** $7.82
9. a) r = 3.8 cm, h = 7.6 cm **b)** $14.70
10. a) r = 43.0 cm, h = 86.0 cm **b)** $348.53
11. A cube will have a surface area of 269 cm^2, and a cylinder will have a surface area of 244 cm^2. A cylinder is more cost efficient.
12. a) r = 7.26 cm, h = 7.25 cm **b)** 496 cm^2
c) Answers will vary. Example: The only cardboard needed is used to enclose the required volume so there is no wastage.
13. a) Answers will vary.
b) prism: 712.9 cm^2, cylinder: 656.2 cm^2, sphere: 581.1 cm^2; The sphere has the least surface area.

Chapter 9 Review, pages 165–166
1. a)

Rectangle	Width (units)	Length (units)	Perimeter (units)	Area (square units)
1	1	14	30	14
2	2	13	30	26
3	3	12	30	36
4	4	11	30	44
5	5	10	30	50
6	6	9	30	54
7	7	8	30	56

b) There are seven possible rectangles when the side measurements are whole numbers.
c) I would choose the 7 m by 8 m shape, because it has the greatest area.
2. a)

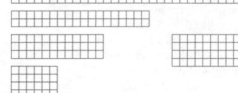

b)

Rectangle	Width (units)	Length (units)	Perimeter (units)	Area (square units)
1	1	36	74	36
2	2	18	40	36
3	3	12	30	36
4	4	9	26	36
5	6	6	24	36

c) I would choose the 6 m by 6 m shape, because for the same enclosed area, it has the least perimeter. Thus, fewer edging bricks will be required.
3. 2 m by 2 m
4. a) 1600 m^2 **b)** 3200 m^2
5. a) 28.3 m by 28.3 m
b) Answers will vary. Example: A square parking lot may not be best design for convenient parking of cars.

6. 9.8 m by 9.8 m by 9.8 m

7. a) 9.3 m by 9.3 m by 9.3 m

b) Answers will vary. Example: The surface area of a cylinder that contains the same volume will be less than the surface area of the box. The manufacturer could save on packaging costs.

8. 953 cm^2

9. 0.71 m by 0.71 m by 0.71 m

10. 22.4 cm by 22.4 cm by 22.4 cm

11. It is not possible to cut six 22.4 cm by 22.4 cm pieces from a 30 cm by 100 cm piece of cardboard because only four such pieces fit.

12. $r = 5.74$ cm, $h = 11.48$ cm; volume 1188.27 cm^3

13. Answers will vary. Example A cylinder will have a greater volume using the same amount of cardboard but the square-based prism may be easier for customers to store.

14. a) 324.64 cm^2, when $r = 4.15$ cm, $h = 8.30$ cm

b) Answers will vary. Example: There is not waste while making the pop can.

Challenge Questions

Challenge Questions 1, page 167

1. The first number in each pair represents a number from the first set, the second a number from the second set. (1, 8), (2, 2), (3, 13), (4, 12), (5, 11), (6, 10), (7, 9), (8, 1), (9, 7), (10, 6), (11, 5), (12, 4), (13, 3)

2. forty

3. 5 times

4. 126 cm

5. 79, 80, 81, 82, 83

6. 0, 4, or 8

7. a) 14, 16 **b)** $2n + 6$ **c)** 58 **d)** 43rd

8. 112 cm

9. 7

10. 20, 22, or 26

Challenge Questions 2, page 168

1. 32 cm

2. 8

3. 1; 3; 5; 8; 19; 39; 199; $2n - 1$

4. 1, 5, 15, 30, 45, 51, 45, 30, 15, 5, 1;
1, 6, 21, 50, 90, 126, 141, 126, 90, 50, 21, 6, 1;
1, 7, 28, 77, 161, 266, 357, 393, 357, 266, 161, 77, 29, 7, 1

5. 84

6. 11

7. Answers will vary

8. Answers will vary

Challenge Questions 3, page 169

1. 1 unit: 17; 2 units: 6; 3 units: 3; 4 units: 1; 5 units: 1

2. A is 4, B is 2, C is 3, and D is 1

3. 15, 21, 28

4. $593.75

5. 2 cm

6. 2, 1; 3, 4, 5; 7, 6

7. 9

8. Answers will vary.

Challenge Questions 4, page 170

1. a) 14 **b)** $t = 2p + 2$

2. 542.5 km

3. $5\dfrac{9}{28}$

4. 4

5. a) 17, 21

b) The number of toothpicks is one more than four times the diagram number.

c) $4n + 1$ **d)** 201, 321

6. Tuesday

7. 05:55

8. 13

9. Answers will vary.

Challenge Questions 5, page 171

1. 1 cm^2

2. 1, 3, 4, 7, 8, 9

3. 17

4. Saturday

5. 4 quarters; 3 quarters, 5 nickels; 2 quarters, 10 nickels; 1 quarter, 15 nickels; 20 nickels

6. 20

7. $\dfrac{5}{2} + \dfrac{4}{3}$

8.

Spend	Change
$1.85	$8.15
$3.65	$6.35
$4.55	$5.45
$5.45	$4.55
$6.35	$3.65
$7.25	$2.75
$8.15	$1.85

9. 15:00

10. yes

11. Answers will vary.

Challenge Questions 6, page 172

1. Answers will vary. For example:

$$\left(9 + \frac{9}{9}\right) \times \left(9 + \frac{9}{9}\right) = 100$$

2. 47, 48, 49

3. $277.\overline{7}$

4. a) 6 **b)** 4 **c)** 2

5. 3 nickels, 2 dimes, 5 quarters

6. 27

7. a) 180 **b)** 8 **c)** 44 **d)** 48

8. 11, 12, 13

9. 35, 12, 23
10. Answers will vary.
11. 06:35
12. Answers will vary.
13. 7 cm
14. Answers will vary.

Challenge Questions 7, page 173
1. 10 201, 40 804, 91 809, 404 × 404 = 163 216,
505 × 505 = 255 025
2. 6
3. a) 25 **b)** 51
4. Answers will vary.
a) yes; 20, 9, 6, 6 **b)** yes; seven 6s
c) no **d)** yes; 20, four 6s
5. $\dfrac{1}{24}$
6. 2 $5 bills, 1 $2 coin, 1 quarter, 1 dime, 1 nickel,
and 3 pennies
7. Answers will vary.
8. Answers will vary.
9. 212, 213
10. Answers will vary. Example: 154, 42, or 126

Challenge Questions 8, page 174
1. Answers will vary. For example:
a) 6 + 7 + 8 + 9 + 10 + 11 + 12
b) 33 + 34 + 35 + 36
2. 3, 5; 7, 1, 8, 2; 4, 6
3. Wednesday
4. 1125 m
5. Answers will vary.
6. 14
7. 4624
8. Answers will vary.
9. Answers will vary.
10. a) 22, 26 **b)** $4l - 6$ **c)** 50, 154
11. 11, 12, 13, 15, 17, 19

Challenge Questions 9, page 175
1. January 1, December 31
2. 2.5 min, assuming the animals can keep up that
speed for 1 km.
3. 63
4. Answers will vary.
5. February and March
6. 34
7. Answers will vary.
8. 49
9. a) Lauryn wins by 1 m.
b) Lauryn and Yolanda run at the same average speed
as in the first race.
10. 16
11. thirty-one or thirty-three
12. 78
13. Answers will vary.

Challenge Questions 10, page 176
1. 19
2. 48.5 square units
3. a) $4 \times 5 - 12 = 8$ **b)** $3 + 14 - 7 = 10$
c) $6 + 7 + 8 \div 4 = 15$ **d)** $5 + 6 + 11 - 3 = 19$
4. three 15-year-olds and two 14-year olds
5. 43
6. a) 13 + 15 + 17 + 19 = 64
b) 21 + 23 + 25 + 27 + 29 = 125
c) 31 + 33 + 35 + 37 + 39 + 41 = 216
d) It is the mean of the numbers.
e) 43 + 45 + 47 + 49 + 51 + 53 + 55 = 343
7. Answers will vary.